Strategic Alliances

KU-395-494

Strategic Alliances
Governance and Contracts

Edited by

Africa Ariño

and

Jeffrey J. Reuer

Anselmo Rubiralta Center
for Globalization and Strategy

University of Navarra

Selection and editorial matter © Africa Ariño, Jeffrey J. Reuer 2006
Individual chapters © contributors 2006

All rights reserved. No reproduction, copy or transmission of this
publication may be made without written permission.

No paragraph of this publication may be reproduced, copied or transmitted
save with written permission or in accordance with the provisions of the
Copyright, Designs and Patents Act 1988, or under the terms of any licence
permitting limited copying issued by the Copyright Licensing Agency,
90 Tottenham Court Road, London W1T 4LP.

Any person who does any unauthorised act in relation to this publication
may be liable to criminal prosecution and civil claims for damages.

The authors have asserted their rights to be identified
as the authors of this work in accordance with the Copyright,
Designs and Patents Act 1988.

First published 2006 by
PALGRAVE MACMILLAN
Houndmills, Basingstoke, Hampshire RG21 6XS and
175 Fifth Avenue, New York, N.Y. 10010
Companies and representatives throughout the world

PALGRAVE MACMILLAN is the global academic imprint of the Palgrave
Macmillan division of St. Martin's Press, LLC and of Palgrave Macmillan Ltd.
Macmillan® is a registered trademark in the United States, United Kingdom
and other countries. Palgrave is a registered trademark in the European
Union and other countries.

ISBN-13: 978-1-4039-9592-6 hardback
ISBN-10: 1-4039-9592-3 hardback

This book is printed on paper suitable for recycling and made from fully
managed and sustained forest sources.

A catalogue record for this book is available from the British Library.

Library of Congress Cataloging-in-Publication Data
Strategic alliances:governance and contracts/edited by Africa Ariño and
    Jeffrey J. Reuer.
        p.   cm.
Based on a conference held in Barcelona, Spain at IESE Business School,
University of Navarra, in June 2005.
Includes bibliographical references and index.
ISBN 1-4039-9592-3 (cloth)
    1. Strategic alliances (Business)—Congresses.   I. Ariño, Africa.
    II. Reuer, J. J. (Jeffrey J.)
    HD69.S8S775 2007
    658'.044—dc22   2006047635

10   9   8   7   6   5   4   3   2
15   14   13   12   11   10   09   08   07

Printed and bound in Great Britain by
Antony Rowe Ltd, Chippenham and Eastbourne

Contents

Notes on the Contributors

Rajshree Agarwal (agarwalr@uiuc.edu) is Associate Professor of Strategic Management at the University of Illinois at Urbana–Champaign. She received a PhD in economics from SUNY-Buffalo. Her research interests focus on knowledge transfer among firms and the implications of entrepreneurship and innovation for industry/firm evolution.

Jaideep (Jay) Anand is Associate Professor of Corporate Strategy and International Business at the Fisher College of Business, Ohio State University. Previously, Jay held positions at Michigan and Ivey. He earned a BTech from the Indian Institute of Technology, and Master's and PhD degrees from the Wharton School. His research interests are in the areas of mergers and acquisitions, strategic alliances and international strategies.

Nicholas S. Argyres is Associate Professor of Strategy and Policy at the Boston University School of Management. His research interests include technology strategy; internal organization and coordination; vertical integration; interorganizational relationships and contracting; and organizational politics. His research has been published in major management and economics journals.

Africa Ariño is Professor of General Management at IESE Business School, University of Navarra, where she serves as Academic Director of the Anselmo Rubiralta Center for Globalization and Strategy at IESE. She holds a PhD from the Anderson School of Management at UCLA. Her research interests include process and dynamic aspects of strategic alliances, as well as their governance mechanisms and performance measurement.

Xavier Castañer is an Assistant Professor in the Strategy Department at HEC School of Management (Paris). His research centres on corporate strategy and value creation. He has published on strategic planning and organizational integration in the *Administrative Science Quarterly*. Professor Castañer holds a PhD in Business Administration from the University of Minnesota.

Rachel Croson is an Associate Professor at the Wharton School of Business at the University of Pennsylvania. Her research uses the methods of experimental economics to investigate strategic interaction and to test game-theoretic models. She received her PhD in Economics from Harvard University.

Ilya R. P. Cuypers is a PhD candidate in Strategic Management and International Business at Tilburg University (the Netherlands). His research focuses on joint venture formation, stability and performance from a number of theoretical perspectives, including real option theory and transaction cost theory.

Pierre Dussauge is a Professor of Strategic Management at HEC School of Management, Paris. His current research focuses on the topic of global strategic alliances. He is the co-author of *Cooperative Strategy: Competing Successfully through Strategic Alliances* (Wiley & Sons, 1999).

Marco Furlotti works for the Centre for Research on Business Organization at Bocconi University where he is in the process of obtaining a PhD in Business Administration. He holds an MSc degree in Economics from the Hitotsubashi University of Japan. His business experience includes executive positions at an investment bank.

Bernard Garrette is Associate Professor of Strategic Management at HEC, Paris. He has been an executive with Valeo (1987–88), a Visiting Professor at the London Business School (1997–9) and a consultant (Senior Practice Expert in Corporate Finance and Strategy) with McKinsey & Company (2000–1). His research focuses on strategic alliances between competitors.

Anna Grandori is Professor of Business Organization, Director of the Research Centre of Business Organization at Bocconi University, and Editor of the *Journal of Management & Governance*. With a background and BA in economics, she has developed an integrative approach across economic and organization sciences, applied to decision-making, knowledge, networks and governance.

Glenn Hoetker is Assistant Professor of Strategic Management at the University of Illinois, Urbana–Champaign. He earned his doctorate in International Business from the University of Michigan. His research interests include interfirm relationships, technology management and the economic and institutional environment of Japan.

Daniel C. Indro is Associate Professor of Finance, Penn State University–Great Valley, Pennsylvania, USA. His current research interests are in the areas of corporate bankruptcy, behavioural finance and strategic alliances.

Prashant Kale is Assistant Professor of Corporate Strategy at the University of Michigan. He examines issues related to 'alliance capability', 'choice of governance forms', and 'alliance and acquisition dynamics in emerging markets'. He has published his work in leading academic and managerial journals and has also received several awards for it.

Franziska Koenig is PhD candidate at the Deutsche Telekom Foundation Distinguished Chair of Strategic Knowledge Management, Institute for Management, Freie Universität Berlin. She focuses on uncertainty-governance choice relationships from three theoretical perspectives, including transaction cost theory, resource-based view and real options theory, with a focus on different uncertainty dimensions.

Mitchell P. Koza is Distinguished Professor of Management and Dean, Rutgers University School of Business, USA.

C. Jay Lambe (PhD, The Darden School at University of Virginia) is an Assistant Professor of Marketing in the Albers School of Business and Economics at Seattle University. Prior to his academic appointment he engaged in business-to-business marketing for Xerox and AT&T, and his research on the relational aspect of this area has been widely published.

Arie Y. Lewin is Professor of Business Administration and Sociology at Duke University. He is Director of the Center for International Business Education and Research (CIBER) and Editor-in-Chief (July 2002–) of the *Journal of International Business Studies* (*JIBS*) and founding Editor-in-Chief of *Organization Science* (1989–98). He is the Lead Principal Investigator of the multi-year international Global Sourcing Research Initiative of administrative and technical work in the USA, Benelux countries, Germany, Scandinavia, Spain and the UK. His overall research interests centre on strategic renewal of organizations and adaptive capabilities that distinguish between innovating and imitating organizations. (http://faculty.fuqua.duke.edu/ciber/center/arie.html).

Xavier Martin is Professor of Strategy and International Business and a Fellow of the Centre for Economic Research at Tilburg University. Published in *ASQ, AMJ, SMJ, JIBS, Organization Science* and other journals, his research examines how corporate strategies, interfirm relationships and knowledge-based assets affect each other and jointly affect firm performance.

Kyle J. Mayer is Assistant Professor at the Marshall School of Business in the University of Southern California. He received his PhD from the University of California at Berkeley. His research examines interorganizational governance, with an emphasis on the strategic use of contracts to manage interorganizational relationships.

Thomas Mellewigt is a Professor of Management and holds the Deutsche Telekom Foundation Distinguished Chair in Strategic Knowledge Management at the Free University of Berlin. His research interests include contractual design and governance mechanisms of strategic alliances, determinants and management of outsourcing relationships and organizational economics. His research has been published in the *Journal of Business Venturing* and other journals and has been presented at many meetings of the Academy of Management and the Strategic Management Society.

Will Mitchell is Professor of Strategy and the J. Rex Fuqua Professor of International Management at Duke University's Fuqua School of Business. He studies business dynamics, focusing on how businesses overcome constraints to change and, in turn, how business changes influence performance.

Louis Mulotte is a doctoral candidate at HEC School of Management, Paris. His research interests focus on the mode firms choose to expand into new product areas (licence purchases, alliances and internal developments) and on the influence of this choice on subsequent growth and survival.

Joanne E. Oxley is Associate Professor of Strategic Management at the Rotman School of Management, University of Toronto, where she teaches international management and strategy. Her research focuses on international collaborative strategies for technology development and commercialization.

Anupama Phene is Assistant Professor of Strategy at the University of Utah. She received her PhD from the University of Texas. Her research examines firm innovation strategy in high technology industries. Her research has been published in the *Strategic Management Journal* and the *Journal of International Business Studies*.

Laura Poppo (lpoppo@vt.edu) is Associate Professor of Organization and Strategy at Virginia Tech University and holds her PhD from the Wharton School, University of Pennsylvania. She is currently on the editorial board of *Organization Science* and *International Journal of Strategic Change Management*. Her research interests include formal and informal governance institutions, emerging economies and knowledge.

Phanish Puranam is Assistant Professor in the Strategy and International Management Area at the London Business School. His research focuses on coordination in interorganizational relationships, and has been published in the *Academy of Management Journal*, *Strategic Management Journal* and *California Management Review*. He is a member of the Editorial Board of the *Academy of Management Review*.

Dr Ragozzino joined the faculty at the University of Central Florida in May 2004, after earning his PhD at the Fisher School of Business at the Ohio State University. His research is in the area of corporate strategy and entrepreneurship and his work has been published in several scholarly journals such as the *Strategic Management Journal*, the *Journal of International Business Studies*, and the *Journal of Economic Behavior and Organization*, among others.

Jeffrey J. Reuer is Associate Professor at the Kenan-Flagler Business School at the University of North Carolina. His research is in the area of corporate strategy, and his current work examines corporate investments such as alliances and acquisitions using information economics and options theory. He holds a PhD from the Krannert Graduate School of Management at Purdue University.

Malika Richards is Assistant Professor of Management, Penn State University–Berks, Pennsylvania and USA. Her research interests are in the areas of comparative management, management of multinationals, cross-cultural issues, and strategic alliances.

Peter Smith Ring (PhD, University of California, Irvine; LLB Georgetown University Law Center) is Professor of Strategic Management in the College of Business Administration at Loyola Marymount University, Los Angeles. His research focuses on alliance processes, and the roles of contracts and interpersonal trust in economic exchanges.

Michael D. Ryall is currently Associate Professor at the Melbourne Business School, University of Melbourne. Professor Ryall is a game theorist whose primary research focus is on the theoretical foundations of strategy. His recent work establishes formal, necessary and sufficient conditions for an agent to enjoy performance advantage in a very general competitive context.

Rachelle C. Sampson is currently Assistant Professor at the R. H. Smith School of Business, University of Maryland. Professor Sampson's research focuses on strategic alliances and the organization of corporate R&D. Her recent studies examine alliance structure and partner selection in the telecommunications equipment industry, legal contracting for alliances and optimal organization for innovation.

Silviya Svejenova is Assistant Professor of Strategy and Entrepreneurship at ESADE Business School in Barcelona, Spain. Her work has appeared in academic journals and book chapters. Her recent co-authored book *Sharing Executive Power: Roles and Relationships at the Top* is published by Cambridge University Press (2005).

Stephen Tallman is the E. Claiborne Robins Distinguished Professor of Business at the University of Richmond. He holds a PhD in International Business and Comparative Management from UCLA. His research interests include global outsourcing, international diversification, industry clusters, and international alliances and joint ventures.

Frans A. J. Van Den Bosch is Professor of Management at the Department of Strategic Management and Business Environment of RSM Erasmus University. His research interests include strategic renewal, and interorganizational and corporate governance. He has published in journals such as *Academy of Management Journal, Journal of Management Studies, Long Range Planning, Organization Science* and *Organization Studies*.

Paul W. L. Vlaar is Assistant Professor at the Department of Strategic Management and Business Environment of RSM Erasmus University. His research interests include the management of interorganizational relationships, interfirm contracting practices, and alliance capabilities. He holds an MSc (Cum Laude) in economics and obtained his PhD (Cum Laude) at RSM Erasmus University.

Henk W. Volberda is Professor of Strategic Management and Business Policy, Chairman of the Department of Strategic Management & Business Environment, and Vice Dean of RSM Erasmus University. He is director of the Erasmus Strategic Renewal Center, senior editor-in-chief of the *Journal of International Business Studies and Long Range Planning*, and member of the Editorial Boards of *Journal of Management Studies* and *Organization Science*. His research on strategic renewal, strategic flexibility, co-evolution of firms and industries, knowledge flows and innovation has been published in many books and journals, among others: *Academy of Management Journal, Management Science, Journal of Management Studies, Long Range Planning, Organization Science* and *Organization Studies*.

Testsuo Wada is Professor of Business Economics at Gakushuin University, Tokyo, Japan. He has also held positions at research institutions of the Japanese government, including the National Institute of Science and Technology Policy. He obtained a PhD in Business Administration from the University of California, Berkeley, and an LLB from the University of Tokyo.

Simon Wakeman is a PhD candidate in the Haas Business School at the University of California, Berkeley. He has an MA in Economics from UC Berkeley and LLB (Hons) and BA (Hons) degrees from the University of Otago, New Zealand. Simon's research focuses on the economics of contracts and intellectual property rights in the commercialization of new technology.

1
Introduction: Governance and Contracts in Strategic Alliances

Africa Ariño[1] and Jeffrey J. Reuer[2]

Alliance research and practice have developed considerably in the last decade, and this book focuses on the governance and contractual foundations of alliances. This general topic has always been central to the alliance literature (Reuer, 2004; Shenkar and Reuer, 2005) and has been the subject of many of the seminal writings in the field. It is also an area that has recently seen interesting contributions as scholars have developed new theories on the design and management of collaborative agreements, and as empirical evidence has accumulated from progressively more detailed investigations of strategic alliances.

While alliance governance and contractual forms are very much related, they are also distinct in scope as well as in the purposes they serve. *Governance* refers to 'alternative institutional modes for organizing transactions' (Williamson, 1979: 234), and prior research in the alliance literature has developed many insights into the problem of governance in this business context. Considerable research, for instance, has been devoted to the question of when firms should use alliances over acquisitions in order to enhance organizational efficiency. A second, related stream of research has examined when various forms of non-equity, or purely contractual, alliances are preferable to equity alliances such as joint ventures or partial acquisitions. By contrast, a *contract* determines 'the specific exchanges negotiated by trading partners and the allocation of risks and trading gains resulting from them' (James, 2000: 48). Governance form solves the broader boundary of the firm problem, whereas contractual form specifies terms of trade and the allocation of decision rights.

Although related, there is not necessarily a one-to-one relationship between governance and contractual forms, although this is commonly the assumption in alliance and other studies on organizational governance over the years. On the one hand, there is substantial contractual heterogeneity within particular governance forms. On the other hand, some contractual clauses are as likely to appear in some governance structures as in others, such as in equity and non-equity alliances. Furthermore, it appears that alliance governance and contractual forms share few determinants (for a revision of empirical work that supports these statements, see Ariño and Reuer, 2005). The two are distinct features of alliance design that deserve more research attention, and only recently have scholars begun to assemble the data necessary to understand the details of alliances' contractual foundations and consider how dimensions of alliance contracts relate to broader governance modes, informal mechanisms of governance, and other aspects of alliance design and management.

This volume results from a conference on 'Strategic Alliances: Governance and Contracts' held in Barcelona, Spain at IESE Business School, University of Navarra, in June 2005. The aim of the conference was to gather a group of distinguished scholars to discuss papers and ideas around firms' investment decisions related to alliances as well as the design and management of collaborative agreements. The conference followed a format that provided more room for extended, focused discussion than is often the case at large conferences. The call for papers was deliberately centred around a few major themes related to the governance mechanisms and contractual underpinnings of alliances. We invited a group of scholars known for work on these topics across a wide array of disciplinary perspectives.

The conference was kicked off with a practitioner panel on the content and process issues associated with alliance contracting. This panel offered managerial and legal practice perspectives to which subsequent discussions related. So as to incite discussion around the conference's themes, we decided to depart from the customary format of paper presentation followed by discussion. Instead, the paper presentations were grouped around common themes and had a panel-like format. One person served as a facilitator for each panel, setting the stage for a fruitful discussion of the papers presented, and offering an integrated view of the set of papers that highlighted the intriguing aspects the papers offered when considered jointly. Twenty-three papers were presented at the conference. After a process of self-selection and revision overseen by the facilitators, this volume includes twenty of the papers. Aiming to reach a broader audience than specialized journals, we asked the authors to remove technical details that would be appropriate in other outlets and – within space limits – to be more extensive in discussing their research questions and theoretical ideas.

Overview of the volume

The structure of this volume reflects the two major conference themes: alliance governance (Part I) and alliances' contractual underpinnings (Part II). The different weight of the two parts is but a reflection of the relatively less research attention that alliance contracts have received. Below we offer some highlights from these two parts of the volume and point out some of the broader themes that emerged from the conference.

Chapters in Part I on the governance of strategic alliances reflect a number of important topics, or sub-themes, that exist in the alliance literature and are topics of considerable on-going research. The first one that is explored in Chapters 2–4 concerns alliances as discrete governance structures. All three chapters focus on the alliance itself and the project underlying the collaboration as the unit of analysis:

- Garrette, Dussauge and Castañer reflect on the case in which firms' overall resource endowment is too limited for them to undertake a desired project on their own. The opportunity for collaboration through scale alliances stems from the existence of potential partners with similar needs. They suggest that scale alliances are most likely formed by weaker firms for whom the alliance is an alternative to carrying out a project autonomously. Their chapter is part of a series of papers that carefully distinguish alliance types and motives rather than aggregating together very different types of collaborations.
- Mulotte, Dussauge and Mitchell consider the project of entering a new business domain, be it a new industry or a new geographic market. In line with the previous chapter, the authors argue that the choice between autonomous and alliance-based entry is affected by pre-entry resources. Because alliance-based entry requires a lesser effort, it may inhibit a firm's ability to create a full set of the new resources required to succeed in the long run, however.
- Grandori and Furlotti broaden the spectrum of governance choices and suggest that strategic, project-based alliances involve a nexus of legal, organizational and social mechanisms. They argue that alliances are not well framed along the continuum of hierarchical versus market governance or along the continuum of relational versus obligational contracting. In line with our earlier claim that there is not necessarily a one-to-one relationship between governance and contractual forms, they propose that contracts are not necessarily coordination devices that are close, similar or consubstantial to markets; rather, contracts contribute to defining and protecting important features of interfirm organizational configurations.

A second sub-theme revolves around the governance mechanisms underlying strategic alliances. Chapters 5–8 are related to this topic. While the first two chapters focus on factors driving the choice of ownership level, the latter two examine how governance choices influence technology exchange and knowledge transfer:

- Kale and Puranam assess the extent to which choice of equity ownership level in exchange partners is influenced by considerations related to resource and exchange attributes. Their findings show that the influence of the former is stronger than that of the latter.

- Richards and Indro also consider ownership characteristics in the context of alliances that involve the government as a partner. In addition to offering empirical evidence of conditions under which a government is more likely to be a partner in a joint venture, they suggest that when governments do get involved in alliances, those in developed countries are more likely than governments in emerging economies to take a dominant role.
- Tallman and Phene examine characteristics of partners and alliances in order to explain the choice of governance mechanisms in the biotechnology industry. Coordination issues appear to be more relevant that appropriation concerns, maybe because of the strength of intellectual property protection mechanisms in this sector. Cooperative arrangements with technologically similar partners may be an effective way to exchange technology in industries with characteristics similar to those of biotechnology.
- Oxley and Wada provide evidence that indeed alliance governance and contract structure have a significant influence on knowledge flows. Interestingly, while alliance-related knowledge transfers increase the more hierarchical the alliance structure is, unrelated knowledge flows are reduced when licensing occurs within the context of a joint venture.

The discussion naturally moves into the dynamics of governance choices, the third sub-theme around which Chapters 9–12 revolve. Governance-related choices constitute a sequence, and early choices influence subsequent ones:

- Agarwal, Anand and Croson assess the effect of previous alliances on acquisition performance based on an experiment they reported. On the one hand, they find that alliances may not be beneficial to a subsequent acquisition because replacing confrontational routines that develop in an alliance setting is more difficult than creating appropriate new routines once an acquisition has taken place. On the other hand, they find that the prior social contact that an alliance enables has a positive impact on acquisition performance.
- Vlaar, Van Den Bosch and Volberda challenge the notion that alliances are a discrete governance decision. They introduce the concept of *governance trajectories*, which implies that partners align firm and transaction characteristics with a series of governance decisions in order to optimize alliance performance throughout its entire lifetime.
- Cuypers and Martin look at international joint ventures from an options perspective. They discuss empirical evidence that real option logic applies when uncertainty is exogenous, but not when uncertainty resolves endogenously. They compare real options arguments about the role of exogenous uncertainty with other theories (e.g. transaction cost theory, agency theory and bargaining).

- Koenig and Mellewigt argue for the need to clarify the relationships between uncertainty and governance. Toward this end, they provide a classification of uncertainty types, uncertainty effects, and governance mechanisms, and this classification allows them to offer a number of propositions on how uncertainty affects governance choice using transaction cost economics, real option theory, and the resource-based view of the firm.

Finally, the fourth sub-theme concerns relational governance. Chapters 13–15 relate to the emergence and use of relational norms:

- Poppo and Lambe explain the development of relational norms as a mechanism that eases adaptation to unexpected changes and events. They argue that the processes and factors that influence perceptions of relational norms change over time. They propose and test a theoretical framework that considers the differential influence of uncertainty reduction factors and emotional factors in the development of relational norms in younger and older exchange relationships.
- Hoetker and Mellewigt examine the conditions under which the use of formal, contractual mechanisms and the use of relational mechanisms are preferable. The nature of the assets involved in an alliance – in terms of property-based versus knowledge-based assets – is a key contingency that determines the optimal configuration of those mechanisms. They find that while the two types of mechanisms may coexist, they are not interchangeable as the most effective means of governing an alliance depends upon the type of assets involved.
- Svejenova, Koza and Lewin propose an enforcement framework that differentiates between trust and trust-like mechanisms that can generate reliability and predictability of partners' cooperative behaviour. These mechanisms include partners' social and legal embeddedness, and the existence of ownership relationships, and may allow the initiation of a relationship in the absence of a common relational history.

Chapters in Part II take up the contractual underpinnings of strategic alliances. This set of chapters collectively suggests that reliance on relational norms is compatible with reliance on detailed contracts, and the papers examine some of the implications of the interplay between relational and formal governance:

- Ring identifies a number of economic and psychological dimensions that define different kinds of contracts, and he discusses the contracting processes that produce these kinds of contracts. Given the uncertainty involved in strategic alliances, the contracts that govern them have to provide for means for governing conduct in the uncertain future, as well as evidence of the intentions of the parties about these matters at the time of contracting.

- Mayer suggests that the role of contracts goes beyond protecting the parties and ensuring enforcement of an exchange, as conventional views of contracts would emphasize. Contracts allow the parties to share enough information that they can understand each other's needs and ensure that their interests are protected. In this way, more detailed contracts can help facilitate relationship development.
- Wakeman focuses on patent rights in the context of alliances involving biotechnology start-ups. He examines how the strength of patent rights affects the timing, choice of partner, and structure of the alliance contract as reflected by financial terms and allocations of control rights.
- Ryall and Sampson examine the question of whether prior relationships complement or substitute for formal governance. They do so by exploring if and how formal terms in technology alliance contracts vary with prior alliances – either with a specific partner or more generally. Their empirical results suggest that the informal governance inherent in interfirm relationships has different effects on formal governance depending upon whether these relationships are on-going or past.
- Argyres and Mayer discuss how firms learn to design their contracts, a process that can take a long time for firms in young, high-technology industries. Patterns of learning to contract are reflected in the evolution of contractual provisions over time, and this learning may result in the development of firm-specific contract design capabilities that may become a source of competitive advantage.
- Ariño, Ragozzino and Reuer examine the experiences of small firms in renegotiating their alliance contracts. Their findings show that although small firms are no more or less likely to renegotiate alliances than other firms, they tend to adjust their alliances less in the face of governance misalignments. In addition, small firms make higher levels of transaction-specific investments without introducing appropriate contractual safeguards, which can trigger contractual renegotiations at later stages of an alliance development.

Conclusions

Several themes emerge from this collection of papers, and they all deserve more attention in future research. First, we see more and more studies that offer detailed investigations into the governance mechanisms supporting interfirm collaborations. This partially reflects growing maturity in the alliance field more generally, and it contrasts the comparatively broad treatments of alliance governance in some of the seminal works in the field. As noted earlier, alliance governance was typically examined through the use of coarse categories such as alliances versus M&A, equity versus non-equity alliances, and the like. Addressing these alliance investment and design choices has been, and will remain, very important in the literature, yet studies are increasingly examining specific features of alliance governance such as ownership levels, allocations of control rights, and so forth. Studies appearing in this volume have begun to examine what explains why firms use particular governance mechanisms in alliances, and in future research scholars might examine the implications of these choices and how they relate to other alliance phenomena such as process dimensions of collaboration and the organizational and managerial context of alliance formation and management (e.g. the structure of the alliance group, knowledge management tools, use of third party experts, etc.).

Second, we see a greater emphasis on the dynamic aspects of alliance governance decisions. For instance, in this volume several chapters examine a number of questions such as how alliances might be used as sequential investment vehicles to enter new markets or acquire another firm, how governance mechanisms change as partners develop multiple alliances over time with each other or others, and how individual dyads are renegotiated in the face of governance misalignments or opportunities to hold up a partner who has made investments specific to a relationship. Several opportunities to extend this research stand out. This work might be connected to process studies of alliances in order to study alliance contracting as well as its effects on the costs of negotiating alliances and the evolution of collaborations. There is also a question of whether the dynamics of a single alliance reflect or prompt changes in the direct and indirect ties a firm has through its interorganizational network, so it may be important to situate individual alliances' governance dynamics in this broader context. There is a dearth of studies on alliance implementation, so studies by scholars studying human resource management or organizational behaviour would be welcome to examine the causes and consequences of various types of alliance dynamics at the individual or group level by investigating managerial capabilities to manage alliances, career considerations, and the functioning of teams within and across organizations, to name a few.

Finally, research on relational governance and work on formal governance have often been conducted by different authors with different assumptions about managerial behaviour, and we are seeing the benefits of studies that empirically investigate the interplay between formal and relational governance mechanisms supporting alliances. Conventional wisdom has held that the two substitute for one another, yet there is emerging evidence presented in this volume that there are opportunities for complementarities, and longitudinal research is beginning to show how formal governance mechanisms might stimulate relational norms or vice-versa. Future research would be valuable that disentangles the benefits or costs of the various mechanisms underlying relational governance such as different forms of trust, the development of interorganizational routines, reduction of information asymmetries, expectations for future exchange, and so forth.

Let us close by thanking several people without whose help this volume, and the conference that helped develop the ideas contained in it, could not have been possible. Generous financial support for this project was provided by the Anselmo Rubiralta Center for Globalization and Strategy at IESE Business School, University of Navarra. We would also like to thank John Bell (Philips International BV) and Antoni Valverde (Freshfields Bruckhaus Deringer) for sharing their experiences and expertise on the managerial and legal aspects of alliance contracting. During the conference and preparation of the book, a number of staff members and doctoral students at IESE offered their assistance, for which we are grateful: Gemma Golobardes, Elena Golovko, Kerem Gurses, Caterina Moschieri, Guillermo Nesi, Giovanni Valentini and Hugo Zarco. We also wish to offer special thanks to several scholars who served as facilitators during the conference and offered developmental reviews on the chapters contained in the volume: Tina Dacin (Queens' University), Estaban Garcia-Canal (University of Oviedo), Carlos Garcia-Pont (IESE Business School, University of Navarra), Arvind Parkhe (Temple University), Brian Silverman (University of Toronto) and Stephen Tallman (University of Richmond). Last, but not least, we are especially grateful to Francisco and José Mª Rubiralta whose generosity has made this project possible, as well as other activities of the Anselmo Rubiralta Center at IESE.

Notes

1. Africa Ariño, Avda. Pearson, 21, 08034, Barcelona, Spain, E-mail: afarino@iese.edu
2. Jeffrey J. Reuer. Kenan-Flagler Business School, University of North Carolina, Campus Box 3490, McColl 4603, Chapel Hill, NC 27599-3490. USA. E-mail: reuer@unc.edu

References

Ariño, A. and Reuer, J. J. (2005) 'Alliance Contractual Design', in O. Shenkar and J. J. Reuer (eds), *Handbook of Strategic Alliances*, Newbury Park, CA: Sage Publications.

James, H. S., Jr. (2000) 'Separating Contract from Governance', *Managerial and Decision Economics*, 21: 47–61.

Reuer, J. J. (2004) *Strategic Alliances: Theory and Evidence*, Oxford: Oxford University Press.

Shenkar, O. and Reuer, J. J. (2005) *Handbook of Strategic Alliances*, Newbury Park, CA: Sage Publications.

Williamson, O. E. (1979) 'Transaction-cost Economics: the Governance of Contractual Relations', *Journal of Law and Economics*, 22: 233–61.

Part I
Governance of Strategic Alliances

2

The Need for Scale as a Driver of Alliance Formation: Choosing Between Collaborative and Autonomous Production

Bernard Garrette,[1] *Xavier Castañer*[2] *and Pierre Dussauge**[3]

Introduction

In this chapter, we reconsider why firms choose to form horizontal alliances when launching a new product rather than to undertake such a project on their own. We observe that past work on alliance formation has focused on resource complementarity as the main driver for interfirm collaboration and, on this basis, has identified firm characteristics that induce them to collaborate. We propose that scale-related motives are also a major driver of alliance formation and argue that firms forming scale alliances exhibit different profiles than those forming complementary alliances.

Recent work on alliance formation claims that a firm's propensity to collaborate results from both need and opportunity (Eisenhardt and Schoonhoven, 1996; Ahuja, 2000). Indeed, firms will consider collaborating when they do not possess the full range of resources required to carry out an activity alone; conversely, they will only have opportunities to collaborate provided they possess valuable resources that make them attractive to potential partners. In other words, firms tend to collaborate when their strengths compensate for a potential partner's weaknesses while their weaknesses are compensated by the partner's strengths. A typical example is a start-up firm having developed a breakthrough innovation teaming up with an established industry incumbent possessing strong marketing capabilities (Teece, 1986). This view of alliance formation suggests that the main driver of interfirm collaboration is the complementarity in the resources owned by the various partners (Shan, 1990; Mitchell and Singh, 1992). Recent empirical work on alliance formation finds indeed that a firm is most likely to form alliances when it is simultaneously strong in some resource categories and weak in others (Ahuja, 2000). We claim that this result stems from the type of alliances studied in most existing research, i.e. predominantly complementary alliances.

We propose that the complementarity view of interfirm collaboration does not apply to all types of alliances. As suggested by prior literature (Hennart, 1988; Kogut, 1988; Sakakibara, 1997; Dussauge et al., 2000, 2004), we argue that alliance formation can also be motivated by the pursuit of scale benefits. In other words, firms may be led to collaborate not so much because they lack one kind of resource altogether but because, regardless of any resource type in particular, their overall resource endowment is too limited in quantity for them to undertake the considered project on their own. In this perspective, firms do not form alliances only to exploit complementary resources but may also decide to collaborate in order to pool similar resources. In this view, alliance formation is still motivated by a need, i.e. a lack of sufficient critical resources. The opportunity to cooperate, however, is quite different in nature: it stems from the existence of potential partners with similar needs rather than from the availability of potential partners with complementary resources.

Thus, in this chapter, we focus on scale alliances and examine the factors that lead a firm to undertake a project in collaboration rather than autonomously. This different focus leads us to formulate predictions on alliance formation that differ from most previous work which we claim has largely overlooked such scale alliances. As argued, in scale alliances, the benefit of collaborating is to jointly overcome the common need for critical resources. However, collaborating also has a cost (Kogut, 1989; Hamel et al., 1989) and, logically, firms will engage in alliances only when the benefits of collaboration exceed its cost (Contractor and Lorange, 1988; Gulati, 1998). We argue that weaker firms have a greater need than larger ones to form scale alliances and will therefore find greater relative benefits in collaboration. Indeed, firms with limited resource endowments will often be faced with the dilemma of either collaborating or not undertaking the project altogether. Stronger firms will generally have the option of carrying out the project on their own and have little incentive to incur the cost associated with collaboration. As a consequence, we predict that the firms most likely to form scale alliances are weaker firms.

Background

Early theoretical work on alliance formation suggested that two main motivations lead firms to enter into alliances within their industry: (i) increasing efficiency and/or market power, and (ii) exploiting asset complementarity and/or acquiring new capabilities (Mariti and Smiley, 1983; Ghemawat et al., 1986; Porter and Fuller, 1986; Kogut, 1988; Hennart, 1988; Nohria and Garcia-Pont, 1991). These motivations are necessary drivers of alliance formation but could be achieved through other means (market transactions or industry consolidation). Transaction cost arguments have thus been introduced to justify when alliances become the preferred option (Hennart, 1988; Kogut, 1988).

Early empirical studies tried to discriminate between the two above-mentioned motivations. Results showing that larger firms had a greater propensity to form alliances provided support for a market power argument (Berg and Friedman, 1978) while the observation that firms forming alliances operated in slightly different industry segments supported the complement-arity/capability acquisition rationale (Berg and Friedman, 1981).

More recently, numerous empirical studies have examined how these motivations are related to both industry-level (Ghemawat et al., 1986; Harrigan, 1988; Nohria and Garcia-Pont, 1991; Burgers et al., 1993; Gulati, 1998) and firm-level factors conducive to the formation of alliances. Studies on firm-level factors have focused on the following characteristics of those firms likely to have the highest propensity to form alliances: firm size, competitive position, product portfolio and resource endowment (Shan, 1990; Mitchell and Singh, 1992; Eisenhardt and Schoonhoven, 1996; Ahuja, 2000).

Shan (1990) examined firm-level determinants that lead high-technology start-up firms to team up with established companies to commercialize an innovation rather than to go to market alone. The results of this study show that smaller firms and industry followers are more likely to collaborate, while larger competitors and technology leaders tend to favour independent market entry. This suggests that the main driver of alliance formation is an insufficient stock of critical resources. All the firms examined in this study are high-tech start-ups that provide their established partner with a valuable innovation, thus creating new business opportunities for this partner.

Mitchell and Singh (1992) focused on the other party in alliances, i.e. industry incumbents that choose to collaborate with innovators to expand into a new technical domain. Their results demonstrate that stronger competitors are more prone than weaker players to form pre-entry alliances, suggesting that more attractive partners are presented with more alliance opportunities and can therefore more easily enter into promising partnership agreements. This appears to contradict Shan's (1990) conclusions. However, Mitchell and Singh (1992) also found, like Shan (1990), that latecomers into the new domain are more likely to collaborate. This suggests that alliance formation is induced by both a need, as argued previously by Shan (1990), and opportunities stemming from a firm's attractiveness as a potential partner.

Eisenhardt and Schoonhoven (1996) have explicitly built on this view, claiming that alliance formation is driven by both strategic needs and social opportunities. In a study on entrepreneurial semiconductor firms, they have shown that firms tend to enter alliance agreements when they are in a vulnerable strategic position, either because they are competing in emergent or highly competitive industries or because they are pursuing pioneering technical strategies, which the authors interpret as denoting a strategic need. Eisenhardt and Schoonhoven (1996) also found that the studied firms were more likely to collaborate when they were in 'strong social positions', i.e led by large, experienced and well-connected top management teams, which they interpret as creating greater opportunities for collaboration.

The above-mentioned studies examine alliances formed by small innovative firms with established industry incumbents. Such an endeavour creates a high degree of complementarity between potential partners, suggesting in turn that this complementarity is the primary driver of alliance formation (Teece, 1986). The general conclusion of these studies is twofold: those small innovating start-ups most likely to collaborate are the weaker or more vulnerable firms; in contrast, those industry incumbents most likely to cooperate with such start-ups are the stronger competitors. Indeed, all start-ups are potentially attractive partners because of the innovation they can contribute to the alliance; those most likely to cooperate are the firms that are the least able to exploit their innovation on their own. Conversely, most established incumbents seek innovations with which to expand their business, those most likely to cooperate are those in a position to cherry-pick and exploit the most promising innovations thanks to their manufacturing and commercial capabilities.

Ahuja (2000) extended the same line of reasoning to alliance formation among leading incumbents in a mature industry. Consistent with the above argument, he found that industry incumbents with the highest propensity to collaborate are those that have greater technical or commercial capital. Based on the argument that alliance formation is driven by both inducements and opportunities, he also found that simultaneous ownership of strong technical and commercial capital reduced a firm's propensity to collaborate. In other words, firms most likely to collaborate are those that are strong in some resource categories and seek a complement in some other resource category. Again, Ahuja (2000) finds that opportunities to collaborate are a function of the firms' attractiveness and that collaboration is induced by some resource need.

In sum, all these studies on firm-level factors driving alliance formation have in fact focused on complementary (link) alliances. However, as mentioned earlier, theories on motivations for alliance formation argue that access to complementary resources is only one of two possible alliance motivations (e.g. Hennart, 1988). Empirical work on alliance activity in various industries bears this distinction by showing that both scale and link alliances coexist in most industry settings, are formed by firms pertaining to different strategic groups and lead to contrasted outcomes (Nohria and Garcia-Pont, 1991; Dussauge et al., 2000, 2004). Little is known, however, on the firm-level factors that drive firms to form scale alliances. While one of the main findings of studies on complementary alliances is that those industry incumbents most likely to collaborate are the leading competitors in the industry, we argue that focusing on scale alliances leads to opposite predictions: those industry incumbents most likely to form scale alliances are competitors in a weaker position.

Theory development

Following Hennart (1988), we use the scale-link typology of alliances. This typology categorizes alliances according to the partners' contributions to the joint activity. Scale alliances, in which partners contribute similar resources for the same stages in the value chain, aim at producing economies of scale for those activities that firms carry out in collaboration. Link alliances, in contrast, aim at combining different skills and resources from each partner. Link alliances include partnerships in which one partner provides market access to products or technologies that the other firm has developed. Scale alliances primarily produce efficiency gains by pooling similar assets from the partners, carrying out business activities in which both firms have experience.

The classical resource-based approach (Penrose, 1959) suggests that a firm's resource endowment determines its growth. Indeed, according to Penrose (1959), most resources are fungible, that is, they can be redeployed to additional uses, other than the current one. The same argument has been applied to more intangible competences (Prahalad and Hamel, 1990; Teece et al., 1997: 529).

Building on this resource-based view of firm growth, we propose that scale alliances are formed primarily within the partner firms' core business, while link alliances are formed to pursue expansion opportunities at the frontiers of the partner firms' current businesses. Combining different resources through link alliances is unnecessary in business areas where firms are already active because, by definition, such firms possess all the categories of discrete resources needed to operate. Combining different resources may in contrast create innovation opportunities (Brown and Eisenhardt, 1995) that allow the partner firms to extend the limits of their existing business, either by entering adjacent product-market areas or by substituting existing products and technologies with innovative ones. On the contrary, pooling greater quantities of similar resources in scale alliances favours growth within the boundaries of the core business by enhancing efficiency on current product lines or by mobilizing sufficient resources to fuel the ongoing renewal of product lines. Innovation in scale alliances is not radically different from what each partner would have achieved on its own, had it had sufficient resources. In contrast, innovation in link alliances stems from the combination of different resources contributed respectively by each partner and could not be achieved by any partner on its own: such innovation is likely to take place outside the scope of the core business of either partner. Indeed, most empirical research on alliances, which we argued focuses on link alliances, conceptualizes these alliances as mechanisms to take advantage of business opportunities that would have been outside the reach of each partner on its own: Mitchell and Singh (1992) examine how alliances between incumbents and innovators allow entry into new technical sub-fields of the industry;

Shan (1990), as well as Eisenhardt and Schoonhoven (1996), study how start-ups and established competitors collaborate in order to market new technologies. The few studies that explicitly consider scale alliances (Nohria and Garcia-Pont, 1991; Dussauge and Garrette, 1995; Dussauge et al., 2000, 2004) show that such alliances are formed by direct competitors exhibiting similar features (size, geographic origin, etc.), all facing similar issues, which choose to collaborate in order to maintain or enhance their position in their core business.

Because of these distinctive resource features of scale and link alliances, the decision to form one or the other type of alliance is an alternative to radically different baseline strategies. Scale alliances are essentially an alternative to autonomous production in the firm's core business. Link alliances, in contrast, are formed primarily to pursue new business developments that would be left aside if no partnering opportunities were available. In other words, in scale alliances, partnering firms face the choice of collaborating or going it alone; in link alliances, partnering firms face the choice of collaborating or forgoing a new business opportunity.

In a context where it might consider forming a scale alliance, a firm possessing resources (assumed here to be fungible) in sufficient quantities is more likely to choose autonomous production over collaboration because of the financial, organizational and strategic cost of cooperating with a competitor (e.g. Hamel, 1991). If, on the contrary, the focal firm lacks sufficient resources and rejects collaboration, it will be forced to give up the considered investment altogether and therefore compromise growth or even on-going presence in entire areas of its core business, the only other choice being to merge.

In contrast, in a position where firms might consider forming a link alliance, most of them will not have the option of pursuing the same new business opportunity on their own, at least in the short run. In such a context, a firm can choose not to form the alliance and not to implement the considered project, without jeopardizing its position or growth in its core business. In this case, taking advantage of such a business opportunity alone will require the acquisition of different resources, and therefore lead to either long-term investments to develop such resources internally or to the acquisition of an existing firm that possesses the needed resources. Overall, scale alliances are primarily defensive in nature while link alliances support more offensive strategies. It can be noted here that scale and link alliances are not substitutes for one another. In other words, a firm is almost never confronted with the choice of forming either a scale or a link alliance. Instead, firms face one of the following two choices: (i) forming a scale alliance or producing autonomously, or (ii) forming a link alliance or not engaging in the considered project.

Given the differences between scale and link alliances outlined above, it is unlikely that those factors leading firms to form link alliances will also motivate the formation of scale alliances. As most past research on alliance formation has implicitly focused on link alliances, their conclusions may not be generalizable to all alliance types. Research focusing specifically on the formation of scale alliances would contribute to a broader understanding of collaboration as an alternative to other strategic and organizational choices. In addition, most existing research has examined the propensity of firms to collaborate, and has thus compared collaboration to non-collaboration, which implicitly includes both producing alone and not engaging in the considered project. Our focus on scale alliances leads us to contrast firms choosing to collaborate with firms choosing to produce autonomously.

In scale alliances, the very coexistence of similar needs in multiple industry incumbents creates the opportunity for collaboration. Indeed, if several firms are simultaneously limited in their growth by a constrained stock of resources, they have a mutual incentive to pool their resources in order to undertake activities jointly. While the benefits of scale advantages can theoretically accrue to all industry incumbents, the costs of collaboration create a disincentive to collaborate. Collaboration costs include coordination costs, the risks associated with mutual dependence as well as a competitive risk (Hamel, 1991). Only those firms that most need additional stocks of a given resource contributed by other partners will engage in scale alliances. Stronger competitors have the option to produce on their own. Moreover, stronger firms will be reluctant to enter into scale alliances because the costs and risks involved will more than outweigh the expected benefits. Hence, the following proposition:

> *Scale alliances are predominantly formed by weaker competitors seeking to maintain or enhance their position in their core business.*

Evidence from aircraft production

To provide empirical support for the above proposition, we examined new product development project launches in the aircraft industry worldwide between 1949 and 2000. We studied 334 new aircraft projects undertaken either through alliances or on a single-firm basis by all 130 major aircraft manufacturers in the Western hemisphere. In this industry, we considered as horizontal alliances those projects that were carried out by several firms sharing the prime contracting responsibility. In contrast to collaborative projects, we defined as autonomous projects those projects that were implemented under the authority of a single prime contractor. This definition of autonomous production does not preclude outsourcing large parts of the project to suppliers, including through vertical partnerships.

Sharing the prime contracting responsibility in aircraft production results in the formation of scale alliances since all prime contracting partners contribute resources in all major functional areas: R&D, manufacturing, marketing and sales. Because the industry is characterized by considerable and ever-increasing economies of scale (Hartley, 1991), new aircraft projects require the mobilization of substantial resources that may be beyond the reach of any individual company even when the company in question has produced similar products in the past (Hartley and Martin, 1990; Dussauge and Garrette, 1995). The resources required to launch a new project include both tangible and intangible resources such as R&D facilities and capabilities, manufacturing assets, and access to large enough markets.

As expected, we find that aircraft manufacturers are more likely to form scale alliances rather than to autonomously undertake a new aircraft project when:

• they are small relative to their industry peers;
• they have access to a smaller market base; and
• their experience in the considered product category is more limited.

These results support the idea according to which scale alliances are primarily formed by weaker competitors.

Conclusion

Overall, the extant literature on link alliances and our results on scale alliances suggest that scale and link alliances exhibit more radical differences that usually thought. They differ in their motivations: scale alliances are formed to pool resources that all partners possess but in quantities too limited to achieve their goals; link alliances are formed to complement one partner's set of resources with a different set of resources possessed by the other partner. Firms enter into scale alliances in order to maintain or grow their position in their core business while they form link alliances to seize new business opportunities. Because of this, scale and link alliances are alternatives to contrasted baseline strategies: scale alliances are essentially an alternative to autonomous production, while link alliances are an alternative to forgoing the considered new business opportunity altogether. Scale alliances are formed primarily for defensive purposes while link alliances support expansion strategies. Logically, scale alliances are formed by firms in a weaker and more vulnerable position while those firms best positioned to take advantage of opportunities afforded by link alliances are the dominant competitors in the industry. Finally, as shown in prior work, scale and link alliances raise different management issues, create different levels of risk and lead to contrasted outcomes (Dussauge et al., 2000, 2004). Indeed, scale alliances primarily raise efficiency issues while link alliances create mutual dependence between the partners and can result in potentially damaging interpartner learning (Hamel, 1991).

Notes

*We would like to acknowledge the research support of the Atos-Origin Chair on 'Growth Strategies and Integration Management' and the HEC-GREGHEC-CNRS pole on growth as well as the research assistance of Louis Mulotte. We are also grateful to participants at the HEC EMO research seminar, the 2004 Strategic Management Society Conference, the 2005 IESE workshop on alliances, and the 2005 Academy of Management, for their insightful comments and encouragement. All remaining errors are ours.

1. Bernard Garrette, Atos-Origin Associate Professor, HEC School of Management, Paris, Département Stratégie et Politique d'Entreprise, 78351 JOUY-EN-JOSAS cedex, E-mail: garrette@hec.fr
2. Xavier Castañer, HEC School of Management, Paris, Département Stratégie et Politique d'Entreprise, 78351 JOUY-EN-JOSAS cedex, E-mail: castañer@hec.fr
3. Pierre Dussauge, HEC School of Management, Paris, Département Stratégie et Politique d'Entreprise, 78351 JOUY-EN-JOSAS cedex, Tel: +33 1 39 67 72 79, Fax: +33 1 39 67 70 84, E-mail: dussauge@hec.fr

References

Ahuja, G. (2000) 'The Duality of Collaboration: Inducements and Opportunities in the Formation of Interfirm Linkages', *Strategic Management Journal*, 21(3): 317–43.

Berg, S. and Friedman, P. (1978) 'Technological Complementarities and Industrial Patterns of Joint Venture Activity, 1964–1975', *Industrial Organization Review*, 6: 110–16.

Berg, S. and Friedman, P. (1981) 'Impacts of Domestic Joint Ventures on Industrial Rates of Return: a "Pooled Cross-Section Analysis"', *Review of Economics and Statistics*, 63: 293–8.

Brown, S. and Eisenhardt, K. (1995) 'Product Development: Past Research, Present Findings, and Future Prospects', *Academy of Management Review*, 20: 343–79.

Burgers, W. P., Hill, C. W. L. and Kim, W. C. (1993) 'A Theory of Global Strategic Alliances: the Case of the Global Auto Industry', *Strategic Management Journal*, 14(6): 419–32.

Contractor, F. J. and Lorange, P. (1988) 'Why Should Firms Cooperate? The Strategy and Economics Basis for Cooperative Ventures', in F. J. Contractor and P. Lorange (eds), *Cooperative Strategies in International Business*, Lexington, MA: Lexington Books: 3–31.

Dussauge, P. and Garrette, B. (1995) 'Determinants of Success in International Strategic Alliances: Evidence from the Global Aerospace Industry', *Journal of International Business Studies*, 26(3): 505–30.

Dussauge, P., Garrette, B. and Mitchell, W. (2000) 'Learning from Competing Partners: Outcomes and Durations of Scale and Link Alliances in Europe, North America and Asia', *Strategic Management Journal*, 21(2): 99–126.

Dussauge, P., Garrette, B. and Mitchell, W. (2004) 'Asymmetric Performance: the Market Share Impact of Scale and Link Alliances in the Global Auto Industry', *Strategic Management Journal*, 25(7): 701–11.

Eisenhardt, K. M. and Schoonhoven, C. B. (1996) 'Resource-Based View of Strategic Alliance Formation: Strategic and Social Effects in Entrepreneurial Firms', *Organization Science*, 7(2): 136–50.

Ghemawat, P. et al (1986) 'Patterns of International Coalition Activity', in M. E. Porter (ed.), *Competition in Global Industries*, Boston, Harvard Business School Press: 345–66.

Gulati, R. (1998) 'Alliances and Networks', *Strategic Management Journal*, 19(4): 293–317.

Hamel, G. (1991) 'Competition for Competence and Inter-Partner Learning Within International Strategic Alliances', *Strategic Management Journal*, 12 (Special Issue: Global Strategy): 83–103.

Hamel, G., Doz, Y. and Prahalad, C. K. (1989) 'Collaborate with Your Competitors – and Win', *Harvard Business Review*, 67(1): 133–9.

Harrigan, K. R. (1988) 'Joint Ventures and Competitive Strategy', *Strategic Management Journal*, 9(2): 141–58.

Hartley, K. (1991) *The Economics of Defence Policy*, London: Bassey's.

Hartley, K. and Martin, S. (1990) 'International Collaboration in Aerospace', *Science and Public Policy*, 17: 143–51.

Hennart, J.-F. (1988) 'A Transaction Costs Theory of Equity Joint Ventures', *Strategic Management Journal*, 9(4): 361–74.

Hergert, M. and Morris, D. (1987) 'Trends in International Collaborative Agreements', *Columbia Journal of World Business*, 22: 15–21.

Kogut, B. (1988) 'Joint Ventures: Theoretical and Empirical Perspectives', *Strategic Management Journal*, 9(4): 319–32.

Kogut, B. (1989) 'The Stability of Joint Ventures: Reciprocity and Competitive Rivalry', *Journal of Industrial Economics*, 38(2): 183–98.

Mariti, P. and Smiley, R. H. (1983) 'Cooperative Agreements and the Organization of Industry', *Journal of Industrial Economics*, 31(4): 437–51.

Mitchell, W. and Singh, K. (1992) 'Incumbents' Use of Pre-entry Alliances before Expansion into New Technical Subfields of an Industry', *Journal of Economic Behavior and Organization*, 18: 347–72.

Nohria, N. and Garcia-Pont, C. (1991) 'Global Strategic Linkages and Industry Structure', *Strategic Management Journal*, 12 (Special Issue: Global Strategy): 105–24.

Penrose, E. T. (1959) *The Theory of Growth of the Firm*, London: Basil Blackwell.

Porter, M. E. and Fuller, M. B. (1986) 'Coalitions and Global Strategies', in M. E. Porter (ed.), *Competition in Global Industries*, Boston, Harvard Business School Press: 315–43.

Prahalad, C. K. and Hamel, G. (1990) 'The Core Competence of the Corporation', *Harvard Business Review*, 68(3): 79–92.

Sakakibara, M. (1997) 'Heterogeneity of Firm Capabilities and Cooperative Research and Development: an Empirical Examination of Motives', *Strategic Management Journal*, 18 (Summer 1997 Special Issue: Organizational and Competitive Interactions): 143–64.

Shan, W. (1990) 'An Empirical Analysis of Organizational Strategies by Entrepreneurial High-Technology Firms', *Strategic Management Journal*, 11(2): 129–39.

Teece, D. J. (1986) 'Profiting from Technological Innovation', *Research Policy*, 15: 285–305.

Teece, D. J. Pisano, G. and Shuen, A. (1997) 'Dynamic Capabilities and Strategic Management', *Strategic Management Journal*, 18: 509–33.

3
Do Alliances Provide Effective Entry Into a New Line of Business? The Short-Term vs. Long-Term Effects of Entering a New Line of Business Through Alliances

Louis Mulotte,[1] *Pierre Dussauge*[2] *and Will Mitchell*[3]

Introduction

Firms frequently use alliances with incumbents as a means to enter new industries (Ingham and Thompson, 1994; Mitchell and Singh, 1992) or new geographic markets (Kogut and Singh, 1988; Hennart, 1991; Hennart and Reddy, 1997; Barkema and Vermeulen, 1998; Chang and Rosenzweig, 2001; Makino and Neupert, 2000). Scholars have long debated how such entry alliances might influence a firm's subsequent performance. One argument suggests that initial alliances with incumbents contribute to later performance because they help a firm gather the resources required to operate in the targeted business (Hamel, 1991; Simonin, 1999; Mitchell and Singh, 1996; Anand and Khanna, 2000; Inkpen, 2000). A second view emphasizes the risks of alliances: they provide only incomplete access to resources, they create a dependence on partners, they are difficult and costly to manage and, finally, they entail profit sharing (Hamel et al., 1989; Balakrishnan and Koza, 1993; Park and Russo, 1996). Traditionally, much of the performance debate has focused on identifying circumstances that benefit from alliance entry and those that suit independent entry.

A third possibility, though, is that the alliances themselves have little impact on performance, but instead firms with different capabilities choose different entry strategies and it is the differences in initial capabilities that cause most differences in post-entry performance. In a parallel literature, Shaver (1998) showed that survival differences that appeared to arise from the choice between greenfield and acquisition entry strategies actually stemmed primarily from differences in firm capabilities that influenced firms' entry strategy choices. Recent studies have begun to examine this question in the context of alliances. Singh and Mitchell (2005), for instance, show that business growth that follows entry by alliance is at least partly an endogenous outcome of the factors that influence firms' choice of alliance or independent entry. Despite such initial studies, there is still only limited understanding of how much alliances themselves contribute to firm performance.

This chapter addresses two questions: what factors drive newcomers to choose between autonomous and alliance-based entry to enter into a new business area and, in turn, do the entry strategies influence subsequent success in the new area of business?

Background

Many studies on new market entry distinguish between wholly-owned operations and joint ownership of a venture with a partner (Hennart, 1991; Makino and Neupert, 2000; Brouthers, 2002). There is a reasonable consensus on the fact that firms favour wholly-owned entry when expansion takes place in highly related domains. In the case of international expansion, this leads to choosing wholly-owned entry when host and home country are culturally and institutionally similar (Hennart, 1991; Hennart and Park, 1993; Hennart and Reddy, 1997; Barkema and Vermeulen, 1998; Brouthers and Brouthers, 2000; Makino and Neupert, 2000; Chang and Rosenzweig, 2001). In the case of diversification, firms tend to favour wholly-owned investments when the resource gap between existing and targeted activities is small (Ingham and Thompson, 1994; Chang and Singh, 1999). In contrast, though, Mitchell and Singh (1992) found that stronger competitors are more likely to use pre-entry alliances when considering diversification into a new emerging technical sub-field of their industry. In doing this, Mitchell and Singh shift the definition of what are considered wholly-owned versus jointly-owned operations. Contrary to prior studies, they do not focus on ownership of the business unit carrying out the new activity, but examine the governance of pre-entry operations: they compare firms that first collaborated in the new area before fully entering, with firms that enter on their own without prior collaboration.

Most studies of entry strategies focus on the first foothold that firms establish in the new business area. Thus, when examining factors that favour the choice of one entry strategy over another, scholars have compared firms that immediately establish an autonomous presence in the business by entering independently to firms that form an initial alliance in the new business, whether or not the entry alliance eventually results in an autonomous presence. Such studies do not distinguish between alliances that firms form as a first step towards an autonomous presence and alliances that firms form to implement a short-term project, without planning on subsequent independence. Mitchell and Singh (1992) are among the few who explicitly address this issue, by exploring factors favouring the use of pre-entry alliances by firms that later undertook independent activity within emerging technical sub-fields of their industry. In line with this approach, our study explores the effectiveness of alliances as entry mechanisms that firms use as initial steps towards autonomous activity.

An extensive stream of research has investigated how entry mode choice influences firms' subsequent performance in their new domain. When examining international expansion, much of this research has found that the degree of ownership has little influence on performance (Delios and Beamish, 2001; Vermeulen and Barkema, 2002). When significant results do appear, they are often contradictory. Vermeulen and Barkema (2001) and Pan and Chi (1999) found that partial ownership led to greater perform-ance than full ownership, for instance, while Woodcock et al. (1994) and Brouthers (2002) found that wholly-owned operations out-performed equity joint ventures.

Several scholars have suggested that the ambiguity surrounding the performance impact of different entry modes stems from the endogeneity of mode choice (Shaver, 1998; Hamilton and Nickerson, 2003). Building on this approach, Brouthers (2002) and Brouthers et al. (2003) found that the apparent performance benefit of entering a new market through wholly-owned ventures became insignificant when accounting for endogeneity. By contrast, a recent study by Singh and Mitchell (2005) found that, even controlling for endogeneity, entry alliances with industry incumbents influenced the entrants' business growth, initially enhancing their growth and then constraining it. As in the literature on determinants of entry mode choice, however, most studies that examine how entry mode influences performance have compared the performance of wholly-owned operations to that of alliances in the targeted domain, without determining whether the alliances led to independent entry into the new business area. Thus, these studies do not determine whether entry through alliance influences firms' ability to compete independently.

Our own research aims to extend how we consider the effectiveness of alliances as mechanisms for entry into new business domains. We propose that alliances help weaker competitors overcome entry barriers but that the pre-entry alliances, while creating a short-term advantage, do not enhance long-term performance.

Theory development

While firms often use alliances as an entry mechanism to a new domain, only some firms that form initial alliances later create independent operations in the new business. We define independent entry as the point at which a firm begins to operate on a stand-alone basis in the new business area. In this approach, the alliance itself is an entry device but its formation is not an independent entry. Rather, independent entry occurs when a firm starts operating in the targeted business outside the scope of the alliance and often after dissolution of the alliance. Some firms might choose to continue collaborating on all new products, and would then never achieve independent entry. We consider two possible strategies towards independent entry, which we refer to as direct entry and sequential entry. Direct entry occurs when a firm carries out its first venture into the new business on its own, without prior cooperation with another firm. In contrast, sequential entry involves creating an independent presence in a new business area only after having cooperated with another firm to establish an initial foothold in the targeted business. Based on these definitions, we now turn to developing two sets of arguments: on the factors that drive the choice of entry strategies, and on the influence of entry strategy on subsequent performance of the new business.

Determinants of entry strategy choice

When assessing entry into a new area, all potential entrants lack domain-specific resources in the targeted line of business. However, different potential entrants differ in their ability to mobilize and redeploy the necessary resources. Following Barney (1986) we consider two main types of resources: (1) domain-specific resources, and (2) generic resources, such as financial assets.

Domain-specific resources are competences and assets that are required to operate successfully in a particular business area, and which cannot be easily redeployed from other business areas. Such resources encompass basic technical skills and assets, market knowledge, product development capabilities, production and sales capabilities. Domain-specific resources are idiosyncratic to the business area and must be purposely developed or at least significantly adapted to the considered business.

We define generic resources as those assets and competences that are readily redeployable across business areas. Generic resources include financial assets, unspecialized labour, facilities and equipment that firms can easily reallocate to different uses. Though such resources theoretically can be easily obtained through open market mechanisms, market imperfections even for such generic factors often make them easier to mobilize rapidly within firms.

Of course, these two types of resources – domain-specific and generic – are not mutually exclusive resource categories, but rather opposite extremes on the same continuum. In addition, although they cannot be substituted for one another, the availability of generic resources can facilitate and speed the development of domain-specific resources, making it easier for firms rich in generic resources to compensate for their lack of domain-specific resources. Likewise, resources are domain-specific in a relative way: some resources can be more easily redeployed into a new business area than others. In other words, a firm's resources can be more or less related to the domain-specific resources required in the new business area it seeks to enter.

We propose that a firm will be more likely to enter a new business domain through pre-entry alliances when:

(1a) the resource gap between the firm's resource endowment and the domain-specific resource requirements is greater;
(1b) the firm's generic resource endowment is more limited, thus decreasing its ability to develop or obtain the necessary domain-specific resources.

Influence on performance of entry strategy choice

We now turn to considering how entry strategy will influence post-entry success. Based on our definition of independent entry, we cannot examine entry strategy success by comparing the relative performance of collaborative versus autonomous activities. Instead, we need to compare the performance of firms that operate on their own following either direct or sequential entry.

When assessing how entry strategy might influence post-entry success, we need to recognize that the factors we argue are driving entry strategy choice might also influence success directly. Indeed, the resources that a firm possesses will have a strong impact on the success of any venture it undertakes. If we want to meaningfully compare post-entry success of direct versus sequential entry strategies, we need to take into account the endogeneity of entry mode choice.

Sequential entry provides a firm with business domain experience before independent entry occurs. Numerous scholars have argued that experience is an effective learning mechanism. Nerkar and Roberts (2004: 781) found that firms with previous product–market participation enhance their new products' success, concluding that 'experience leads to better understanding of market conditions and customer needs'. Similarly, Mitchell and Singh (1992) concluded that previous experience increases technological knowledge, which also translates into more valuable new products. Consequently, products that firms introduce after undertaking prior collaborative participation may benefit from the firms' previous product–market experience.

In contrast, though, another stream of literature suggests a different view of the impact of experience on subsequent success. Zollo and Winter (2002) argue that experiential learning is essentially of a tacit nature and thus primarily useful when a firm's environment, and thus conditions for success, are relatively static. According to them, learning through experience leads to little understanding of the causal relationships between actions and performance. Thus, experiential learning suits contexts in which the replication of past actions results in similar outcomes, that is, environments in which the conditions for success remain unchanged. In the particular case of new product introduction, these observations suggest that experiential learning will produce its greatest benefits in the short term, when environmental, technical and competitive conditions remain fairly stable, while it will be

Inappropriate when conditions change substantially, i.e. over several generations of new products.

In addition, Zollo and Reuer (2003) argue that experience can have detrimental effects on performance. Indeed, learning through experience may give firms a false sense of confidence that can jeopardize the success of future products and endanger the very survival of the operation in the new business line (Balakrishnan and Koza, 1993; Park and Russo, 1996). More specifically, alliances generate only partial learning that may prove insufficient to successfully carry out stand-alone activities. Previous experience gained through alliances may thus cause superstitious learning (Levitt and March, 1988; Levinthal and March, 1993; Zollo and Reuer, 2003) and over-confidence in a firm's own capabilities (Hayward and Hambrick, 1997; Durand, 2003) that will hinder future long-term success.

To push these arguments further, we distinguish between short-term performance and long-term survival. We expect that pre-entry experience that a firm acquires through alliances will enhance the firm's chances of successfully launching a first new product on its own. Therefore, we argue that sequential entry will increase short-term post-entry success.

Over-confidence, in turn, will primarily arise as a consequence of past success, especially if the firm achieves the success with the assistance of a partner and without confronting all the related hurdles and difficulties. Therefore, a firm with pre-entry alliance experience, which subsequently introduces an autonomously developed product, may tend to become over-confident in its own abilities relative to the new market, may over-extend its investments and its exposure in the new business line and, as a result, may be more vulnerable to environmental shocks that affect the business at a later date. On the contrary, firms entering directly will have had to overcome greater hurdles without the support from partners, will have encountered more limited success with their first product introduction, and will therefore be more perceptive in their future ventures in the considered business line.

Firms that enter sequentially might also be more prone to attempt to replicate past routines that they adopted from their partner, which in the short term can prove effective but in the long term make it more difficult to successfully adjust to changes in the environment because they do not understand the basis of the routines. Firms entering directly, in contrast, will have had to progressively develop new resources on their own from the start, which may be detrimental in the short term but will provide better abilities to adjust to changes in the medium and long term.

Based on these arguments we propose that:

(2a) firms using sequential entry will achieve greater short-term success than firms using direct entry;
(2b) firms using direct entry will achieve greater long-term success than firms using sequential entry.

Empirical evidence from the aerospace industry

We tested our predictions on a sample of 159 firms that entered one of the four sub-fields of the aircraft industry (fighter aircraft, turboprop aircraft, rotorcraft, and jet transport aircraft) between 1944 and 2000.

In the first step of our analysis we analysed the factors driving the choice of direct entry over sequential entry. In the second stage of our model, we analysed the influence of entry strategy on post-entry success while accounting for the endogeneity of the choice. Because we needed to distinguish between short-term and long-term success, we used two dependent variables: (1) we assessed short-term performance by recording the cumulative sales of the firm's first autonomously developed aircraft programme and (2) we assessed long-term performance by recording how long the firm's independent operation in the new line of business survived. In both models, our independent variable was the *entry strategy* dummy variable; we also took into account the possible endogeneity of the entry strategy choice.

Results

The results support our predictions. First, both types of resources influence entry mode choices, such that a firm's domain-specific resource endowment (proposition 1a) and a firm's stock of generic resources (proposition 1b) favour the choice of direct entry over sequential entry.

Second, entry mode strategy affects short-term and long-term performance. Moreover, as we expected, we found that the endogeneity of entry strategy choice should be assessed when studying post-entry performance. In turn, experience gained through the use of alliances has a significantly positive influence on short-term performance in the form of the cumulated sales of the first autonomously developed product (proposition 2a). Pre-entry alliances detract from long-term performance, however, because firms that enter a new sub-field directly enjoy a longer post-entry presence when compared to firms that use a sequential entry (proposition 2b).

Overall, several results stand out. We found that weaker competitors select sequential entry in order to overcome entry barriers, as compensation for limited domain-specific and generic resources. We also verified that entry strategy is endogenous and should be taken into account when studying the performance impact of entry strategy. Finally, we found that the use of pre-entry alliances enhances short-term success but has a negative influence on long-term success, even when endogeneity of strategy choice is accounted for.

Conclusion

This research suggests that initial choices at the time of entry, which are affected by pre-entry resources, are critical for post-entry success and survival

(Helfat and Lieberman, 2002). In line with Zollo and Winter (2002) and Zollo and Reuer (2003), this research highlights that experience accumulation is less effective compared to other more deliberate forms of learning (such as autonomous product development in the case of this study). Indeed, we argued and found empirical evidence that experience accumulated may develop over-confidence in one's own competence and does not replace the intentional autonomous development of the required routines needed to effectively develop new products in a high technology context. This illusion of control negatively affects post-entry long-term performance as such intentionally obtained routines are required when changes in the competitive environment call for the introduction of products adjusted to radically new customer needs or incorporating radically new technologies. The illusion of control may also result in unforeseen development problems that lead to time-consuming redesign and ultimately cancel out the benefits of whatever advantage may have been acquired through the use of pre-entry alliances.

In addition to contributing to the alliance literature, our research also adds to the more general literature on dynamic capabilities. This emerging literature is extending resource-based theory by identifying means by which firms create new resources (Teece et al. 1997; Eisenhardt and Martin, 2000; Helfat and Raubitschek, 2000; Karim and Mitchell, 2000). In the context of dynamic capabilities, the choice of sequential or direct entry is a mode choice that is part of the process by which firms create resources that they need to operate in a new environment. That is, sequential entry provides a mechanism by which weaker firms can gain access to other firms' resources. The alliance choice offers short-term benefits but may inhibit the understanding and control that a firm needs to develop a full suite of new resources that it requires for long-term success. By contrast, direct entry forces a firm to develop new resources primarily through its own efforts, leading both to greater understanding of the resources and greater control over them. The most direct implication of this comparison is that the alliance process provides a jump-start in resource creation but may inhibit a firm's ability to create a full set of the new resources, if a firm does not already have sufficient understanding of the resource base on which it is building.

Notes

1. Louis Mulotte, HEC School of Management, Paris, Département Stratégie et Politique d'Entreprise, 78351 JOUY-EN-JOSAS cedex, Tel: +33 1 39 67 72 68, Fax: +33 1 39 67 70 84, E-mail: mulottel@hec.fr
2. Pierre Dussauge, HEC School of Management, Paris, Département Stratégie et Politique d'Entreprise, 78351 JOUY-EN-JOSAS cedex, Tel: +33 1 39 67 72 79, Fax: +33 1 39 67 70 84, E-mail: dussauge@hec.fr
3. Will Mitchell, The Fuqua School of Business, Duke University, Durham, NC 27708-0120, Tel: 919.660.7994, Fax: 919.681.6244, E-mail: Will.Mitchell@duke.edu

References

Anand, B. and Khanna, T. (2000) 'Do Firms Learn to Create Value? The Case of Alliances', *Strategic Management Journal*, 21(3): 295–315.

Balakrishnan, S. and Koza, M. (1993) 'Information Asymmetry, Adverse Selection and Joint Ventures, Theory and Evidence', *Journal of Economic Behavior and Organization*, 20: 99–117.

Barkema, H. and Vermeulen, F. (1998) 'International Expansion Through Start-up or Acquistion: a Learning Perspective', *Academy of Management Journal*, 41(1): 20–7.

Barney, J. (1986) 'Strategic Factor Markets: Expectations, Luck, and Business Strategy', *Management Science*, 32(10): 1231–41.

Brouthers, K. (2002) 'Institutional, Cultural and Transaction Cost Influences on Entry Modes Choice and Performance', *Journal of International Business Studies*, 33(2): 203–21.

Brouthers, K. and Brouthers, L. (2000) 'Acquisition or Greenfield Start-up? Institutional, Cultural and Transaction Cost Influences', *Strategic Management Journal*, 21(1): 89–97.

Brouthers, K., Brouthers, L. and Werner, S. (2003) 'Transaction Cost-enhanced Entry Mode Choices and Firm Performance', *Strategic Management Journal*, 24(12): 1239–48.

Chang, S. and Rosenzweig, P. (2001) 'The Choice of Entry Mode in Sequential Foreign Direct Investment', *Strategic Management Journal*, 22(8): 747–76.

Chang, S. and Singh, H. (1999) 'The Impact of Modes of Entry and Resource Fit on Modes of Exit by Multibusiness Firms', *Strategic Management Journal*, 20(11): 1019–35.

Delios, A. and Beamish, P. (2001) 'Survival and Profitability: the Roles of Experience and Intangible Assets in Foreign Subsidiary Performance', *Academy of Management Journal*, 44(5): 1028–38.

Durand, R. (2003) 'Predicting a Firm's Forecasting Ability: the Roles of Organizational Illusion of Control and Organizational Attention', *Strategic Management Journal*, 24(9): 821–38.

Eisenhardt, K. and Martin, J. (2000) 'Dynamic Capabilities: What Are They?', *Strategic Management Journal*, 21(10–11): 1105–21.

Hamel, G. (1991) 'Competition for Competence and Inter-partner Learning with International Strategic Alliances', *Strategic Management Journal*, 12(SI): 83–103.

Hamel., G., Doz, Y. and Prahalad, C. K. (1989) 'Collaborate With Your Competitors – and Win', *Harvard Business Review*, 67(1): 133–9.

Hamilton, B. and Nickerson, J. (2003) 'Correcting for Endogeneity in Strategic Management Research', *Strategic Organization*, 1(1): 51–78.

Hayward, M. and Hambrick, D. (1997) 'Explaining Premium Paid for Large Acquisitions: Evidence of CEO Hubris', *Administrative Science Quarterly*, 42(1): 103–27.

Helfat, C. and Lieberman, M. (2002) 'The Birth of Capabilities: Market Entry and the Importance of Pre-history', *Industrial and Corporate Change*, 11(4): 725–60.

Helfat, C. and Raubitschek, R. (2000) 'Product Sequencing: Co-evolution of Knowledge, Capabilities and Products', *Strategic Management Journal*, 21(10): 961–80.

Hennart, J.-F. (1991) 'The Transaction Costs Theory of Joint Ventures: an Empirical Study of Japanese Subsidiaries in the US', *Management Science*, 37(4): 483–97.

Hennart, J.-F. and Park, Y.-R. (1993) 'Location, Governance and Strategic Determinants of Japanese Manufacturing Investment in the US', *Strategic Management Journal*, 15(6): 419–36.

Hennart, J.-F. and Reddy, S. (1997) 'The Choice between Mergers/Acquisitions and Joint Ventures: the Case of Japanese Investors in the United States', *Strategic Management Journal*, 18(1): 1–12.

Ingham, H. and Thompson, S. (1994) 'Wholly-owned vs. Collaborative Ventures for Diversifying Financial Services', *Strategic Management Journal*, 15(4): 325–34.

Inkpen, A. (2000) 'A Note on the Dynamics of Learning Alliances: Competition, Cooperation, and Relative Scope', *Strategic Management Journal*, 21(7): 775–9.

Karim, S. and Mitchell, W. (2000) 'Path-dependent and Path-breaking Change Reconfiguring Business Resources Following Acquisitions in the US Medical Sector, 1978–1995', *Strategic Management Journal*, 21(10): 1061–81.

Kogut, B. and Singh, H. (1988) 'The Effects of National Culture on the Choice of Entry Mode', *Journal of International Business Studies*, 19(3): 411–32.

Levinthal, D. and March, J. (1993) 'The Myopia of Learning', *Strategic Management Journal*, 14(8): 95–112.

Levitt, B. and March, J. (1988) 'Organizational Learning', *Annual Review of Sociology*, 14: 319–40.

Makino, S. and Neupert, K. (2000) 'National Culture, Transaction Costs, and the Choice between Joint Ventures and Wholly Owned Subsidiary', *Journal of International Business Studies*, 31(4): 705–13.

Mitchell, W. and Singh, K. (1992) 'Incumbents' Use of Pre-entry Alliances before Expansion into New Technical Subfields of an Industry', *Journal of Economic Behavior and Organization*, 18(3): 347–72.

Mitchell, W. and Singh, K. (1996) 'Survival of Businesses using Collaborative Relationships to Commercialize Complex Goods', *Strategic Management Journal*, 17(3): 169–95.

Nerkar, A. and Roberts, P. (2004) 'Technological and Product-market Experience and the Success of New Product Introductions in the Pharmateutical Industry', *Strategic Management Journal*, 25(8–9): 779–99.

Pan, Y. and Chi, P. S. K. (1999) 'Financial Performance and Survival of Multinational Corporations in China', *Strategic Management Journal*, 20(4): 359–74.

Park, S. and Russo, M. (1996) 'When Competition Eclipses Cooperation: an Event History Analysis of Joint Venture Failure', *Management Science*, 42: 875–90.

Shaver, M. (1998) 'Accounting for Endogeneity When Assessing Strategy Performance: Does Entry Mode Choice affect FDI Survival', *Management Science*, 44(4): 571–85.

Simonin, B. (1999) 'Ambiguity and the Process of Knowledge Transfer in Strategic Alliances', *Strategic Management Journal*, 20(7): 595–623.

Singh, K. and Mitchell, W. (2005) 'Growth Dynamics: the Bidirectional Relationship between Interfirm Collaboration and Business Sales in Entrant and Incumbent Alliances', *Strategic Management Journal*, 26(6): 497–521.

Teece, D., Pisano, G. and Shuen, A. (1997) 'Dynamic Capabilities and Strategic Management', *Strategic Management Journal*, 18(7): 509–30.

Vermeulen, F. and Barkema, H. (2001) 'Learning Through Acquisitions', *Academy of Management Journal*, 44(3): 457–76.

Vermeulen, F. and Barkema, H. (2002) 'Pace, Rhythm, and Scope: Path Dependencies in Benefiting from Internationalization', *Strategic Management Journal*, 23(7): 637–53.

Woodcock, P., Beamish, P. and Makino, S. (1994) 'Ownership-based Entry Strategies and International Performance', *Journal of International Business Studies*, 25(2): 253–73.

Zollo, M. and Reuer, J. (2003) 'Superstitious Learning in Corporate Acquisitions', *INSEAD Working Paper*: 3–31.

Zollo, M. and Winter, S. (2002) 'Deliberate Learning and the Evolution of Dynamic Capabilities', *Organization Science*, 13(6): 701–13.

4
The Bearable Lightness of Interfirm Strategic Alliances: Resource-Based and Procedural Contracting

Anna Grandori[1] and Marco Furlotti[2]

Introduction

Alliances and networks have been analysed along many dimensions and through a variety of theoretical lenses.[3] Nevertheless, a precise characterization of the 'ingredients' of that broad class of governance solutions is still missing. In fact, most analyses of networks and alliances, being disciplinarily bounded, typically consider only a limited set of governance mechanisms. Some studies only concern themselves with broad legal forms (albeit 'extended' to various types of contracting modes, as obligational and relational contracting[4]); others with specific juridically defined contractual schemes (e.g. joint-ventures, franchising, licensing etc.); others still with structures defined simply on property rights (e.g. equity/non-equity alliances), on the organizational mechanisms sustaining cooperation and exchange (brokers, liaison roles, joint decision-making, arbitration, programmes etc.), or on the social mechanisms that embed and affect economic transactions. These 'partial analyses', useful as they are, cannot but overlook the importance of the *combinations* between mechanisms of different nature in effective governance. In previous work, we have opted for a combinative analysis of legal, economic and organizational mechanisms as a way of characterizing and assessing network forms more precisely (Grandori, 1997), arguing that forms of network and alliance can be specified according to the partition and differentiated allocation of property rights, complemented by a selection of coordination mechanisms. On that track, the present chapter takes a step further, inquiring into the mode of formalizing and enforcing those combinations into both private and public documents or 'contracts'.

The specific focus of the analysis is that of alliances that are strategic and project-based, as a sub-class of interfirm networks of special interest in a 'combinative' analysis perspective. In fact, we do not want to deny that there are interfirm collaborations that are almost entirely regulated by some homogeneous sub-class of mechanisms, such as merely social and informal ties (like long-term supply relationships in industrial districts) or merely formal and legal means (like some forms of licensing). But the nature of the most important, 'strategic', collaborations, precisely because they are broad-ranging, is typically not entirely captured in those partial perspectives, as they involve a nexus of legal, organizational and social mechanisms. In addition, strategic alliances are often complex to regulate because they are neither of the long, open-ended, repeated game, highly socially embedded, routine-helped variety (like long-term marketing and purchasing networks); nor of the short-term, market-like, highly obligational, largely court-enforceable variety (like licence and concession contracts). Hence, strategic alliances are typically not well framed along the most familiar 'continua' of hierarchy versus market mechanisms, and of relational versus obligational contracting. Finally, strategic alliances – especially in innovative, knowledge-intensive, strategic industries – are quite often project-based. Therefore they entail truly contrasting demands – such as task complexity limiting extensive formalization, high levels of risk demanding proper guarantees, needs for 'swift' establishment of agreements and common interests with distant or new partners, eventually long time horizons but also the awareness that an end or a 'completion' stage has to be reached – which can be governed only by using a wide range of mechanisms.

Another distinguishing feature of the approach taken here in analysing the contractual foundations of alliances is to acknowledge that almost any coordination mechanism can be agreed upon and formalized into contracts. In other terms, contracts are not necessarily coordination devices that are close, similar, or consubstantial to markets. The use of authority, democracy, plans, rules and procedures can be stipulated by explicit, court-enforceable contracts, as much as prices are.[5] Hence, contracts can and do contribute to define and protect important features of organizational configurations (both intra- and interfirm).

This chapter contributes a framework for analysing contracts in this perspective, and applies it to characterize the contractual bases of strategic, project-based alliances. A result of our analysis will be to give a response to the puzzling question: how can complex matters be regulated by 'light' contracts, as it is, in fact, observed?

Dimensions and antecedents of contractual configurations

According to juridical definitions, contracts are 'agreements that institute or modify reciprocal obligations between parties'. Hence, understanding contract variety entails understanding to what extent and by what means obligations are instituted and enforced: whether formal or informal, self-enforceable or externally enforced, a definitional feature of a contract is the extent to which it institutes obligations, the degree or intensity of its obligational effect. Some more operational attributes of contracts, that substantiate their obligational intensity, have also been identified.

The most commonly employed dimension is the degree of *formalization*: to what extent contracts are written as a basis for third-party enforceability or kept informal and enforced by some other, 'relational' mechanism. Formalization is undoubtedly an important first attribute, but it does not capture, per se, the 'extension' of the regulated matters, nor their type.[6]

Another important dimension of contracts, therefore, is their *complexity*, i.e. their articulation and detail on a larger rather than smaller number of matters (Ariño and Reuer, 2004). A higher degree of articulation and detail of organization (either formal or informal) involves a specification of actions and behaviours to be constrained in their most operative and particular rather than general features (Grandori, 2001a). As applied to contracts, though, complexity is often not distinguished from, and even considered an indicator of, 'completeness' (Ryall and Sampson, 2003).[7] We depart from this view and highlight that *completeness* is a different concept: actually complete contracts can be very 'simple', rather than very long and detailed. Complete contracts constrain action unequivocally (Bernheim and Winston, 1998). Hence when there is uncertainty, what may make a contract complete under uncertainty, i.e. under lack of knowledge of possible relevant alternatives and relevant states of the world, can never be, by definition, a complete description of 'all possible actions and states of the world'. However, this does not mean that complete contracting is impossible, as is usually concluded. The way out is to devise clauses specifying a procedure for selecting action 'no matter what', or 'in any *non*-considered contingency' (Grandori, 2005). Hence, if there are uncertainties, and a list of actions cannot be completely specified, what may make a contract complete is a contract on a procedure through which actions are selected in unforeseen contingencies, through entitlement of some parties to decide (be it a private joint-decision system, a private authority or a public court) or by means of reference to impersonal rules and norms to be applied. So, we can have both very articulated and very simple complete contracts.

Fourth, the dimension of completeness is linked to the *type* of matters or actions on which a contract is stipulated. On this ground the relevant distinction is between rights and obligation over *behaviours* (tasks or services to be delivered) – the most obvious elements on which contracts can be stipulated – and rights and obligations over the *resources* that generate behaviours and services. Associational contracting over resource commitments, we submit, defines a 'constitutional order', the 'core' of alliance contracts. As a dimension, we can conceive of a degree of *associativeness* of a contract. Contracts need not be only about actions and tasks to be performed and prices and compensations to be corresponded in exchange. Actually both task and price specifications are difficult, when dealing with complex and uncertain matters. As a response, a shift of the matter of contracting to something that is capable of generating actions and settling terms of exchange is both possible and empirically observed (Grandori, 2005): resource commitments (and the property right allocations that define and protect them), and decision procedures and rights that state ways of selecting actions, rather than specifying which action should be carried out under what circumstances. This possibility stays at the core of the explanation offered here of why contracts on complex matters can be 'light' rather than 'heavy', 'simple' rather than 'complex'.

What other elements do we expect to be applied, as complements of the associational core, and when? To what extent will they be built into contracts, or will they be kept as extra-contractual elements? There is a wide array of coordination mechanisms that have been defined in general terms. They include: price-like coordination; governance by teams, communities and democratic voting; brokers, intermediaries and integrators; hierarchy (both authority-based and agency-based); rules and procedures; plans, programmes and job descriptions. All of them can be applied not only to intrafirm but also to interfirm governance (Grandori, 1997) and, we especially highlight here, all of them can also be incorporated into contracts. The specific collection of coordination mechanisms that complements an associational contract (and their degree of inclusion in the contract itself) defines some further important features of the mode of governance.

The conditions under which each specific mechanism is relatively more effective and efficient are now reasonably well understood both in general terms and as applied to interfirm coordination.[8] Synthesizing and stylizing, which coordination mechanism is superior (least cost, both in terms of opportunity cost and process cost) depends on the degree of *uncertainty* and of *conflict of interests*. Higher levels of uncertainty and conflict potential are expected to call for 'higher-powered' integration devices, with higher mutual adjustment capacity (more information exchange devices and more conflict resolution devices). Hence, we expect the associational contract instituting an alliance to be complemented by a selection of coordination mechanisms that respond to those conditions.

To what extent do we expect to find them formalized into the contract(s) regulating the alliance? Again both information complexity and conflict of interests are expected to affect the formalization of agreements into contracts. Complex tasks coordination needs formal supports because the number of elements that can be memorized and agreed upon mentally is limited, as in the case of the extensive 'technical specifications' included in the contracts for large industrial projects. The coordination of action is sustainable without the formalization of authorities and task descriptions, or of rules and procedures, only if the best actions to take are known and if the advantages of taking them are superior to those of not cooperating. Finally, the joint exposure of resource investments to risk demands reciprocal protection from withdrawal and protection of the rights to recover investments, whatever the type of resources invested. Hence, in general, in strategic alliances, we expect to find contracts that formalize property rights, but also, to a good average extent, complementary coordination mechanisms.

Evidence from R&D project-based alliances

In what follows we shall examine the content of a few successful project-based alliance contracts. The purpose of this investigation is to provide preliminary evidence on the predictive power of our framework. These alliances proxy conditions of high uncertainty about the possible results of the collaboration. Hence we expect highly formal, highly associational contracting over resources and resource commitments. The three cases vary, however, as to task complexity and conflict between interests on tasks. Hence, around the core associational clauses, we expect different belts of coordination mechanisms: democratic and team-like, whenever activities are particularly research-intensive; price-like when activities are well defined and uncertainty only relates to different levels or quantities to be exchanged; more hierarchy and rules-intensive for intermediate uncertainty levels. To explore these variations, we consider some R&D contracts, as well as some alliances where collaboration was contracted over more downstream tasks.

3M and Polycom Inc.[9]

The objective of this collaboration was the development of an improved version of Polycom's communicating overhead projection system. Polycom contributed hardware and software design capabilities directly related to the focal product, while 3M had technologies suitable for certain sub-systems of the product and greater experience in manufacturing. Contingent clauses are almost completely absent from the contract. By far the largest part of the agreement deals with the allocation of rights to the parties and with the creation of procedures for decision and action, rather than with the prescription of specific actions. Without pretence of being exhaustive the following recaps a few of the covenants in the contract that express such features.

RESOURCE COMMITMENT OBLIGATIONS
– Polycom agrees to annually expend funds for research and development of the [Product] in an amount meeting or exceeding [Amount]

DECISION AND CONTROL PROCEDURES
– Mutual agreement of the Parties shall be required for Engineering Changes. In the event that the combined demand for [Product] (. . .) should exceed such manufacturer's manufacturing capacity in any given month, Polycom and 3M agree to allocate the available capacity between them pro rata

In order to allow the Parties to assess whether adequate manufacturing capacity will be available (. . .) each Party agrees to provide the other, by the first day of each calendar quarter, with a non-binding, written forecast of its anticipated requirements

– To resolve any disputes among the Parties, 3M or Polycom must first provide written notice to the other (. . .) If the dispute is not then resolved, there shall follow (. . .) a meeting (. . .) to discuss and negotiate in good faith

– Should the procedure outlined above not bring about a resolution of the dispute, then (. . .) the Party first sending the notice shall initiate a voluntary, non-binding mediation conducted at a mutually-agreed location (. . .) by a mutually-agreed mediator

While the contract is rife with associational elements, it contains some obligational contracting features as well. Indeed certain clauses articulate in somewhat more specific terms the duties of the parties, namely, the technical areas to which the parties have to contribute technical and support staff and the amount and timing of payment of 3M's financial support to product development.

As to the contingencies considered in the contract, they tend to be related to the parties' behaviour, rather than to the environment:

– FAILSAFE PRODUCTION In the event that Polycom (i) suspends for more than [Period], or terminates its dataconferencing business, (ii) becomes subject to any bankruptcy or insolvency proceeding (. . .) or (iii) becomes insolvent (. . .) 3M shall have the right to have [Product] manufactured by a party of its choosing

– ENHANCEMENTS (. . .) should Polycom fail to meet its funding commitment for research and development in any given year, the Parties agree to meet (. . .) to review the actual level of Polycom's funding and to reduce the amount of 3M's future royalty and/or future sales volume commitment accordingly. With respect to the royalty requirement for the then current calendar year, the royalty shall be reduced to a percentage determined by multiplying (. . .)

and usually they concern the parties' actual or potential *contribution of resources* to the relationship, rather than specific actions.

Finally, the agreement offers us a clear example that before being a sensible theoretical model of contracting, the idea that a pooling of resources and effort can be beneficial, regardless of specific contingencies, indeed reflects the way the parties themselves perceive the problem:

– FURTHER BUSINESS ARRANGEMENTS The Parties recognize that the market for audioconferencing (. . .) is not fully developed at this time, and that their respective areas of technological expertise and marketing abilities suggest that collaboration in the further development of Conferencing Products (. . .) could prove to be mutually beneficial. Therefore, the Parties agree to reasonably cooperate with each other in exploring the possible advantages of additional business arrangements.

From the contract, some fundamental traits of the profile of organizational coordination can also be reconstructed. The coordination mechanisms are centred on decision–right sharing and guarantees that no party can go alone, but communication obligations and fair conflict resolution procedures, based on negotiated joint decision-making, are also specified.

Lucent Technologies Inc. and Broadband Technologies (BBT)[10]

Technically this contract is a Master Agreement, regulating a stream of future projects, each of which requires Project Letters for actual implementation. The relationship is a 'fee for services' one, whereby the researching party (BBT) offers specialist expertise that the commissioning party lacks, but which is available from a number of competing suppliers.

The contract has a strong associational tone. The specific task to be carried out by the research partner is described in very general terms. The agreement establishes a procedure for determining task content:

– As soon as practicable (. . .) the Parties shall agree on a preliminary list of possible Projects, and associated fees (. . .) The Parties recognize that the list of potential Projects on such list is subject to additions and deletions, by mutual agreement, and shall not bind either Party until an appropriate Project Letter for any given Project is executed by both Parties (. . .)

and envisages a process of progressive discovery and specification.[11]

However, despite the fact that at the time of drafting the agreement the tasks can be specified only in very general terms, the parties already commit to each other rather forcefully.[12] Overall, the agreement is configured as Lucent 'hiring' the development firm, for a still vague technical purpose, basing on a prior assessment that BBT will be able to deliver what Lucent will detail in due time.

While the associational elements dominate, this agreement also includes clauses that establish bilateral governance devices to ease disengagement from the relationship upon a change of circumstances, thus acknowledging that at times the expected benefits may not justify continuing cooperation.[13] To deal with such case, that implies an increase in the conflict of interests, the parties envisage a change in the type of contract, with the logic of exchange and obligational contracting superseding the logic of associational and relational contracting.

Around the association contract, a thin belt of organizational mechanism is provided for. This consists essentially of team-like governance, complemented by the assignment of some authority to one of the parties.[14] Paragraphs 2.02 and 2.03 provide that each Project Letter shall specify 'the name [one per party] (...) of the Lucent's and BBT's representatives assigned to administer the Project' and assign the representatives action rights, decision rights on operational matters, and reporting duties, thereby configuring them as liaison roles. Hence, consistently with our framework, the Lucent–BBT associational contract is complemented by somewhat more bureaucratic mechanisms, in accordance with the more exchange-like and less joint research intensive type of cooperation.

ISS Inc. (Owner) and I.S.T. Partners, Ltd. (Representative)[15]

This agreement was entered by Integrated Security Systems (ISS), a producer of industrial security and traffic control products, and an unaffiliated partner, to fund the Owner's Intelli-Site software sales and marketing efforts. Reporting from ISS indicates that both resource constraint and uncertainty about market acceptance of Intelli-Site stood in the way of ISS effecting its own investment in Intelli-Site's market development.

With this agreement the parties created a situation of strong bilateral dependence. On one side, ISS granted exclusive worldwide sales and marketing rights to the Representative (i.e. the licensor agreed that he could not exploit the product himself). On the other side, the Representative agreed to provide various engineering services and application development for the sake of improving marketability, and to automatically assign to the Owner all rights in enhancements and inventions that he might develop.

The agreement described the task of the parties very concisely and in quite general terms. The associational character of the agreement was further strengthened through a clause establishing the duty of the Owner to supplement the Representative's own funds to accomplish large projects:

- PROJECT INDEMNIFICATION Owner agrees that if the aggregate capital accounts of I.S.T. Partners, Ltd. are not sufficient to complete any project or sales contract relating to the Code or Documentation, that Owner has the sole and exclusive obligation to meet any additional funding obligations to complete the project for sales contract.

While the parties expected that the pooling of some of their assets and capabilities would be beneficial, at the same time they expressly circumscribed the collaboration to the particular transaction and, through a no-joint-venture clause, they explicitly underscored the limited depth of their relationship:

- INDEPENDENT CONTRACTOR STATUS Sales Representative is an independent contractor under this Agreement, and nothing herein shall be construed to create a partnership, joint venture or agency relationship between the parties hereto.

In short, it is clear that what made the agreement viable was not the planning for contingencies, but the fact that it aptly allocated rights and incentives. The Representative was made an almost full residual claimant (he was allocated 85 per cent of the sales revenues) after 'renting' the job (he agreed to pay up front a non-refundable amount of $250 000 for existing contracts). In other terms, the association contract is here complemented by price-like mechanisms, in accordance with the actions to be taken, uncertain mostly in terms of realized amounts of sales.

The agreement proved successful. After the capabilities and market acceptance of the product became clear, ISS decided to increase its own investment in market development and accelerated the termination of the agreement through the repurchase of the worldwide sales and marketing rights of the product.

Conclusions

The expectations based on our framework were broadly supported by the three case studies. Differently from what the usual 'market + hierarchy' notion of hybrids implies, an analysis of the content of alliance contracts confirms that they are not, emphatically, a mixture of price-like and authority-based coordination, although these mechanisms are sometimes employed. If there is a chief coordination mechanism always found to complement the associational contracts constituting alliances, that is multi-party 'democratic' decision-making (through voting, negotiation and specification of discretion areas). This is prominent in the first case, which arguably entails the higher uncertainty. Bureaucratic mechanisms are more present in the second, and market-like in the third contract.

The contracts constituting and regulating strategic alliances comprise an associational core, focused on resource commitments and on the specification of property rights, broadly intended; and a belt of contractual clauses incorporating coordination mechanisms of various kinds. We have also specified that associational and procedural contracting is the way in which formal contracts can deal with conditions of high uncertainty. We have also made precise in which sense proprietary alliance contracts are more 'firm-like' than the interfirm contracts. Not because they make more use of hierarchy – which in fact is not the case – but because they are associational and procedural contracts (Grandori, 2005) instituting 'continued associations among co-specialized, dedicated assets, coordinated by conscious direction' (Demsetz 1991).

Hence, our discussion on alliance contracts here, as well as our previous inquiries into extra-contractual coordination mechanisms employed between and within firms (Grandori, 2001b), conclude that internal and external forms of organization seem not to be so 'discrete' and fundamentally different 'in kind' as it is usually assumed. Contracting on resources rather than on tasks provides a foundation for any 'proprietary association', of which a firm may be seen as a particular case.

Notes

1. Anna Grandori, Università Bocconi - Via Sarfatti 25 - 20136 Milano, Italia. E-mail:anna.grandori@uni-bocconi.it
2. Marco Furlotti, Università Bocconi - Via Sarfatti 25 - 20136 Milano, Italia. E-mail:marco.furlotti@uniboccconi.it
3. See Grandori and Soda (1995), Oliver and Ebers (1998) for reviews of network literature enlightening that feature.
4. We use the term 'obligational contracting' in the sense of formal 'contingent claim contracting', as in Williamson (1975, 1981).
5. In this direction, see Stinchcombe (1990), Sobrero and Schrader (1998).
6. Nor, actually, whether formalization is private or court-enforceable.
7. This view descends from Williamson's idea that as uncertainty increases contracts are expected to become more and more contingent and articulated, in order to take into account as many contingencies as possible, and, where that is no longer possible or it is too costly, to be complemented by extra-contractual mechanisms such as authority or norms.
8. This synthesis of the antecedents of coordination forms is based on the wider treatments offered in Grandori (1997, 2001a).
9. This and the other contracts discussed were obtained from the EDGAR database, maintained by the SEC. The contract is dated 28 March 1997.
10. Contract dated 4 February 1998.
11. In fact the contract requires that the project letters at a minimum include a detailed description of the project and a statement defining all deliverables, milestones and their associated due dates.
12. For instance, the agreement establishes an obligation for Lucent to pay BBT a certain amount, which cannot be waived even if Lucent deems it appropriate to purchase the agreed deliverables from alternative sources. Additionally, the agreement states that Lucent can refuse delivery of a deliverable that meets specifications only if delivery delay extends for more than six months. This is indeed not a trivial period, in view of the fact that the collaboration is expected to last about three years, and is an implicit acknowledgement of the uncertainty of the tasks.
13. For instance, the agreement establishes that for each project a 'reusability value' of the project deliverables to BBT be negotiated. Such value would be an input to a formula and would help reduce the amount due by Lucent in the event of earlier termination of the agreement.
14. Various clauses establish that decisions at the strategic as well as the organizational and operational levels of the alliance will be taken 'by mutual agreement'.
15. Contract dated 1 September 1996.

References

Ariño, A. M. and Reuer, J. J. (2004) 'Alliance Contractual Design', IESE Business School Working Paper No. 572.

Bernheim, D. and Winston, M. (1998) 'Incomplete Contracts and Strategic Ambiguity', *American Economic Review*, 88: 902–32.

Demsetz, H. (1991) 'The Theory of the Firm Revisited', in O.Williamson and S.Winter (eds), *The Nature of the Firm: Origins, Evolution and Development*, Oxford: Oxford University Press: 159–78.

Grandori, A. (1997) 'An Organizational Assessment of Interfirm Coordination Modes', *Organization Studies*, 18(6): 897–925.

Grandori, A. (2001a) *Organization and Economic Behavior*, London, Routledge.

Grandori, A. (2001b) 'Neither Hierarchy Nor Identity: Knowledge Governance Mechanisms and the Theory of the Firm', *Journal of Management and Governance*, 5(3-4): 381–99.

Grandori, A. (2005) 'Firm-like Contracts: From Task Contingencies to Resource Commitments', Università Bocconi, Crora papers.

Grandori, A. and Soda, G. (1995) 'Inter-firm Networks: Antecedents, Mechanisms and Forms', *Organization Studies*, 16: 183–214.

Oliver, A. and Ebers, M. (1998) 'Networking Network Studies: an Analysis of Conceptual Configuration in the Study of Inter-organizational Relationships', *Organization Studies*, 19(4): 549–84.

Ryall, M. D. and Sampson, R. C. (2003) 'Do Prior Alliances Influence Contract Structure? Evidence from Technology Alliance Contracts', Simon School of Business Working Paper No. FR 03–11.

Sobrero, M. and Schrader, S. (1998) 'Structuring Inter-firm Relationships: a Meta-analytic Approach', *Organization Studies*, 19(4): 585–615.

Stinchcombe, A. (1990) 'Organizing Information Outside the Firm: Contracts as Hierarchical Documents', Ch. 6 of A. Stinchcombe, *Information and Organizations*, Berkley, CA: University of California Press: 194–239.

Williamson, O. E. (1975). *Markets and Hierarchies: Analysis and Antitrust Implications – A Study in the Economics of Internal Organization*, New York: Free Press.

Williamson, O. E. (1981). 'The Economics of Organization: the Transaction Cost Approach', *American Journal of Sociology*, 87(3): 548–77.

5
Why Managers Choose Equity Ownership in Interfirm Relationships

Prashant Kale[1] and Phanish Puranam[2]

Introduction

In interfirm relationships, companies often seek equity ownership in their exchange partner. With an explosive increase in such relationships in recent years, scholars have applied various theories to highlight the role of certain resource and exchange attributes to explain why firms seek equity ownership in their exchange partners (Schilling and Steensma, 2002; Poppo and Zenger, 1998). Theories about resource attributes emphasize the perceived benefits due to certain types of resources, and argue that firms seek ownership in their partner to access the private value of such partner resources (Peteraf, 1993). On the other hand, theories about exchange attributes (Hennart, 1993) state that absent impediments to exchange, ownership of the underlying resources is unnecessary to access their benefits; instead a firm's ownership in its exchange partner is a response to market failure (Williamson, 1985). These theoretical explanations are not necessarily opposing – they mainly provide different or alternate insights into the mechanisms that might underlie firms' equity ownership choices in their partners.

While extant resource- and exchange-based theories provide valuable insights into this phenomenon, several questions about the role of managerial choice in these theories remain unexplored. Do managers *actually* make ownership decisions in interfirm relationships as described by these theories? If yes, what relative importance do they assign to these respective attributes? Do they view resource and exchange attributes independently or interdependently? Extant studies do not provide satisfactory answers to these questions. Hence, in this chapter we assess whether managers choose ownership in their partner firms in accordance with the logic of the resource-based view (RBV) and transaction cost economics (TCE), two exemplars of the resource- and exchange-based approaches to theorizing about ownership. We do it by using a field-experimental technique known as 'policy-capture' (Tyler and Steensma, 1995) that allows us to experimentally manipulate criteria suggested by these theories, and observe their relative influence.

Improving our understanding about the role of managerial choice in theories of economic organization serves three purposes. First, such theories can be made more precise. Theories about the optimal choice of organizational form rely on two alternative mechanisms: they assume that either managers actually choose the optimal organizational form that is observed, or that the external environment in which firms operate selects them (Williamson, 1985). Thus, correspondence between theoretical predictions and observed outcomes could arise either because managers act in conformance with theory, or because selection forces eliminate choices inconsistent with the theory's normative guidelines. By evaluating the extent to which managerial choice conforms to theoretical assumptions, we can assess the extent to which theories should rely on managerial choice or selection pressures as their key underlying mechanism. Second, we can make the theories more behaviourally plausible by incorporating systematic aspects of behaviour into them to improve their explanatory power. Third, we can educate managers to make better decisions because if their choice does not correspond to normative theory, we can point out such discrepancies.

Theory

In this section, we first briefly highlight some of the limitations of extant research in examining the influence of research and exchange attributes on equity ownership choices in interfirm relationships. Both resource-based and transaction cost theorizing generally assume that managers select an appropriate organizational form to optimize net benefits of conducting related economic activity (Williamson, 1991). For example, transaction cost economists assume that exchange performance is maximized by matching transactions, which differ in exchange attributes, to governance structures that differ in their capacity to address them. Thus, exchanges are organized under common ownership when exchange-specific investments are required and the idiosyncratic nature of these investments might create a hold-up problem. Empirical analysis often uncovers a positive relationship between (a) investment in exchange-specific assets, and the probability of that exchange being organized under common ownership, and (b) the 'appropriate' ownership choice (from a TCE cost minimization perspective) and performance (David and Han, 2004). But we argue that such evidence does not necessarily tell us whether decision-makers actually used a logic based on the prevention of hold-up to make the observed ownership choice.

Consider the evidence linking choice and performance first. Managers might choose ownership structures for diverse reasons, but only those decisions that are 'appropriate' given the level of exchange-specific investments required will perform well as long as there are adequate selection pressures. Similar arguments apply for the resource-based view. Empirical

evidence of positive association between the prescribed choice and performance supports the argument that the theory describes optimal behaviour in
a strong selection environment. But we cannot infer that higher performing
decisions were taken by managers actually aware of, and acting in conformity
with, the theory. Observed ownership choices in interfirm relationships may
also reflect several different considerations arising from similar antecedents.
From the perspective of any theory of economic organization, a 'correct'
choice may not have been made for the 'correct' reason. For instance, the
need for exchange-specific investments in interfirm relationships can signal
to managers not only the hazards of hold-up, but also the opportunity to
create a unique source of competitive advantage through partnership (Dyer
and Singh, 1998). Alternately, it could also signal the need for close coordination between partners (Monteverde, 1995). Thus it is difficult to decide
which of these interpretations characterizes managers' decision-making in
studies that do not control for such alternative explanations (Schilling and
Steensma, 2002). While we can account for such alternative mechanisms
by simultaneously including different variables that represent them in the
empirical analysis (Poppo and Zenger, 1998), obtaining such extensive field
data and ensuring their orthogonality is difficult.

For these reasons, studies featuring observed ownership structures in interfirm relationships shed limited light on managerial choice. Hence, in this
study we use a technique (policy-capture) that allows us to assess the extent
to which criteria identified by RBV and TCE actually influence managerial
decision-making. We now present arguments showing how managers might
make equity ownership decisions if they were to behave according to these
theories. Further, we highlight how managers might make these choices if
they were jointly influenced by both theoretical considerations.

RBV and TCE considerations and equity ownership: direct effects

According to the resource-based view, firms enjoy a competitive advantage
if they have resources (including tangible and intangible) that are valuable,
that generate unique value in conjunction with existing resources, and are
difficult for other firms to imitate (Barney, 1991). The resource-based view on
economic organization assumes that generation of competitive advantage
is the primary motivation for choosing ownership structures in exchange
relationships (Steensma and Corley, 2000). Competitive advantage manifests
itself through improvement in a firm's own performance relative to rivals,
or by worsening rivals' performance (Porter, 1980).

Equity ownership in partners can help achieve both kinds of competitive
advantage. First, by owning equity in a partner with relevant resources, a
firm has the authority to control the usage of those resources through mechanisms such as board representation and administrative oversight (Gulati
and Singh, 1998). The RBV suggests that value attached to such decisions

is greater when the resources in question can enhance a firm's competitive position. This leads to the prediction that managers will seek ownership of partner firms that possess resources capable of enhancing the competitive position of the focal firm, as long as the price of said resources does not exceed expected benefits (Barney, 1989). Second, ownership, and resulting property rights, also enables the focal firm to exclude rivals from gaining access to such resources (Porter, 1980). Thus, the more attractive the resources in question are to a firm's rivals, the greater the competitive advantage the firm derives by blocking rivals from gaining access to them. Thus, based on RBV arguments, we also expect managers to seek ownership in partner firms that possess resources valued by rivals.

According to TCE, Williamson (1985) suggests that exchanges with high transaction costs are better organized within a firm than across markets. By conducting transactions internally, a firm can control transaction costs by providing cooperative incentives, monitoring and punishments. But a move into the firm also has costs in terms of low powered incentives, and bureaucratic decision-making. Thus a rational decision about where to locate a transaction, 'in the market' or 'in the firm' (through complete ownership), involves a comparison of the costs and benefits of ownership in a given transaction.

The need for relationship-specific investments by one of the parties is an important source of anticipated transaction costs. If one partner has to invest in assets that are specific to the relationship, the other partner might 'hold-up' the former and force a contract renegotiation along terms favourable to itself. But in such cases, ownership of the partner provides a firm with the necessary hierarchical control to monitor such behaviour and mitigate contractual hazards that might arise (Gulati and Singh, 1998). Equity stakes also alleviate the hazards of opportunistic behaviour by aligning incentives through creation of mutual hostages (Williamson, 1985). Further, transaction cost theorizing also considers the effect of uncertainty on ownership choices. It predicts that uncertainty about market conditions requires adaptation between partners but such adaptation is costly in terms of cooperative effort. However, it is easier to manage such adaptation processes within a firm because of superior cooperation through monitoring, sanctions and collaborative incentives (Williamson, 1991). While some other determinants of transaction costs have also been investigated, relationship-specific investments and uncertainty have been the most widely studied antecedents of observed ownership structures (David and Han, 2004).

To summarize the TCE arguments, we expect that managers are more likely to seek equity ownership in their partner when there is a need for relationship-specific investments to benefit from exchange with the partner, and when there is uncertainty about demand conditions relevant to the exchange.

RBV and TCF considerations and equity ownership: joint effects

Although academic studies distinguish between resource and exchange attributes, practitioners may not necessarily maintain this distinction. While the former is a resource attribute in terms of RBV, the latter is an exchange attribute in TCE analysis. Thus, we examine how managers may perceive joint effects of these attributes while making equity ownership choices. Basically, we argue that gaining access to resources that enhance a firm's own competitive position or blocking rivals from accessing them, enhances the value of resource ownership, but makes these relationships stronger (or weaker) depending on the exchange attributes in question.

Relationship-specific investments may enhance the value of owning resources that strengthen the competitive position of a firm, because they might allow partner firms to customize their resources to create synergies. For instance, by adopting a common standard, or changing technical specifications to enhance inter-operability, the technologies of partner firms may be worth more together. Such co-specialization of resources is a necessary condition for resources to generate competitive advantage (Peteraf, 1993). Thus, relation-specific investments may not only signal potential hold-up problems as TCE reasoning suggests, but also indicate the prospect of creating a bundle of co-specialized resources, thereby enhancing competitive advantage through their ownership. But a different logic might operate when a firm desires ownership over its partner's resources not because of their significance to its competitive position, but because it needs to exclude rivals from accessing them. Then, co-specialization is perceived as a cost, rather than an investment, if the resources are not valued in use by the focal firm. Thus, all else being equal, we expect managers to avoid seeking ownership of such resources. In summary, we expect the need for relationship-specific investment (an exchange attribute) and significance of partner's resource to the focal firm (a resource attribute) to have a joint positive impact on managers' likelihood to seek ownership of such resources. But we expect need for relationship-specific investments and value of partner's resources to rival firms to have a joint negative impact on this decision.

Further, as mentioned before, demand uncertainty reflects a need for adaptation between partners (Gulati et al., 2005). For the same degree of uncertainty, adaptation is more difficult when the resources in question enhance the competitive position of the focal firm. For example, consider a company like Cisco partners with Crescendo to access the latter's technology (resources). Cisco may anticipate the need for adaptation through renegotiation with Crescendo if there is significant uncertainty about demand conditions for the goods generated by its resources. However, this renegotiation may be more difficult when both parties know the criticality of Crescendo's resources to Cisco's own competitive position. Therefore, the adaptation advantages of ownership will be perceived as greater when the partner's resources enhance the competitive position of the focal firm. But when a partner's resources are sought primarily to keep them from falling into the hands of rivals, and not for their intrinsic worth to the focal firm, demand uncertainty may diminish the benefits of ownership. For instance, Cisco may see no particular value for Crescendo's resources for its own competitive position, but may nonetheless seek to deny its rivals from accessing them. In this case, adaptation pressures arising from demand uncertainty signal additional costs associated with owning Crescendo. Put simply, when the focal firm values the partner's resources in use, adaptation pressures due to demand uncertainty enhance the value of ownership. But they diminish the value of ownership when those resources are not intrinsically valuable to the focal firm. In summary, we expect demand uncertainty and significance of a partner's resources to the focal firm's competitive position to have a joint positive effect on a manager's decision to seek equity ownership in the partner, but demand uncertainty and value of a partner's resources to rival firms to have a joint negative effect on this decision.

Data, methods and analysis

Policy-capture methodology

Policy-capture is a technique used in decision-making research to understand individuals' decision processes (Pablo, 1994). In this methodology, we present managers with a series of decision-making situations that are experimentally designed by manipulating the level of relevant theoretical decision criteria. After reviewing the criteria, managers have to make a decision (in our case, the level of equity ownership they choose in a partner) that represents their judgement in a situation based on the information available (in our case, the levels of various resource and exchange attributes). We can infer how managers consider, weight and combine data on theoretically important decision criteria by studying the statistical relationships between the decision (dependent variable), and criteria (independent variables). For this study, we developed a policy-capturing instrument using a hypothetical example of 'Company A' seeking resources from 'Company B' through a formal partnership, and managers had to decide how much equity ownership managers of Company A would like to have in Company B. We created 30 different partnering scenarios between these two companies by manipulating various decision criteria reflecting different resource and exchange attributes. We randomly assigned ratings to each decision criterion on a scale of 1–5 (1 = Very Low and 5 = Very High) to create these scenarios. Sixty-six managers, each of whom made such decisions in their own companies, from different industries completed this instrument.

Dependent variable: equity ownership

The dependent variable is 'Equity Ownership' which is coded '0' for rela tionships with zero equity ownership, and '1' for relationships with some degree of equity ownership in its partner.

Independent variables

In policy-capture studies we provide data on independent variables to respondents by randomly assigning levels of the variables such that they are as close to being orthogonal as possible, while ensuring that scenarios are realistic. To capture the extent to which a partner's resources could generate competitive advantage for the focal firm, we used the item 'Extent to which the technology is significant to our business/competitive position' and we rated it 'Low or High' using the 1–5 scale. We used an item 'Extent to which our competitors are likely to gain benefit from or be interested in this technology' to reflect the value of the partner's resources to rivals.

We used an item 'Extent of investments required by both parties to fully benefit from the partnership (e.g. investments in R&D, production, marketing, etc.) that are specific to the technology being accessed and cannot be used for other purposes', to represent the construct 'relationship-specific investments' (Poppo and Zenger, 1998). Lastly, we used the item 'Extent to which we understand and can assess the market potential for the technology being accessed' to reflect the extent of uncertainty about the demand for the goods/services generated by the partner's resources. We selected the above items based on prior research, and we modified them based on fieldwork where necessary. Prior research suggests that managers sometimes don't respond to TCE-based criteria since they don't fully understand them. Thus in our fieldwork we paid specific attention to test the robustness of these criteria. We also pre-tested the instrument with 25 managers and found that they generally exhibited satisfactory understanding of the TCE criteria we had used. Finally, we also controlled for industry and respondent attributes (e.g. respondents' experience) in our analysis.

Analysis

We estimated a logit model to assess which factors managers considered in choosing between 'non-equity partnerships' and 'partnerships with at least some equity ownership'. We find that factors representing 'resource significance to the focal firm's competitive position', as well as 'resource value to rivals', were statistically significant in influencing managers to choose at least some degree of equity ownership in their partner. This provided support for the direct relevance to 'resource attributes' in impacting managers' equity ownership decision. The results for exchange attributes were mixed. The effect of relationship-specific investments on managers' decision to choose equity ownership in their partner is positive and significant as expected. On the other hand, uncertainty about market conditions features significantly in managers' decision models, but in the opposite direction to that predicted by TCE theory – thus there is mixed support for the direct relevance of exchange attributes.

To examine the joint effects of resource and exchange attributes, we constructed interaction terms between these two sets of attributes, and we assessed their significance in logit models following Ai and Norton's approach (2003). In terms of their significance, we found no evidence for the expected 'joint positive effect between relationship specific investments and resource significance', and the expected 'joint negative effect between demand uncertainty and value of resource to rivals'. However, we found strong support for the expected 'negative joint effect of the need for relationship-specific investment and resource exclusivity'. On the other hand, we found support for a strong 'negative interaction between demand uncertainty and resource significance', which was contrary to expectations.

Among the control variables, significance of industry effects suggested that equity ownership choices also varied systematically across industries. We also found that respondents with greater tenure in their firms are more likely to choose higher levels of equity ownership in their partnerships. This might indicate greater responsibility assigned to them, as well as more confidence on their part about using equity ownership to organize exchange relationships.

Discussion and conclusion

Our two principal findings can be summarized as follows: managerial choices are strongly influenced strongly by resource attributes that indicate scope for establishing competitive advantage and only weakly by exchange attributes that signal transactional hazards. We also observe that managers view resource and exchange attributes interdependently when making equity ownership decisions.

Implications for research and practice

First, while field studies generate mixed results for the RBV proposition that competitive advantage considerations motivate equity ownership in interfirm relationships (see for instance Folta and Miller, 2002; Schilling and Steensma, 2002), our results suggest that managerial choices of equity ownership are influenced primarily by the significance of the partners' resources to the focal firm's competitive position, as well as their value to rivals. Our results may be stronger because we have been able to isolate the influence of resource attributes on managerial choices more precisely (through orthogonal manipulation) than is typically possible in field studies, and because we observe managerial choices directly, or both.

Second, as predicted by TCE, we find that the need for relationship-specific investments increases managers' likelihood of choosing greater levels of equity ownership. Thus it seems that TCE theorists need not rely on selection forces alone to justify their arguments about the effects of asset specificity on ownership choices, but can invoke managerial choice as well. However, contrary to TCE predictions, demand uncertainty lowers managers' likelihood of seeking equity ownership in their partners – this result is consistent with prior studies. Thus we echo David and Han's view (2004) that the role of uncertainty in influencing ownership structures requires further theoretical refinement.

Third, we find that while both resource and exchange attributes influence managerial equity ownership choices in interfirm relationships, the influence of the former is much stronger. By comparing the sizes of marginal effects as well as added explanatory power to the model, it seems that equity ownership choices in exchange relationships are motivated more by the achievement of competitive advantage, and less by the need to eliminate transactional hazards in interfirm exchange. This finding also might imply that resource (RBV) attributes perhaps have a greater impact on even how/where firms search for resources through interfirm relationships and that they consider exchange attributes only when they might have adverse effects for their ability to assess those resources – research can potentially examine this interesting issue in greater detail in future.

Fourth, we find that managers view resource and exchange attributes interdependently. They seem to view relationship-specific investments as additional costs of ownership, rather than as opportunities to enhance competitive advantage through co-specialization, when they seek a partner's resources primarily to block rivals from accessing them. Further, the perceived adaptation advantages of ownership appear to depend on both anticipated need for adaptation in the relationship (demand uncertainty) and the value of resources themselves. Prior research has not considered such interaction effects between antecedents of ownership advanced by RBV and TCE, but has instead viewed them as competing explanations (though see Folta and Miller, 2002 for interaction effects between technological uncertainty and other antecedents of ownership). By explicitly modelling such interactions, future research can progress towards greater integration between these two important theories and also develop more precise empirical specifications to test that. Fifth, this study's implications for practice are straightforward: managers can improve their decision-making quality about equity ownership levels in interfirm relationships by becoming aware of criteria that may not currently feature in their decision calculus, or may feature only implicitly.

In conclusion, we state that while assumptions about managerial choice are common in theories explaining equity ownership in interfirm relationships, they are rarely assessed for their realism. In this study, we use the strengths of the policy-capture technique to establish that both resource and exchange attributes influence managerial choices of equity ownership in such relationships. We also find that resource attributes have a stronger influence than exchange attributes, and they may also jointly influence managerial choice over and above their independent effects. Our results suggest how the resource-based and transaction cost theories of economic organization can be refined in terms of their assumptions about theoretical mechanisms, as well as in terms of how they are tested empirically.

Notes

1. Prashant Kale, Assistant Professor of Corporate Strategy and International Business, Stephen M. Ross School of Business, University of Michigan, D4209E, 701 Tappan Street, Ann Arbor, MI 48109, Tel: 734-764-2305, E-mail: kale@umich.edu
2. Phanish Puranam, Assistant Professor of Strategy and International Management, London Business School, Sainsbury 317, Sussex Place, Tel: 44 (0) 20-7262-5050, E-mail: ppuranam@london.edu

References

Ai, C. R. and Norton E. C. (2003) 'Computing Interaction Effects in Logit and Probit Models', *Economic Letters*, 80(1): 123–9.

Barney, J. (1989) 'Asset Stocks and Sustained Competitive Advantage: a Comment', *Management Science*, 35(12): 1511–13.

Barney, J. (1991) 'Firm Resources and Sustained Competitive Advantage', *Journal of Management*, 17(1): 99–120.

Conner, C. and Prahalad, C. K. (1996) 'A Resource Based Theory of the Firm: Knowledge vs. Opportunism', *Organization Science*, 7(5): 477–502.

David, R. J. and Han S.-K. (2004) 'A Systematic Assessment of the Empirical Support for Transaction Cost Economics', *Strategic Management Journal*, 25(1): 39–58.

Dyer, J. H. and Singh, H. (1998) 'The Relational View: Cooperative Strategy and Sources of Interorganizational Competitive Advantage', *Academy of Management Review* 23(4): 660–79.

Folta, T. B. and Miller, K. D. (2002) 'Real Options in Equity Partnerships', *Strategic Management Journal*, 23(1): 77–88.

Gulati, R., Lawrence, P. and Puranam, P. (2005) 'Adaptation in Vertical Relationships: Beyond Incentive Conflict', *Strategic Management Journal*, 26(5): 415–40.

Gulati, R. and Singh, H. (1998) 'The Architecture of Cooperation: Managing Coordination Costs and Appropriation Concerns in Strategic Alliances', *Administrative Science Quarterly*, 43: 781–94.

Hennart, J.-F. (1993) 'Explaining the Swollen Middle: Why Most Transactions are a Mix of "Market" and "Hierarchy"', *Organization Science*, 4(4): 529–47.

Monteverde, K. (1995) 'Technical Dialog as an Incentive for Vertical Integration in the Semiconductor Industry', *Management Science*, 41(10): 1624–38.

Pablo, A. L. (1994) 'Determinants of Acquisition Integration Level: a Decision-making Perspective', *Academy of Management Journal*, 37(4): 803–36.

Peteraf, M. A. (1993) 'The Cornerstones of Competitive Advantage: a Resource-Based View', *Strategic Management Journal*, 14(3) (March): 179–91.

Poppo, L. and Zenger, T. (1998) 'Testing Alternative Theories of the Firm: Transaction Cost, Knowledge Based and Measurement Explanations for Make or Buy Decisions in Information Services', *Strategic Management Journal*, 19: 853–77.

Porter, M. E. (1980) *Competitive Strategy*, Cambridge and New York: Free Press.
Schilling, M. A. and Steensma, H. K. (2001) 'The Use of Modular Organizational Forms. an Industry-Level Analysis', *Academy of Management Journal*, 44(6): 1149–68.
Schilling, M. A. and Steensma, H. K. (2002) 'Disentangling the Theories of Firm Boundaries: a Path Model and Empirical Test', *Organization Science*, 13(4): 387–401.
Steensma, H. K. and Corley, K. G. (2000) 'On the Performance of Technology-Sourcing Partnerships: the Interaction between Partner Interdependence and Technology Attributes', *Academy of Management Journal*, 43(6): 1045–67.
Tyler, B. B. and Steensma, H. K. (1995) 'Evaluating Technological Collaborative Opportunities: a Cognitive Modeling Perspective', *Strategic Management Journal*, 16(5): 43–70.
Williamson, O. E. (1985) *The Economic Institutions of Capitalism*, New York: Free Press.
Williamson, O. E. (1991) 'Comparative Economic Organization: the Analysis of Discrete Structural Alternatives', *Administrative Science Quarterly*, 36: 269–96.

6
Government as an Alliance Partner

Malika Richards[1] and Daniel C. Indro[2]

Introduction

In their study of 3000 transnational corporations, Desai et al. (2004) find that these companies increasingly chose to venture out alone when operating overseas. Nevertheless, popular media still document many occurrences of alliance formations. For example, a casual search from the Thomson Financial database returns 3974 instances of alliance formations announced between 1 January 2004 and 31 December 2004. Perlmutter and Heenan (1986) recognize the importance of alliances as organizational forms to conduct global businesses.

In general, an alliance is formed to enhance the economic interests of the partners. Contractor and Lorange (1988) mention several rationales for interfirm cooperation. They further note that it is not just lesser developed nations or centrally planned economies that make it 'easier' to do business through a joint venture with a local partner. Many companies have found that the most practical way to sell products in the Japanese market is through a joint venture.

When joint ventures are formed between two companies, both tend to be driven by common profit consideration. In such a case, division of the alliance's profits depends on the partners' relative ownership shares of the venture. But what if one of the partners is a government? Prior research suggests that the search for an ideal partner depends on the complementarity in the partners' products, geographical presence or functional skills (Bleeke and Ernst, 1993; Harrigan, 1985; Lynch, 1989). In addition to complementary strengths, compatibility and trust between partners are critical as they contribute to the success of the alliance (BenDaniel and Rosenbloom, 1998). When a government is an alliance partner, it may pursue other national goals that may not necessarily be compatible with the multinational's profit motive. As a result, partnering with a government may require the multinational to offer an ownership concession, especially when entry is restricted. In addition, the types of international joint ventures a government engages in could be different from those taken on by private or publicly traded companies.

Lane and Beamish (1990) document the importance of joint venture partner selection in developing countries. Due to the possibility of drastic changes in the government of a developing country, these authors recommend against having a local politician or government official as a partner. Nevertheless, alliances where one of the partners is a government may be the only way to go because of legal requirements or because of a scarcity of local private companies for the multinational firms to partner with. This situation is particularly relevant in countries undergoing economic transformation, such as China, Vietnam and transitional Eastern European countries. The new strategies and initiatives developed in the 1990s through alliances with multinationals and other national governments offer a remarkable testimony to the successful working relationship between the government and the private sector in Singapore (Goh et al., 1993).

In this study, we examine the conditions under which a government is likely to be a partner in a joint venture. In addition, in ventures where one of the partners is a government, we attempt to answer why some multinationals partner with the host government while in other cases it is a local company that partners with a foreign government. We also examine how their ownership characteristics differ in these instances.

Partner selection criteria

Prior research identifies two dimensions of partner selection criteria: task-related and partner-related (Geringer, 1991). The task-related dimension includes factors pertinent to the operational skills and resources that are necessary for the joint ventures to achieve their goals. The partner-related dimension encompasses issues of partners' cooperation. Building on previous studies on partner selection, we examine four factors that can potentially explain why a government engages in a joint venture.

Task-related factors

Task-related factors include those pertaining to the availability of skills and resources, such as financial resources, technical expertise, and access to unique distribution systems, to achieve the joint venture's goals. The availability of these resources is likely to vary depending on the type of joint venture agreement that the partners enter into. For example, when two partners establish a marketing joint venture, it is common to expect that one partner has knowledge about the market while the other possesses a valuable product to sell in that market.

In the case of a manufacturing joint venture, a multinational is likely to form a joint venture in a developing country in order to secure access to raw materials or cheap local labour. While Lane and Beamish (1990) recommend against using a government official as a partner, it may not always be possible for a multinational to find a compatible local company. At the same time, the government of a developing country is also likely to be interested in establishing a manufacturing base in an effort to modernize the economy. Hence, while the multinational and the government may be motivated by two seemingly different goals – much like situations described in the game theory literature – their mutual needs provide a common ground to create a workable joint venture.

For an R&D joint venture, it may be tempting to say that companies from developed countries would like to keep their operations within the national boundary. However, the paucity of skilled human resources in a country, coupled with the increasing availability of capable human resources abroad, may prompt a multinational from a developed country to establish R&D operations beyond its national border. Indeed, Gergen (2005) argues that 'U.S.-based companies are finding it increasingly attractive to build not only their manufacturing plants abroad but their R&D operations as well.'

Partner-related factors

In their analysis of joint ventures in developing countries, Lane and Beamish (1990) argue that the most common reason for joint venture failure is inadequate understanding of cross-cultural cooperative behaviour. They also assert that major differences in the performance of joint ventures in developing countries can be explained by the presence of long-term need and commitment between the partners. Lane and Beamish (1990) describe need as the requirement for skills and resources in a venture (complementary strengths).[3]

While it is necessary for each partner to bring complementary strengths to the partnership, it is also important for a partner not to acquire the other partner's strength, because such action can undermine any mutual trust that has been developed (BenDaniel and Rosenbloom, 1998). Trust is absolutely essential in an international joint venture agreement. Nevertheless, because trust cannot be written into a contract, cultivating good faith and strong confidence in a partner as early as possible is critical. The degree of trust in a society is likely to vary from culture to culture. As a result, what are considered minor inconveniences if the two partners are co-owners of a company could prove disastrous to the harmonious working relationship between two partners from different cultural backgrounds. Abundant anecdotal evidence points to the importance of understanding the impacts of these seemingly minor blunders on the success of a joint venture (Ricks, 1999).

Country-related factors

Having operations overseas is likely to present a multinational with additional complications not typically found in a domestic business. In addition to dealing with potential language and cultural barriers, overseas market realities are subject to a vastly different regulatory environment than that in a domestic market. As a result, a multinational may find itself ill-equipped to deal with the regulatory complexity of the foreign operations. Finding a suitable local partner to help the multinational deal with such a complexity is critical. A politically well-connected local partner will be tremendously helpful, as it knows the right channel to the government bureaucracy. Finding such a partner takes a lot of time and effort, and requires rigorous exploration. It may be easier to partner with the government directly. Such direct dealing with the government provides the multinational with the ability to negotiate concessions directly with the party having the authority to set forth the regulation. On the other hand, a direct business relationship with the government may expose the multinational to unethical conduct (such as bribes and other corrupt practices) prohibited by the law of the company's home country (e.g. the US Foreign Corrupt Practices Act). Hence, partner selection for a venture abroad requires careful consideration of the above trade-offs.

Industry-related factors

The success of a venture is likely to depend on industry conditions. Luo (1995) finds that industry factors are related to joint venture performance in China. Industry conditions can affect not only firm performance, but also the firm's propensity to invest in that industry. For example, Kogut and Chang (1991) show that Japanese direct investment in the US flows to R&D-intensive industries. Their results also show that joint ventures are used for the sourcing and sharing of US technological capabilities.

It is reasonable to believe that industry characteristics in a domestic operation differ from those in an overseas operation. Differences in industry characteristics of domestic and foreign markets may require a multinational to adopt a different strategy. For example, advertising and promotion suitable for a domestic audience may be considered distasteful by a foreign audience (see Ricks, 1999). Understanding how to adapt to industry conditions is especially crucial for multinationals wishing to enter an emerging market, because while the payoffs from such an entry are likely to be high, there may be daunting challenges that make failure a realistic possibility. Finding a suitable local partner who understands these challenges is therefore critical.

Analysis and results

This study focuses on international joint venture agreements between two partners, where one partner is a foreign entity (a foreign government or a multinational corporation). All joint ventures are within the 'manufacturing' SIC code range of 2000–3999. Our data come from the following sources: *Compustat, Euromoney*, Hofstede (1980, 2001), Thomson Financial, and the

World Economic Forum (1999, 2004). Our final sample contains 1096 global joint venture agreements in 47 countries that were announced between 1999 and 2003. China (340), Japan (78), the United States (76), India (73) and S. Korea (50) collectively compose 56 per cent of the sample (Tables 6.1–6.3).

Table 6.1: Joint venture locations

Location	Industrialized	# of JVs	Gov't partner	Host gov't	Foreign gov't	High tech
Argentina	N	6	0	0	0	2
Austria	Y	2	0	0	0	0
Australia	Y	28	2	1	1	9
Belgium	Y	7	1	1	0	2
Brazil	N	30	1	0	1	20
Bulgaria	N	1	1	1	0	1
Canada	Y	20	3	3	0	12
Czech Rep	N	2	0	0	0	12
Chile	N	2	1	0	1	1
China	N	340	77	57	20	243
Colombia	N	1	0	0	0	0
Denmark	Y	4	0	0	0	2
Finland	Y	3	2	2	0	2
France	Y	28	2	2	0	20
Germany	Y	29	1	0	1	19
Greece	Y	3	0	0	0	1
Hong Kong SAR	N	6	0	0	0	5
Hungary	N	8	1	1	0	4
Indonesia	N	19	0	0	0	13
India	N	73	8	5	3	50
Ireland	Y	3	0	0	0	0
Israel	N	1	0	0	0	0
Italy	Y	15	1	0	1	11
Japan	Y	78	2	0	2	55
Malaysia	N	24	3	3	0	10
Mexico	N	20	3	0	3	8
Norway	Y	5	2	1	1	1
Netherlands	Y	4	0	0	0	3
New Zealand	Y	3	0	0	0	1
Philippines	N	11	0	0	0	3
Poland	N	4	1	1	0	2
Portugal	Y	4	0	0	0	1
Russian Fed.	N	33	6	4	2	23
South Africa	N	9	0	0	0	5
Singapore	N	12	1	0	1	7
S. Korea	N	50	1	0	1	38
Spain	Y	8	1	1	0	4
Sweden	Y	6	3	2	1	3

Table 6.1: (Continued)

Location	Industrialized	# of JVs	Gov't partner	Host gov't	Foreign gov't	High tech
Switzerland	Y	5	0	0	0	2
Thailand	N	18	1	1	0	8
Turkey	N	5	0	0	0	2
Taiwan	N	28	1	1	0	26
United Kingdom	Y	24	0	0	0	16
United States	Y	76	2	0	2	46
Venezuela	N	3	2	2	0	2
Vietnam	N	34	5	4	1	13
Zimbabwe	N	1	1	0	1	0

Table 6.2: Joint venture characteristics

	Total sample	JVs without gov't partners	JVs with host gov't partner	JVs with foreign gov't partner
More than 50% ownership	N/A	N/A	12	8
Less than 50% ownership	N/A	N/A	28	8
Option to buy clause	6	5	0	1
Manufacturing only agreement	885	764	84	37
Marketing only agreement	11	9	1	1
R&D only agreement	11	10	0	1
Combined agreement	189	177	8	4
JV high tech involvement (based on SIC)	231	207	19	5
Advertising intensity (based on SIC) *mean*	0.14%	0.15%	0.08%	0.06%
Total number	1096	960	93	43

To answer our research questions we conducted two logistic regression analyses and a test of differences between means. First, we examined the role of task-related, partner-related, country-related and industry-related factors in explaining the likelihood of a government as a partner in an international

Table 6.3: Joint venture location characteristics

Host country location characteristics (average scores)	Total sample	JVs without gov't partners	JVs with gov't partner
Euromoney country risk[1]	68.21	69.05	62.23
Institutional investor country credit rating[1]	66.05	66.70	61.45
No gov't interference in X-border venture neg.[2]	5.08	5.14	4.72
Gov't has little influence on companies[2]	3.51	3.54	3.31
Mgmt. spends little time on gov't bureaucracy[2]	3.83	3.87	3.51
Few foreign ownership restrictions[2]	4.92	4.95	4.72
Starting a new business is easy[2]	4.52	4.55	4.34
FDI is important source of tech. transfer[2]	4.88	4.89	4.85
Intellectual property protection is stringent[2]	4.25	4.32	3.76
Competition in local market is intense[2]	5.32	5.33	5.22
Cultural dimensions[3]:			
Power distance	66.01	64.96	73.37
Individualism	41.13	42.41	32.10
Masculinity/femininity	59.21	59.35	58.22
Uncertainty avoidance	52.29	53.59	43.18
Total number of JVs	1096	960	136

[1] Lower scores indicate *more* risky countries.

[2] Scores range from $1 = $ low to $7 = $ high.

[3] Scores range from $1 = $ low to $100 = $ high.

joint venture. In this study there are 136 joint ventures where one parent is a government. Then, we looked at those joint ventures involving a government and compared the ones involving a foreign government with those involving a host government partner. Out of 136 joint ventures in which one parent is a government, there are 43 ventures in our sample in which the foreign partner is a government entity. The remaining 93 ventures have the host government as a partner. We eliminated from our sample the few cases in which both the host and the foreign partner were governments. Next, we examined the relationship between a government partner's equity ownership level and the location of the international joint venture (i.e. whether it is in an emerging or an industrialized country). This ownership percentage reflects the government partners' relative control rights of the venture.

We use the type of joint venture activity to operationalize *task-related factors*. We use cultural distance between the two joint venture partners to capture *partner-related factors*. Based on Hofstede's (1980, 2001) four national culture dimensions, we computed the cultural distance between the two joint venture partners for each joint venture agreement, using Kogut and Singh's (1988) method. Cultural distance can be thought of as a *culture-*based measure of trust between two partners from two different cultural backgrounds. Glaeser et al. (2000) find from their experiments that the tendency to cheat one another increases when partners have national and racial differences.

We use five variables to represent host *country-related factors*: country risk, degree of government interference in business, how easy it is to start a new business, the degree to which foreign direct investment (FDI) is an important source of technology transfer, and the degree to which local market competition is intense. We use *Euromoney*'s annual country risk ratings as a proxy for location risk in the country where a joint venture operates.[4] Schnitzer (2002) notes that country risk is alleviated if the host government is a joint venture partner. The other four variables were obtained from the World Economic Forum's (1999, 2004) surveys.

We use technology involvement, and advertising intensity to operationalize *industry-related factors*. Joint ventures in high technology sectors (SIC codes 2800–2999, 3500–3899) are more likely to involve tacit knowledge and transfer of technology or production processes. As a result, this industry variable captures the potential for bargaining frictions and information asymmetry between the transacting parties. Advertising intensity is calculated by dividing an industry's advertising expenditures by its sales. We obtained information on industry advertising intensity from *Compustat*. Because we do not have access to this information for each and every country in our sample, and also because accounting standards do vary across countries, we use US industry-level data (at the 3-digit SIC level, if available, otherwise at the 2-digit level).

Table 6.4 presents a summary of the results examining the likelihood of government as a partner in joint venture agreements. Joint ventures with a government partner are more likely to involve manufacturing only, as opposed to a combination of activities, than are joint ventures without a government partner.

Table 6.4 also shows that joint ventures with a government partner are more likely to have a greater degree of cultural distance between the two partners. Furthermore, in countries where starting a new business is less easy, there is more likely to be a government partner involved in a joint venture. In countries with less intense local competition, a government partner is more likely to be involved in a joint venture. Stated differently, local competitors in these countries make little effort to steal customers away from each other. It may be that there are few local competitors, or that they do not have the resources to aggressively expand market share. In addition, governments

Table 6.4: Summary of results examining the likelihood of government as a partner in joint venture agreements (N = 1096)

- *More likely* to be a government partner if it is a manufacturing-only agreement
- *More likely* to be a government partner if there is greater cultural distance between the two partners (No impact if China is excluded from sample)
- *Less likely* to be a government partner if there is little host government interference in business
- *Less likely* to be a government partner if there is less host country risk
- *Less likely* to be a government partner if starting a new business is easy in the host country
- *Less likely* to be a government partner if competition in host country's market is intense
- No impact: marketing-only agreement
- No impact: R&D-only agreement
- No impact: FDI is an important source of technology transfer in the host country
- No impact: if the JV is in a high-tech industry
- No impact: industry advertising intensity

are *less* likely to be joint venture partners in countries where cross-border ventures are negotiated freely (without government interference), where the government has little influence over the local companies, where senior management of local companies spend little time dealing with government bureaucracy, and where foreign ownership of companies in the country is prevalent or encouraged. Lastly, in riskier countries there is more likely to be a government partner involved in a joint venture. Removing China, which has the most international joint ventures in our sample, rendered cultural distance insignificant. This result suggests that most of the variation in cultural distance is captured by China.

There are 136 joint venture agreements in our sample involving a government partner. Table 6.5 shows a summary of the results examining the

Table 6.5: Summary of results examining the likelihood of foreign (as opposed to host) government as a partner in joint venture agreements (N = 136)

- *Less likely* to be a foreign government if there is greater cultural distance between partners
- *More likely* to be a foreign government if the JV is in a high-tech industry
- No impact: manufacturing- and R&D-only agreement
- No impact: marketing-only agreement
- No impact: level of host government interference in business
- No impact: country risk score
- No impact: starting a new business is easy in the host country
- No impact: competition in the host country local market is intense
- No impact: FDI is an important source of technology transfer in the host country
- No impact: industry advertising intensity

UNIVERSITY OF HERTFORDSHIRE LRC

likelihood of a foreign government partner (as opposed to a host government partner) in joint venture agreements. As in Table 6.4, the base joint venture activity group is those ventures engaged in a combination of activities (e.g. both manufacturing and marketing). However, we had to combine 'manufacturing only' with 'R&D only', as there was only one 'R&D only' joint venture in this sub-sample.

Table 6.5 indicates that foreign governments are less likely than the host governments to engage in international joint ventures when there are large national cultural differences between the two parties. On the other hand, foreign governments are more likely than host governments to be engaged in high-tech joint venture agreements. None of the other variables we examined played a significant role in predicting the likelihood of joint ventures having a foreign versus a host government partner. Removing China from the sample did not alter the results shown in Table 6.5.

Table 6.6 reports the results of a test of differences in mean equity ownership of government partners. This test focuses only on those 136 joint venture agreements involving a government partner. We compare the equity ownership levels of host government versus foreign government partners in industrialized and emerging countries. We relied on Michigan State University's *Market Potential Indicators for Emerging Markets* website for help in categorizing the countries in our sample. The results indicate that host governments are more likely to have majority equity ownership in industrialized countries, but take a minority stake in emerging countries. In contrast, foreign governments are more likely to have a majority equity ownership share in emerging countries, yet a minority ownership share in industrialized countries. Removing China from the sample made the difference in mean equity ownership between host and foreign governments in joint ventures in emerging countries insignificant. So, the differences in mean equity ownership of government partners in emerging countries are driven by international joint ventures located in China.

Table 6.6: Test of differences in mean equity ownership of government partners (N = 136)

JV location	Host government partner		Foreign government partner		T-statistic
	Equity	N	Equity	N	
Emerging countries	47.39	80	51.35	34	−1.70*
Industrialized countries	53.39	13	48.89	9	1.98*

* $p < 0.10$.

Discussion and conclusion

Task-related, partner-related, country-related, and to a lesser extent industry factors, all play a role in predicting the likelihood of a government partner and/or what kind of government partner will be engaged in an international joint venture. Governments are more likely to engage in purely manufacturing agreements, a task-related factor, than in agreements involving a combination of activities. In our sample, 636 (72 per cent) of manufacturing-only joint ventures are located in emerging countries. Of these 636 ventures, 105 involve government partners. Moreover, governments are involved in manufacturing-only joint ventures more in emerging countries than they are in industrialized countries. These results indicate that manufacturing-only joint ventures not only provide the host governments of emerging countries with an opportunity to modernize their economies, but also the multinationals with a means to lower their production costs in order to stay globally competitive.

Cultural distance between the two partners, a partner-related factor, is another key feature that predicts the likelihood of government as a partner. We found that China is the primary reason behind this difference. It is possible that multinational companies, faced with culturally unfamiliar locations, may partner with the host government in the belief that, since the host government writes the laws, that things will go more smoothly if it is co-opted through a partnership. At the same time, it may be the host government that is protectionist, and simply makes it 'easier' for a foreign firm from an unfamiliar culture to enter the country via a joint venture with the government. Indeed, Table 6.5 indicates that the host governments are more likely than foreign governments to be involved with a partner from culturally unfamiliar locations. As the list of countries in Table 6.1 shows, the majority of joint ventures involving host government partners are located in emerging countries, some of which are also formally centrally planned economies.

Industry factors, such as advertising intensity or technology involvement, do not seem to play a significant role in predicting the likelihood that a joint venture has a government partner. However, in high-tech industries, when a government does become involved in an international joint venture, it is more likely to be a foreign government than a host government. In some cases it is possible that the foreign government partners come from smaller, less-developed nations in which the government is the only organization with the resources and credibility to establish overseas high-tech equity partnerships. In other cases it is possible that the foreign government partner comes from an industrialized, or newly industrialized, nation and it is interested in becoming involved in particular technologies for reasons of national security.

Numerous country-level factors are related to the likelihood of a government partner being involved in an international joint venture. For instance, the government partner joint ventures are more likely to be located in risky countries, in countries where it is not easy to start a new business, where local competition is not intense, and where there is a lot of government interference in both local businesses and cross-border ventures. With regard to the protectionist policies of host governments – one of the reasons cited by Contractor and Lorange (1988) for forming international joint ventures – these findings are not surprising. Interestingly, though, none of these country-level factors plays a significant role in explaining why it is a host or foreign government involved. In the case of country risk, it is possible that a foreign government invests in a risky location to obtain access to certain raw materials for national security reasons, while its private companies are unwilling to assume the downside risks. Alternatively, in risky countries, foreign multinationals may be more willing to partner with the host government than with local companies, because the local companies lack the ability to offer contingency assurances provided by the host government.

We found significant differences in joint venture ownership between the host and foreign governments. Specifically, host governments in industrialized countries prefer to hold majority ownership shares when they form a joint venture with a foreign multinational. This is not the case for host governments of emerging countries, in particular China. This is possibly a reflection of the bargaining power that foreign multinationals hold in the emerging countries, despite the argument that host governments have the coercive power of law on their side. These countries may see foreign direct investment as vital to the growth of their economies. In contrast, the governments of industrialized countries are less likely to view foreign direct investment as essential to their economic growth.

The foreign government partners have completely opposite equity ownership patterns to those of the host governments. Bargaining power may play a role in these cases as well. The foreign governments investing in industrialized countries have minority equity ownership stakes, yet those investing in emerging countries have majority ownership shares. Domestic firms in the industrialized countries (e.g. Wal-Mart in the United States) may have annual sales that exceed the total GDP of some nations. This gives the firms considerable clout when negotiating, even with a foreign government. The reverse may be true for domestic companies in emerging countries.

Our findings differ from those of Brouthers and Bamossy (1997). In their eight case studies of international joint venture negotiations in two Eastern European emerging economies, these authors found that governments are key stakeholders who intervened significantly in these joint ventures, thereby altering the balance of power between parties and the bargaining consequences. Our findings indicate that, when governments do get involved in an international joint venture, those in developed countries are more likely than governments in emerging economies to take a dominant role.

In conclusion, we find that partnering with a government, while usually not recommended (Lane and Beamish, 1990), is nevertheless a strategy embarked upon by certain multinational corporations. Our study identifies conditions under which multinational corporations are likely to engage in such an arrangement. The degree to which control rights, as reflected by ownership stake, differ between host and foreign governments, depends on whether the joint ventures are located in emerging or industrialized countries.

Notes

1. Malika Richards, Assistant Professor of Management, Penn State University – Berks, Reading, PA 19610, Tel: (610) 396-6096, Fax: (610) 396-6026, E-mail: mur12@psu.edu
2. Daniel C. Indro, Associate Professor of Finance, School of Graduate Professional Studies, Penn State University – Great Valley, Malvern, PA 19355, Tel: (610) 725-5283, Fax (610) 725-224, E-mail: dci1@psu.edu
3. Drawing from their examination of the US biotechnology industry, Zollo et al. (2002) suggest that the quality of the firm's interorganizational routines developed from past alliances is an important partner selection criterion. In the context of alliances across national borders, their results imply that past history of alliances can be as important as cross-cultural understanding as a partner selection criterion.
4. We provide information on *Institutional Investor*'s Country Credit Rating and the World Economic Forum's intellectual property protection scores in Table 6.3 for descriptive purposes. These two scores are very highly correlated with the *Euromoney* ratings.

References

BenDaniel, D. J. and Rosenbloom, A. H. (1998) *International M&A, Joint Ventures, and Beyond: Doing the Deal*, New York: Wiley.

Bleeke, J. and Ernst, D. (1993) *Collaborating to Compete*, New York: Wiley.

Brouthers, K. D. and Bamossy, G. J. (1997) 'The Role of Key Stakeholders in International Joint Venture Negotiations: Case Studies from Eastern Europe', *Journal of International Business Studies*, 28(2): 285–308.

Contractor, F. J. and Lorange, P. (1988) 'Why Should Firms Cooperate? The Strategy and Economics Basis for Cooperative Ventures', in Contractor and Lorange (eds), *Cooperative Strategies in International Business*, Amsterdam: Elsevier: 3–30.

Desai, M. A., Foley, C. F. and Hines Jr., J. R. (2004) 'Venture Out Alone', *Harvard Business Review*, 82(3): 22.

Gergen, D. (2005) 'Will America Slip from No. 1?' *Newsweek*, 4 April.

Geringer, J. M. (1991) 'Strategic Determinants of Partner Selection Criteria in International Joint Ventures', *Journal of International Business Studies*, 22: 41–62.

Glaeser, E. L., Laibson, D. I., Sheinkman, J. A. and Soutter, C. L. (2000) 'Measuring Trust', *Quarterly Journal of Economics*, 115: 811–46.

Goh, M., Choy, C. L. and Yeoh, C. (1993) 'Strategic Management in Economic Development: the Singapore Experience', *International Journal of Management*, 10(2): 165–73.

Harrigan, K. R. (1985) *Strategies for Joint Ventures*, Lexington, MA: Lexington Books.

Hofstede, G. (1980) *Culture's Consequences: International Differences in Work-related Values*, Beverly Hills, CA: Sage Publications.

Hofstede, G. (2001) *Culture's Consequences: Comparing Values, Behaviors, Institutions and Organizations across Nations*, Thousand Oaks, CA: Sage Publications.

Kogut, B. and Chang, S. J. (1991) 'Technological Capabilities and Japanese Foreign Direct Investment in the United States', *Review of Economic and Statistics*, 73(3): 401–13.

Kogut, B. and Singh, H. (1988) 'The Effect of National Culture on the Choice of Entry Mode', *Journal of International Business Studies*, 19: 411–32.

Lane, H. W. and Beamish, P. W. (1990) 'Cross-cultural Cooperative Behavior in Joint Ventures in LDCs', *Management International Review*, 30 (Special Issue): 87–102.

Lynch, R. P. (1989) *The Practical Guide to Joint Ventures and Corporate Alliances*, New York: Wiley.

Perlmutter, H. V. and Heenan, D. A. (1986) 'Cooperate to Compete Globally', *Harvard Business Review*, 64(2): 136–52.

Ricks, D. A. (1999) *Blunders in International Business*, 3rd edn, Oxford: Blackwell.

Schnitzer, M. (2002) 'Debt vs. Foreign Direct Investment: the Impact of Sovereign Risk on the Structure of International Capital Flows', *Economica*, 69(273): 41–67.

World Economic Forum (1999) *The Global Competitiveness Report 1999*, New York: Oxford University Press.

World Economic Forum (2004) *The Global Competitiveness Report 2003–2004*, New York: Oxford University Press.

Zollo, M., Reuer, J. J. and Singh, H. (2002) 'Interorganizational Routines and Performance in Strategic Alliances', *Organizational Science*, 13(6): 701–13.

7
Coordination, Appropriation and Governance in Alliances: the Biotechnology Case

Stephen Tallman[1] *and Anupama Phene*[2]

Introduction

Why are alliances so popular? They confer many benefits, particularly in knowledge-intensive industries. Why do so many fail? They bring many hazards, particularly in knowledge-intensive industries. From a resource-based (or knowledge-based) perspective, alliances are formed to maximize the benefits of combining complementary operating capabilities and other resources, requiring increasing coordination as capabilities become more complex. However, while alliances theoretically may be structured to enhance synergistic advantages, they also are certainly susceptible to appropriation concerns, with partners possibly acting opportunistically and governance costs incurred to protect capabilities (Heiman and Nickerson, 2004). Thus the choice of an appropriate governance mechanism is critical to both achieving the benefits and reducing the costs associated with an alliance.

Prior research has typically characterized governance structures as contractual or institutional (Doz and Hamel, 1998) based on the proximity of such structures to market or hierarchical forms. Institutional structures replicate the coordination characteristics of a hierarchy (Gulati and Singh, 1998) through equity ownership on the part of the alliance partners, while contractual arrangements are based on written agreements and verbal under-standings between partners that do not involve shared ownership (Gerwin and Ferris, 2004). Theoretical and empirical studies regarding the choice of alliance governance mechanisms have focused on partner firm character-istics such as the risk of opportunistic behaviour by one or both partners (Hennart, 1988), the nature of firm resources and capabilities (Tallman, 1999), ability of partners to engage in appropriation (Pisano et al., 1988), overlap between allying partners in markets (Khanna, Gulati and Nohria, 1998) or technologies (Colombo, 2003), and presence of trust or relational capital between partners (Gulati, 1995) as key determinants of governance choice, and in turn of the risks of influence, misappropriation of rents, and degree of coordination.

We suggest that in addition to partner considerations, the strategic characteristics of the alliance transaction will be useful in explaining the choice of
governance mechanisms, whether institutional or contractual, in technology
alliances. We propose that strategic intent, transactional complexity, and
proximity in the location and technology of its partners will have implications for appropriation, coordination and flexibility, thereby influencing
the choice of governance type. This effort will (1) bring strategy back into
the resource-based argument, which tends to focus only on the potential
of capabilities to generate advantage, and (2) address the actual knowledge
transacted, rather than making assumptions about this knowledge from the
characteristics of the partners.

Theory development

High-technology alliances and governance

Technological dynamism, reflected in an industry environment punctuated
by competence destroying technologies, forces firms to maintain a wide
range of technological knowledge and skills (Tushman and Anderson, 1986).
However, very few firms can develop this wide range of knowledge internally at short notice – outside know-how is needed. Further, technological
know-how is difficult to buy in a pure market transaction due to difficulties associated with its evaluation and transmission – again, particularly
in the short time frames available in dynamic industry sectors (Vanhaverbeke et al., 2002). Alliances offer a viable alternative route for firms to access
external knowledge resources in a dynamic industry environment. This is
demonstrated by the widespread use of strategic alliances in industries like
biotechnology and semiconductors that are characterized by ongoing rapid
technological innovation. Technology alliances are used by firms for various
purposes, such as new product development (Rothaermel and Deeds, 2004),
creation of new capabilities (Colombo, 2003) or transfer of existing knowledge (Khanna et al., 1998). Such objectives naturally create the need for
organizational structures that encourage frequent and close partner interaction in order to facilitate the transmission of new technical knowledge.

However, transaction cost concerns suggest that while a key objective of
the alliance may be to acquire specialized and crucial knowledge resources
from other organizations, this must be balanced with avoiding compromise
of the firm's own skills and capabilities with its partners (Yeheskel et al.,
2001; Heiman and Nickerson, 2004). Firms tend to be protective of their core
knowledge in order to prevent unwanted appropriation by alliance partners
(Norman, 2002). A particular aspect of technology alliances is the potential
competition for ideas; 'learning races' (Khanna et al., 1998; Hamel, 1991)
which result either in the firm absorbing and learning critical capabilities
from its partner or in the firm losing its own capabilities to its partner.
Allying partners must adopt a structure that provides safeguards from opportunistic behaviour, but must do so in a reasonably efficient manner, and

without destroying the sense of cooperation and mutuality necessary to achieve coordination.

One of the mechanisms used by firms in alliances to address the balance of coordination and appropriation concerns in the context of strategic alliances is the choice of governance mechanism. Tallman (1999) proposes that the resources and capabilities of the potential partners drive the choice of alliance governance mechanism, such that technical capabilities that have to deal with greater appropriability issues and higher coordination costs are more likely to result in equity involvement. This view is substantiated by findings (Pisano, 1994; Gulati and Singh, 1998) that alliances with a technological component are more likely to rely on shared equity holdings since they allow firms to deal effectively with appropriation concerns. Alliances that are closer to hierarchies, such as equity joint ventures, perform better at interorganizational learning (Oxley, 1997), especially in the transfer of complex tacit capabilities (Kogut, 1988) than do less formal alliances. Heiman and Nickerson (2004) show that formal mechanisms for knowledge sharing help coordination, and that such mechanisms are supported by equity involvement to reduce the increased risk of opportunism when such mechanisms are in place. Institutional alliances typically entail the revelation of broad product and process technologies, and require active efforts to help the partner to learn about these capabilities, but the institutional mechanism of shared equity also provides an organizational context that aligns partner interests, potentially providing better monitoring and control and thereby preventing appropriation of core assets (Hennart, 1988).

Contractual alliances, on the other hand, can only protect partners from opportunism by strictly limiting cooperation to the specific scope of the alliance. Less technical knowledge is revealed, specific terms for compensation are agreed, and complex process capabilities are typically not revealed. On the other hand, these limitations reduce learning potential and limit the potential benefits from collaboration. Why would contractual alliances ever be used? They are less costly to manage. Institutional governance mechanisms are expensive in both time and investment capital at every stage, from negotiation of the deal, to setting up the equity structure, to staffing an independent venture, to providing strategic oversight, to dividing the assets upon termination. Contracts are less expensive to write, manage and end – if they can suffice to accomplish the necessary tasks. We propose that technology alliances will make a choice between contractual and institutional mechanisms based on the strategic characteristics of the alliance and their effects on appropriation and coordination.

Strategic characteristics of the alliance

Alliance intent. Although alliances with a technological component are characterized by a common motivation to exchange, share or develop knowledge, their intent often varies. Some technology alliances are formed with competitors with a view towards cooperative product development or to create access to complementary knowledge/capabilities, often involving manufacturing and research and development. Such alliances are typically horizontal in nature, that is, the partners participate at the same stage of the same value-added chain or chains, and thus imply considerable similarity of resources and capabilities between the allying partners. We might expect partners in such alliances to demonstrate high levels of absorptive capacity for each other's technical knowledge. However, firms from different industry sectors (as in biotechnology) may actually have somewhat different, even competing, technologies. Overlap between partners' knowledge bases has been found to facilitate shared learning (Dyer and Singh, 1998), but formal mechanisms for alliance management (Kale et al., 2002) or formal knowledge management practices improve the transfer of tacit or complex knowledge (Heiman and Nickerson, 2004). Investment in a formal structure to facilitate coordination of knowledge may be necessary if highly tacit or complex knowledge is involved, and it seems particularly likely that complex process knowledge will be shared in horizontal alliances, where the R&D or manufacturing systems of the partners must mesh.

At the same time, appropriation concerns also will tend to be higher in horizontal transactions due to the ease with which partner firms can appropriate critical knowledge from each other, particularly when they actively encourage integrative learning. Further, these appropriation concerns may extend to most or all areas of the firm's capabilities due to greater overlap – absorptive capacity is not limited to the knowledge covered by the alliance. Contractual agreements can only account for unintended spillovers if the agreement is highly restrictive, which will hinder cooperation in sharing tacit knowledge. An institutional arrangement with equity sharing, on the other hand, should provide a degree of alignment of interests that will limit misappropriation of knowledge. We expect alliances with primary manufacturing or R&D objectives to use institutional governance mechanisms in response to both appropriation concerns and learning coordination needs.

Alliances with a technology component are also formed between partners whose core expertise is at different stages of the value-added chain. In biotechnology, these vertical alliances are often reflected in alliances between biotechnology firms with innovative products and pharmaceutical companies with downstream capabilities in drug testing and marketing or in licensing of technology for sale of products in other markets or supply of financial funds or intermediate products and raw materials. Such alliances are vertical in nature. Appropriation concerns in these alliances are reduced due to the distinctiveness of resources and capabilities that each partner possesses. This distinction and specialization makes it harder for a firm to appropriate a partner's knowledge due to limited absorptive capacity for the other's tacit knowledge. Further, ongoing coordination between partners concerning explicit technology or products is not necessary as there is a clear hand-off between partners with little need for detailed learning. Investment in expensive institutional mechanisms is not necessary, due to limited appropriation and coordination pressures and a contractual arrangement often suits these alliances.

Partner proximity – geographic. Besides the intent of the alliance, we expect the geographic location of the allying partners to influence the choice of governance mechanism. The regional cluster literature points to the benefits of knowledge spillovers that occur through simple physical presence in a geographic location. Geographic proximity enhances the development of local networks that facilitate the transfer of knowledge from one firm to another (Saxenian, 1994). However, Zaheer and George (2004) suggest that simple co-location in clusters is not sufficient to access knowledge. They determine that firms need to develop alliances within clusters and outside clusters to engage in knowledge transfer. We suggest that the governance mechanisms for alliances with geographically proximate partners and geographically distant partners will vary primarily due to the differences in the social networking relationships that exist within clusters and outside clusters. Informal social relationships between allying partners in proximate locations create relational capital, engender similar structural understandings of the industry, and permit the development of trust, which allays appropriation concerns. The benefits provided by an institutional mechanism are substituted by the relational capital created due to geographical closeness. Alliances between geographically proximate firms therefore can use contractual mechanisms more effectively than can partners from different geographic locations.

Partner proximity – technological. Alliance partners that have similar technological profiles and are focused on the same industry niche or pursue similar R&D projects are likely to communicate complex knowledge more easily due to high relative absorptive capacity (Lane and Lubatkin, 1998). Proximity of partners, in contrast to horizontal alliance intent, specifically demonstrates greater overlap technological areas and therefore such alliances are less likely to require investment in an institutional mechanism for the purpose of coordination than others. However, such alliances have potentially higher risks of appropriation since the participants have better understandings of their partner's knowledge and technology, and technological proximity does not necessarily entail social networking. Whether in horizontal or vertical alliances, partners in close technological proximity can limit appropriation fears in two ways. Restrictive contracts can explicitly limit the scope of knowledge exchanges, or institutional alliances with shared equity can reduce the incentives for misappropriation. In a situation with relatively low needs for detailed coordination, due to shared understanding of the application of the technology, appropriation concerns will be particularly critical when external IP regimes are loose. However, careful contracting, particularly when patent protection is strong and limits opportunities for misappropriation without consequence, will be less expensive than institutional governance when there is little associated learning benefit. In alliances where partners are technologically distant, appropriation concerns are limited by the inability of participants to effectively absorb partners' knowledge, but close coordination to develop common understandings of the technology being exchanged and thereby to enhance mutual absorptive capacity seems critical and an institutional mechanism would be valuable. This outcome is most likely in industries with strong patent enforcement to further limit the potential for misappropriation of knowledge.

Complexity of the alliance. Another facet of the alliance is the complexity inherent in the knowledge exchange. When alliances involve multidirectional knowledge and technology flows between partners in contrast to unidirectional flows they are likely to raise challenges in the context of both coordination and appropriation. Coordinating multidirectional flows is more complex than arranging for unidirectional flows, and is more likely to need a supporting infrastructure to ensure smooth and timely knowledge flows. An institutional mechanism would be most appropriately equipped to offer the flexibility of modifying the organization structure to support these flows. Multidirectional knowledge flows also require multiple frequent interactions between partners, thus exposing core technologies and knowledge and also creating complex transactions. Consequently appropriation concerns are likely to be high and complete contracts more difficult to write, also favouring an institutional mechanism. In contrast, alliances with unidirectional flows are likely to face lower pressures for coordination and lower risks of knowledge misappropriation and thus can use contractual mechanisms. In general, complex technology alliances will be more likely to use institutional mechanisms.

Analysis

We test our hypotheses in the biotechnology sector, which seems to be an appropriate starting point since innovation and technology development is critical in biotechnology (Sorensen and Stuart, 2000; Kogut and Kim, 1994) and alliances are often used as routes for accessing knowledge external to the firm (Powell et al., 1996). We compiled our sample of alliances from the Securities and Data Company (SDC) Database on Joint Ventures and Strategic Alliances, including all US domestic alliances announced between 1 January 1990 and 31 December 1995, resulting in a sample of 248 alliances, ensuring that alliance partners had to deal with a homogeneous intellectual property regime, providing similar levels of protection.

Dependent variable
Institutional mechanism. Alliances were classified as institutional if partners contributed equity and contractual if there were no equity commitments.

Independent variables
Alliance intent. We coded information about the alliance intent to reflect each purpose for which it was formed, characterized as marketing, licensing, manufacturing, supply (of materials), funding (financial support) and research and development. Alliances often had multiple objectives.

Partner proximity – geographic. A binary variable indicating whether or not all partners in the alliance were located in the same state.

Partner proximity – technological. A binary variable indicating whether all participants in the alliance had the same 3-digit primary SIC code.

Complexity of knowledge exchange. A binary variable that indicates alliances in which there were multidirectional transfers of technology (for example, either from multiple partners to the alliance or from multiple partners to each other, as opposed to alliances with unidirectional technology flows (from only one partner to the alliance).

Findings

Given the binary nature of our dependent variable, we used logistic regression analysis to test our model. In our sample, we find very few instances of alliances using institutional mechanisms, as only 20 alliances in our sample involved equity sharing, while 228 of the alliances were cooperative contractual arrangements. Alliances were formed for multiple objectives; however, more than half of them had R&D, licensing or marketing objectives. Manufacturing was also a significant objective, with a quarter of the sample indicating it as their purpose. Supply and funding arrangements were limited. Participants in the alliances tended to be more proximate geographically than technologically and most alliances did not involve complex knowledge exchanges.

In testing the effects of strategic intent, we find that manufacturing agreements increase the likelihood of using an institutional mechanism over straight R&D alliances, in accordance with our expectations. Downstream types of vertical alliances, such as marketing and licensing, lead to a greater likelihood of a contractual alliance, again as predicted. Supply and funding agreements have no effect on the choice of governance mechanism.

Geographic proximity does not seem to influence the governance mechanism. Partner technological proximity receives weak support when entered separately, but is highly significant in a comprehensive model. Our findings indicate that greater technological proximity leads to a greater use of the contractual mechanism. In the strong patenting regime that is associated with biotechnology in the United States, appropriation concerns are likely to be low for any patent licensing, and a contractual mechanism should be adequate to protect knowledge and less costly to administer than an institutional arrangement (Ernst and Young, 1993; Shan and Song, 1997). Finally, the complexity of the alliance, when tested alone, is found to lead to an increased likelihood of using an institutional mechanism. However, this variable loses its effect in a comprehensive model, possibly due to its strong negative correlations with the variables representing downstream strategic intentions and resulting multicollinearity.

Conclusion

Our analysis of alliances in the biotechnology industry highlights the effects of the strategic characteristics of an alliance on the choice of governance mechanisms. While prior research, typically based on industry character-istics, has suggested that technology alliances are more likely to rely on institutional mechanisms, our findings demonstrate limited use of the insti-tutional mechanism in the biotechnology industry. Further, we find that this decision is contingent on various transactional characteristics – the alliance intent, the technological proximity of partners and the complexity of the alliance. Key findings that emerged were that manufacturing alliances tend to use institutional mechanisms, while marketing, licensing alliances and alliances with technologically proximate partners tended to use contractual mechanisms.

The driving factor in this industry sector behind the choice of governance mechanism appears to coordination issues rather than appropriation concerns. Transaction cost arguments regarding risks of appropriation that make institutional mechanisms the preferred choice for technology alliances do not hold sway in this industry sector, probably due to its strong IP protection regime. Thus, industry environment, in the case of biotechno-logy a strong patent protection regime, may reduce appropriation concerns (Teece, 1986). With coordination issues as the key factor, our findings achieve greater plausibility – manufacturing alliances require more coordin-ation in contrast to marketing or licensing alliances that require limited interaction. Similarly, technologically proximate alliances do not necessarily need supplemental coordination mechanisms but can simply rely on generic shared knowledge and can therefore utilize contractual mechanisms. These findings offer important implications for managers. An effective way to exchange technology in certain industries may be through the creation of cooperative arrangements with technologically similar partners. Substantial investment in an institutional mechanism may be unwarranted to guard against appropriation in industries with strong patent protection and high propensity to patent (Teece, 1986).

However, our study has its limitations. We have focused on alliances in a single industry and our findings may not be representative of other industries with weaker intellectual property regimes. Future research can contrast the usage of governance mechanisms in industries with differing levels of patent protection. We confined our sample to domestic alliances. Perhaps firms are more willing to use a contractual mechanism in alliances with partners from the same country due to a common institutional context reflected in common rules and regulations. Alliances between firms from different countries may rely more on institutional mechanisms due to inherent differences in partners, and their national environments.

Notes

1. Stephen Tallman, Robins School of Business, University of Richmond, Richmond, VA 23173, Tel: 804 287 6589, Fax: 804 289 8878, E-mail: stallman@richmond.edu
2. Anupama Phene, David Eccles School of Business, University of Utah, 1645 East, Campus Center Drive, Salt Lake City, UT 84112, Tel: 801 587 9055, Fax: 801 581 7214, E-mail: mgtap@business.utah.edu

References

Colombo, M. (2003) 'Alliance Form: a Test of the Contractual and Competence Perspectives', *Strategic Management Journal*, 24: 1209–29.

Doz, Y. and Hamel, G. (1998) *Alliance Advantage: the Art of Creating Value through Partnering*, Boston, MA: Harvard Business School Press.

Dyer, J. and Singh, H. (1998) 'Relational Advantage: Relational Rents and Sources of Interorganizational Competitive Advantage', *Academy of Management Review*, 23: 660–79.

Ernst & Young (1993) *Biotech 93*, San Francisco: Arthur Young High Technology Group.

Gerwin, D. and Ferris, J. (2004) 'Organizing New Product Development Projects in Strategic Alliances', *Organization Science*, 15: 22–38.

Gulati, R. (1995) 'Does Familiarity Breed Trust? The Implications of Repeated Ties for Contractual Choice in Alliances', *Academy of Management Journal*, 38: 85–112.

Gulati, R. and Singh, H. (1998) 'The Architecture of Cooperation: Managing Coordination Costs and Appropriation Concerns in Strategic Alliances', *Administrative Science Quarterly*, 43: 781–815.

Hamel, G. (1991) 'Competition for Competence and Interpartner Learning within International Strategic Alliances', *Strategic Management Journal*, Summer Special Issue 12: 83–103.

Heiman, B. A. and Nickerson, J. A. (2004) 'Empirical Evidence Regarding the Tension between Knowledge Sharing and Knowledge Expropriation in Collaborations', *Managerial and Decision Economics*, 25: 401–20.

Hennart, J.-F. (1988) 'A Transaction Costs Theory of Equity Joint Ventures', *Strategic Management Journal*, 9: 361–74.

Kale, P., Dyer, J. and Singh, H. (2002) 'Alliance Capability, Stock Market Response, and Long Term Alliance Success', *Strategic Management Journal*, 23: 747–68.

Khanna, T., Gulati, R. and Nohria, N. (1998) 'The Dynamics of Learning Alliances: Competition, Cooperation, and Relative Scope', *Strategic Management Journal*, 19: 193–210.

Kogut, B. (1988) 'Joint Ventures: Theoretical and Empirical Perspectives', *Strategic Management Journal*, 9: 319–32.

Kogut, B. and Kim, D. (1994) 'Technological Platforms and Diversification', *Organization Science*, 7: 283–302.

Lane, P. and Lubatkin, M. (1998) 'Relative Absorptive Capacity and Interorganizational Learning', *Strategic Management Journal*, 19: 461–77.

Norman, P. (2002) 'Protecting Knowledge in Strategic Alliances – Resource and Relational Characteristics', *Journal of High Technology and Management Research*, 13: 177–90.

Oxley, J. (1997) 'Appropriability Hazards and Governance in Strategic Alliances: a Transaction Cost Approach', *Journal of Law, Economics, and Organization*, 13: 387–409.

Pisano, G. (1994) 'Knowledge Integration and the Locus of Learning: an Empirical Analysis of Process Development', *Strategic Management Journal*, 15: 85–101.

Pisano, G., Russo, M. and Teece, D. (1988) 'Joint Ventures and Collaborative Arrangements in the Telecommunications Equipment Industry', in *International Collaborative Ventures in US Manufacturing*, ed. D. Mowery, Washington, DC: American Enterprise Institute: 23–70.

Powell, W., Koput, K. and Smith-Doerr, L. (1996) 'Interorganizational Collaboration and the Locus of Innovation: Networks of Learning in Biotechnology', *Administrative Science Quarterly*, 41: 116–45.

Rothaermel, F. and Deeds, D. (2004) 'Exploration and Exploitation Alliances in Biotechnology: a System of New Product Development', *Strategic Management Journal*, 25: 201–25.

Saxenian, A. (1994) *Regional Advantage*, Cambridge, MA: Harvard University Press.

Shan, W. and Song, J. (1997) 'Foreign Direct Investment and the Sourcing of Technological Advantage: Evidence From the Biotechnology Industry', *Journal of International Business Studies*, 28: 267–84.

Sorensen, J. and Stuart, T. (2000) 'Aging, Obsolescence and Innovation', *Administrative Science Quarterly*, 45: 81–112.

Tallman, S. (1999) 'The Multiple Roles of Alliances in Competency-Based Multinational Strategies', *Management International Review*, 39: 65–82.

Teece, D. J. (1986) 'Profiting from Technological Innovation: Implications for Integration, Collaboration, Licensing and Public Policy', *Research Policy*, 15: 285–305.

Tushman, M. and Anderson, P. (1986) 'Technological Discontinuities and Organizational Environments', *Administrative Science Quarterly*, 31: 439–65.

Vanhaverbeke, W., Duysters, G. and Noorderhaven, N. (2002) 'External Technology Sourcing through Alliances or Acquisitions: an Analysis of the Application Specific Integrated Circuits Industry', *Organization Science*, 13: 714–34.

Yeheskel, O., Shenkar, O., Figenbaum, A., Cohen, E. and Giffen, I. (2001) 'Co-operative Wealth Creation: Strategic Alliances in Israeli Medical Technology Ventures', *Academy of Management Executive*, 15: 16–26.

Zaheer, A. and George, V. (2004) 'Reach Out or Reach Within? Performance Implications of Alliances and Location within Biotechnology', *Managerial and Decision Economics*, 25: 431–52.

8
Licences and Joint Ventures as Knowledge Acquisition Mechanisms: Evidence from US–Japan Alliances

Joanne E. Oxley[1] and Tetsuo Wada[2]

Introduction

A central theme of economic change during the postwar period has been the global diffusion of technological knowledge, and government efforts to influence international technology flows for national competitive advantage (Freeman, 1987; Nelson, 1993). Examples of countries where externally developed technology has been a critical driver of economic transformation include Japan and the East Asian 'tigers', Korea, Singapore and Taiwan[3] and, more recently, China. Newly industrializing countries are not the only, nor even the primary, recipients of significant international technology flows, however. Long after it has caught up and overtaken many leading Western economies, Japan continues to be a major importer of foreign technology, particularly from the US, even as it has become a leading source of technology flows to other countries around the globe.

Much of the prior research on international technology transfer has focused on the 'absorptive capacity' of local firms, or of the local economy in general, and how this enhances the effectiveness of inward technology transfer (Mowery and Oxley, 1995). In this chapter we refocus attention on the organizational vehicles used for knowledge acquisition in international markets and, in particular, examine the role of alliance governance and contracts in shaping the scope of knowledge transfer from foreign to domestic companies. This is an important area of inquiry since governments continue to differentially support certain types of alliance in an effort to influence international technology flows.

More generally, alliance partners have a clear interest in designing their alliance structures to provide appropriate incentives for the knowledge sharing necessary to achieve alliance objectives, but our knowledge of how different alliance structures affect these incentives and knowledge transfers is still quite limited. We know little, for example, about the *breadth* of knowledge transfers achieved in different types of alliances: are inter-firm knowledge transfers limited to knowledge directly related to alliance activities, or do alliance partners also gain access to apparently unrelated knowledge? Does this vary systematically with alliance type? In instances where pairs or groups of firms are involved in multiple alliances together, does the existence of other alliances linking the same partners affect the scope of knowledge transfers in a focal alliance? If so, how?

Below, we provide more details on the role of alliances in international technology transfer in the latter half of the twentieth century. We present theoretical arguments relating the structure of individual technology alliances and 'dyadic alliance portfolios' to the scope of technological knowledge acquired by a firm from an international alliance partner. We then report data on technology in-licensing by Japanese firms that provide relevant evidence of how different types of alliances shape the knowledge flows realized within an alliance. The findings reveal that alliance governance and contract structure have significant effects on these knowledge flows. We discuss possible implications for government policy and, more directly, for the design and management of interfirm alliances.

The role of alliances in international technology transfer

International technology transfers take place through a variety of channels, including foreign direct investment, joint ventures and other alliances, licensing, and trade in capital goods. Of these, licensing agreements and other technology alliances became increasingly prevalent in the last decades of the twentieth century. During the 1980s, for example, the rate of establishment of international technology alliances roughly doubled and, after a slow-down in the early 1990s, peaked again around 1995 and continued at an elevated level through the turn of the century (Freeman and Hagedoorn, 1994; Hagedoorn, 2002); meanwhile, US royalty receipts grew by more than 75 per cent between 1980 and 1990 (US Department of Commerce data, cited in Mowery and Oxley, 1995: 75) and, as an example of the growth trend on the recipient side, South Korean spending on licences for imports of technology grew tenfold during the 1982–91 period (OECD, 1992).

Government policy has often actively encouraged in-licensing by domestic companies and has sometimes limited foreign companies' ability to invest in equity joint ventures or wholly-owned subsidiaries, in the belief that the high degree of foreign control retained in many joint ventures may limit technology flows to domestic firms (Contractor, 1990). Meanwhile, government officials and commentators in advanced economies such as the US have sometimes expressed concern that joint ventures with foreign companies may result in excessive knowledge transfer and so undermine the competitiveness of domestic firms (Reich and Mankin, 1986; Hamel, 1991). These seemingly contradictory concerns point to a need for greater understanding of the connection between governance structure and knowledge flows in alliances of different types.

Alliance governance and the scope of knowledge transfer

For firms wishing to access technology and related knowledge via an alliance, there are multiple modes of cooperation open to them, each with different costs and performance attributes. Transaction cost theory posits that alliance types range along a market-hierarchy continuum (Oxley, 1997), from the most arm's-length unilateral technology licence agreements, through cross-licensing or other contract-based technology sharing agreements, to equity joint ventures that approach the governance properties of internal organization or hierarchy. The logic underlying this market-hierarchy alliance continuum is the following: moving from a unilateral to a cross-licensing agreement increases incentive alignment because the reciprocal nature of the agreement provides incentives for on-going cooperation. The shared equity and joint returns achieved within an equity joint venture further increases incentive alignment and promotes cooperation and knowledge sharing. Prior research, focusing on the structure of individual alliances, has shown that joint ventures support greater knowledge transfer than arm's-length agreements, providing evidence of the positive relationship between the extent (or rate) of knowledge transfer and the presence of hierarchical structures in an alliance (Kogut, 1988; Mowery et al., 1996).

Joint ventures have an additional feature, however, in addition to shared equity: joint ventures also embody complex administrative structures and joint board membership. The joint board provides a direct communication link with senior managers of the parent companies and provides for greater monitoring of alliance and partner firm activities (Kogut, 1988). Furthermore, joint venture partners have enhanced auditing rights over financial and operational activities related to the alliance (Osborn and Baughn, 1990). In the context of a technology transfer alliance, this enhanced control and monitoring rights that accrue to the partner firm providing the technology may be used to limit the scope of knowledge flows in an attempt to reduce potentially harmful 'leakage' of valuable intellectual property (Oxley and Sampson, 2004). Indeed, the ability to place such controls on unintended knowledge transfers is arguably an important underpinning of the enhanced knowledge sharing (within the domain of the alliance activities) that we associate with the joint venture structure. This logic thus suggests that even as joint ventures result in *higher* alliance-related knowledge transfers, they may produce *lower* knowledge transfers in areas unrelated to alliance activities, relative to contract-based alliances.

In addition to the direct effect of contract/administrative structure on knowledge flows within a focal alliance, we should also consider the potential effect of the 'dyadic alliance portfolio'. A given pair of firms is often involved in multiple alliances together, and their dyadic alliance portfolio may comprise a mix of joint ventures and non-equity agreements such as patent licences.[4] In addition, although the alliances in this portfolio are sometimes intimately related – for example when licensing occurs within the context of a particular joint venture – for diversified and/or multi-unit firms, it is often the case that different alliances are in quite distinct technology domains, operationally unrelated to each other.

There are theoretical reasons to suspect some degree of complementarity between joint ventures and licence agreements for interfirm knowledge transfer even when they are operationally distinct. Joint ventures represent a mutual hostage arrangement (Oxley, 1997), potentially increasing the cost of defection from *any* agreement linking the partner firms. It thus follows that, in addition to enhancing cooperation and knowledge-sharing in the venture itself, the presence of this hostage could reduce the risk of opportunistic behaviour (and hence increase knowledge sharing) in concurrent alliances, even when they are operationally unrelated. In addition, the joint venture structure, by its very nature, increases the density of organizational linkages and personal contacts between the partner firms (Kogut, 1988), possibly increasing 'partner-specific absorptive capacity' (Mowery et al., 2002), as partners learn how to interface and transfer knowledge effectively. This may facilitate subsequent knowledge transfer and absorption in both related and unrelated alliances (Lane and Lubatkin, 1998), particularly if a firm has a centrally managed alliance management structure (Dyer et al., 2001).

In summary, our theoretical arguments suggest that, in comparison with simple unilateral or bilateral licensing agreements, an equity joint venture embodies structures that support greater knowledge transfers within the scope of alliance activities, while also limiting unintended leakage of technological knowledge in unrelated areas. Furthermore, to the extent that partners take into consideration the benefits of maintaining cooperation in other relationships not directly related to the focal alliance activities, then the existence of multiple alliances joining the same partners may enhance realized knowledge flows in a particular alliance.

Empirical context

The empirical context for our study is technology in-licensing from the US by Japanese firms.[5] Particularly detailed data on these in-licensing activities exist because Japanese firms were required to report technology importing contracts (patent and know-how licensing) under Article 29 of the Foreign Exchange Law of Japan (1949 Law 228), in effect until 1998. We were able to gain access to data from the National Institute for Science and Technology Policy (NISTEP), on the content and terms of all patent licence agreements between Japanese and US firms during the period 1988–92. This data encompassed 602 contracts involving 1807 patents. Over 80 per cent of these contracts were in the electronics and machinery sectors. The contracts included a mixture of unilateral and cross-licence agreements, although we have information on the content and terms of the in-licence only.[6] Thus, all of the licensors in our empirical study are US firms and all of the licensees are Japanese firms.

In addition to data availability, Japan provides an attractive context for our study of knowledge acquisition through alliances because, as indicated in the introduction, externally generated technology played an important role in the transformation of the Japanese economy in the post-1945 era, and Japan continues to be a major importer of technology, particularly from the US. Furthermore, Japan kept restrictive policies on inward direct investment until late 1970s, which promoted licensing of technology relative to direct investment by foreign firms. It is important to note, however, that by the time of our study (1988–92) no significant restrictions on establishment of equity joint ventures (even if majority foreign-owned) or on licensing terms remained in place (Aramaki, 2004). As such, we can infer that firms involved in the alliances in our sample freely chose alliance structures to meet the knowledge transfer goals of the partner firms.

To capture other characteristics of our sample firms' 'dyadic alliance portfolio', and to measure the knowledge transfers that were realized in different alliances, we married the NISTEP data with data from two other sources. First, we matched the licensing data with data on joint venture agreements in effect at the beginning of the sample period, documented in the *Toyokeizai Directory of Foreign Subsidiaries in Japan*, and *Toyokeizai Directory of Foreign Subsidiaries by Japanese Firms*. Of the 536 firm dyads in our sample, 27 firm pairs had equity joint ventures in effect at the beginning of the sample period. Of these, 13 joint ventures were directly related to the in-licensing activity – as indicated by the fact that the patent licence was granted to the joint venture rather than to the Japanese parent company itself. We assume that the other 14 joint ventures were unrelated to the in-licensing activity, since it was highly unusual for a US firm to grant a JV-related licence to the Japanese parent company during this period.

Second, following prior research (Almeida, 1996; Mowery et al., 1996) we measure alliance knowledge flows using patent citation data, drawn primarily from the *Micropatent* database, which records details of every patent granted in the US since 1975. Patent citations have been shown to serve as a useful indicator of the technological lineage of new patents, much as bibliographic citations indicate the intellectual lineage of academic research (Jaffe and Trajtenberg, 2002): when a Japanese firm cites its US partner more frequently after establishment of an alliance, this indicates that the Japanese firm has acquired technological knowledge from its US partner; the greater the rate of increased citation, the greater the extent of knowledge transfer.

In addition to measuring the overall extent of knowledge transfer, the citation measures also give an indication of the *breadth* of the flow. Patents are classified by the patent examiner into technology 'classes' that represent different technological areas. These technology classes have been used in prior research as an indication of a firm's areas of technological expertise (e.g. Jaffe, 1986). Thus, by looking at the technology class of the patents that the Japanese firm is citing after the alliance has been established, we can distinguish between citations to patents that belong to the same technology classes as the licensed patents – indicating *alliance-related* knowledge flows – and citations to patents that belong to technology classes not covered by the licensed patents – indications of *unrelated* knowledge flows.

To analyse these data we used a regression technique suitable for analysis of patent data – negative binomial regression – to examine the relationship between alliance and dyadic portfolio structures on overall knowledge flows within the alliance, as well as on alliance-related and unrelated knowledge flows. In addition to the indicators of alliance governance structures and dyadic alliance portfolios that are our primary concern, we also control for other alliance partner characteristics that are likely to affect the knowledge flows within an alliance, and/or our empirical indicator of these flows, that is the extent to which the Japanese licensee cites the US licensor's patents following alliance formation. The elements of our empirical model are summarized in Figure 8.1.

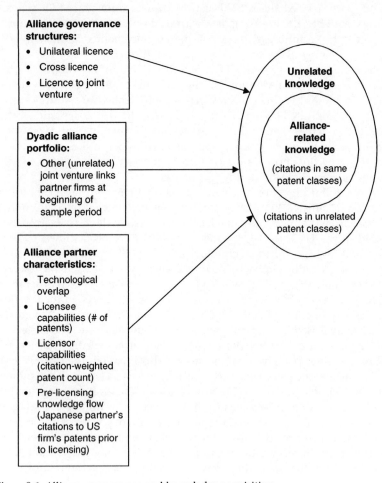

Figure 8.1: Alliance governance and knowledge acquisition

Results

The results from our analysis reveal the following significant findings (summarized in Table 8.1). First, the data show that moving from a unilateral to a cross-licensing arrangement increases both the rate and breadth of knowledge transfers from a licensor to licensee: we see elevated citation rates in technology areas unrelated to the licensed patent as well as in related technology areas. This supports prior research arguing that the bilateral nature of cross-licence agreements leads to greater incentive alignment, infuses the relationship with confidence and reduces concerns regarding misappropriate, so increasing knowledge sharing (Oxley, 1997). Second, we see that the existence of a joint venture linking the two firms at the beginning of the sample period further enhances alliance-related knowledge transfer realized in the focal licence agreement, but with some important caveats: while knowledge transfers directly related to the alliance activity are enhanced (citation rates in the technology classes covered by the patent licence increase), knowledge transfers in other areas are significantly *decreased* (i.e. citation rates in technology classes not covered by the licensed patents are lower than for an equivalent 'bare' licence). Our interpretation of this result is that joint venture participants are actively managing knowledge flows within the venture to limit unintended leakage of valuable technological knowledge that is not directly related to alliance activities. Such limits are likely to be accepted by the Japanese partner, since the US partner will be more open to sharing alliance-related knowledge when they have confidence that knowledge transfers are limited in unrelated domains. Although we do not see evidence here of a positive net impact on *total* knowledge transfers (relative to a 'bare' licensing agreement), this may simply be indicative of the fact that many of the JVs in the sample have been in existence for several years at the time that the licensing agreement is initiated[7] and, as a result, significant knowledge transfers have already been achieved. Since our empirical analysis includes a control variable measuring pre-licence citation rates, the effect of this prior learning is reflected in the positive coefficient on the pre-licence citation variable.

In terms of potential dyadic portfolio effects on knowledge acquisition, we find no evidence of this in our data. In particular, there is no observed empirical relationship between the existence of a JV linking the licensor and licensee firms and the extent or breadth of knowledge transfer in a focal licence except where the JV is directly related to the licensing activity. This is a surprising finding and, if it withstands further scrutiny, suggests that the 'action' in understanding alliance outcomes resides primarily in the structuring and management of individual alliances, rather than in the 'dyadic alliance portfolio', and that managers in diversified firms do not need to take into account the existence of alliances in other divisions of the firm for the design and management of a focal alliance.

Table 8.1: Summary of results

Predictor variable	Impact on overall knowledge transfer	Impact on transfer of alliance-related knowledge	Impact on transfer of unrelated knowledge	Interpretation
Cross licence	+	+	+	Greater incentive alignment in cross licence increases knowledge transfer
Licence to joint venture	None	++	–	Joint venture increases alliance-related knowledge transfer even further, and decreases leakage of unrelated knowledge
Unrelated JV	None	None	None	Dyadic alliance portfolio has no significant effect on knowledge transfer in focal alliance
Technology overlap	+	+	+	Firms are more able to acquire knowledge from alliance partners with expertise in similar technology areas
Licensee patents	+	+	+	More capable firms are more able to acquire technological knowledge from alliance partners
Importance of licensor's patents	+	+	+	Licensees are more likely to cite licensor's patents when these are 'important' patents, with broad applicability
Pre-licence citation rate	+	+	+	Firms that previously cited their alliance partner's patents frequently, continue o do so

Discussion

In summary, the empirical analysis reported here provides confirmation of some previous results regarding the differential impact of different alliance 'modes' on knowledge transfer, and adds significantly to prior research in several respects. Most fundamentally, our research suggests that knowledge flows realized in alliances do not simply increase monotonically as we move along the market-hierarchy continuum: while alliance-related knowledge transfers do increase with each move to a more hierarchical structure, unrelated knowledge flows do not conform to this pattern but are instead reduced when licensing occurs within the context of a joint venture.

Although interesting and provocative, the empirical analysis reported here is clearly subject to limitations. From a policy perspective, without a good model of how the firm-level effects we observe aggregate up to the country level, we can only speculate on the implications of our results for national technology policy. However, the results are consistent with the belief embodied in diffusion-oriented technology policies such as those found in Japan, Taiwan, Switzerland and elsewhere (Ergas, 1986; Chiang, 1995), that significant benefits can be gained from encouraging technology importing via in-licensing by local firms. The results call into question, however, policies promoting in-licensing over equity-based investments, which have sometimes been a part of diffusion-oriented policy regimes, since foreign multinationals appear to be more willing to increase alliance-related technology transfer in instances where the partner firms are also linked in an equity joint venture.

Aside from these level of analysis issues, our study is also subject to some technical limitations. Chief among these is the issue of unobserved heterogeneity, and the potential problems of endogeneity that this introduces. Because we know that firms selectively adopt different modes of cooperation (Oxley, 1997; Colombo, 2003), ignoring this selection process may introduce bias into estimates of the subsequent performance of different modes (Shaver, 1998). We have taken steps in the current empirical design to mitigate the potential impact of such endogeneity, and note that our test of the impact of pre-existing joint ventures on knowledge transfer in subsequent licence agreements is quite conservative: firm dyads with pre-existing joint ventures have already experienced significant knowledge sharing and 'convergence' (Mowery et al., 2002) in their technological portfolios by the beginning of the sample period, and we control for start-of-period citation rates and technological overlap in our analysis. At a minimum, our results indicate that additional research is needed, to explore in greater detail how contract and governance structures in different alliance types shape knowledge-sharing incentives and outcomes.

Notes

1. Joanne E. Oxley, Rotman School of Management, University of Toronto, 105 St.George Street, Toronto ON M5S 3E6, Canada, E-mail: oxley@rotman.utoronto.ca
2. Tetsuo Wada, Gakushuin University, Faculty of Economics, 1-5-1 Mejiro, Toshima-ku, Tokyo 171-8588 Japan. E-mail: tetsuo.wada@gakushuin.ac.jp
3. See, for example, Pack (2001) for an assessment of the role of externally developed technology in explaining Taiwan's rapid growth over the period 1960–90.
4. Note that our focus on 'dyadic portfolio effects' is quite distinct from previous considerations of how a focal firm's position in an overall network of alliances and other interorganizational ties impacts knowledge flows to the firm (e.g. Ahuja, 2000; Powell et al., 1996).
5. For details of the empirical study referred to here, see Oxley and Wada (2005).
6. NISTEP records whether a particular licence is part of a cross-licence agreement, but we do not have information on what patents are out-licensed by the Japanese firm to its US counterpart.
7. The average age of JVs at the beginning of the sample period is 8.5 years, and the oldest JV is 39 years old.

References

Ahuja, G. (2000) 'Collaboration Networks, Structural Holes, and Innovation: a Longitudinal Study', *Administrative Science Quarterly*, 45(3): 425–55.
Almeida, P. (1996) 'Knowledge Sourcing by Foreign Multinationals: Patent Citation Analysis in the US Semiconductor Industry', *Strategic Management Journal*, 17 (Winter): 155–65.
Aramaki, K. (2004) 'Shihon Torihiki Jiyuka No Sequencing' (Sequencing of Liberalization on Direct Investment) *Kaihatsu Kenkyu Shoho* (JBIC Institute Quarterly Reports, in Japanese), 21: 49–77.
Chiang, J.-T. (1995) 'Technology Policy Paradigms and Intellectual Property Strategies: Three National Models', *Technological Forecasting and Social Change*, 49: 35–48.
Colombo, M. G. (2003) 'Alliance Form: a Test of the Contractual and Competence Perspectives', *Strategic Management Journal*, 24(12): 1209–29.
Contractor, F. J. (1990) 'Ownership Patterns of US Joint Ventures Abroad and the Liberalization of Foreign Government Regulations in the 1980s: Evidence from the Benchmark Surveys', *Journal of International Business Studies*, 21(1): 55–73.
Dyer, J., Kale, P. and Singh, H. (2001) 'How to Build an Alliance Capability: the Role of the Alliance Function', *Sloan Management Review* (July).
Ergas, H. (1986) 'Does Technology Policy Matter?' in B. R. Guile and H. Brooks (eds), *Technology and Global Industry*, Washington, DC: National Academy Press.
Freeman, C. (1987) *Technology Policy and Economic Performance: Lessons from Japan*, London: Frances Pinter.
Freeman, C. and Hagedoorn, J. (1994) 'Catching Up or Falling Behind: Patterns in International Interfirm Technology Partnering', *World Development*, 22(5): 771–80.
Hagedoorn, J. (2002) 'Inter-firm R&D Partnerships: an Overview of Major Trends and Patterns since 1960', *Research Policy* (31): 477–92.
Hamel, G. (1991) 'Competition for Competence and Inter-partner Learning within International Strategic Alliances', *Strategic Management Journal*, 12: 82–103.
Jaffe, A. B. (1986) 'Technological Opportunity and Spillovers of R&D: Evidence from Firms' Patents, Profits and Market Value', *American Economic Review*, 76: 984–1001.
Jaffe, A. B. and Trajtenberg, M. (2002) *Patents, Citations and Innovations: a Window on the Knowledge Economy*, Cambridge, MA: MIT Press.

Kogut, B. (1988) 'Joint Ventures: Theoretical and Empirical Perspectives', *Strategic Management Journal*, 9: 319–32.

Lane, P. J. and Lubatkin, M. (1998) 'Relative Absorptive Capacity and Interorganizational Learning', *Strategic Management Journal*, 19(5): 461–77.

Mowery, D. C. and Oxley, J. E. (1995) 'Inward Technology Transfer and Competitiveness: the Role of National Innovation Systems', *Cambridge Journal of Economics*, 19: 67–93.

Mowery, D. C., Oxley J. E. and Silverman, B. S. (1996) 'Strategic Alliances and Interfirm Knowledge Transfer', *Strategic Management Journal*, 17 (Winter): 77–91.

Mowery, D. C., Oxley J. E. and Silverman, B. S. (2002) 'The Two Faces of Partnerspecific Absorptive Capacity: Learning and Co-specialization in Strategic Alliances', in Farok Contractor and Peter Lorange (eds), *Cooperative Strategies and Alliances*, London: Elsevier, 291–320.

Nelson, R. R. (ed.) (1993) *National Innovation Systems: a Comparative Analysis*, New York: Oxford University Press.

OECD (1992) *Industrial Policy in OECD Countries*, Paris: OECD.

Osborn, R. N. and Baughn, C. C. (1990) 'Forms of Interorganizational Governance for Multinational Alliances', *Academy of Management Journal*, 33(3): 503–19.

Oxley, J. E. (1997) 'Appropriability Hazards and Governance in Strategic Alliances: a Transaction Cost Approach', *Journal of Law, Economics and Organization*, 13(2): 387–409.

Oxley, J. E. and Sampson, R. S. (2004) 'The Scope and Governance of International R&D Alliances', *Strategic Management Journal* 25: 723–49.

Oxley, J. E. and Wada, T. (2005) 'Alliance Structure and the Scope of Knowledge Transfer: Evidence from US–Japan Agreements', *Rotman School of Management Working Paper*.

Pack, H. (2001) 'The Role of Acquisition of Foreign Technology in Taiwanese Growth', *Industrial and Corporate Change*, 10(3): 713–34.

Powell, W. W., Koput, K. W. and Smith-Doerr, L. (1996) 'Interorganizational Collaboration and the Locus of Innovation: Networks of Learning in Biotechnology', *Administrative Science Quarterly* 41(1): 116–45.

Reich, R. B. and Mankin, E. D. (1986) 'Joint Ventures with Japan Give Away Our Future', *Harvard Business Review*, 64(2): 78–86.

Shaver, J. M. (1998) 'Accounting for Endogeneity When Assessing Strategy Performance: Does Entry Mode Choice Affect FDI Survival?' *Management Science*, 44(4): 571–85.

9

Are There Benefits from Engaging in an Alliance with a Firm Prior to its Acquisition?

Rajshree Agarwal,[1] Jaideep Anand[2] and Rachel Croson[3]

Theoretical backgroud

Numerous articles in strategy have argued that sequential strategies, i.e. alliances followed by acquisitions, may be superior to outright acquisitions (Reich and Mankin, 1984; Doz et al., 1986; Haspeslagh and Jemison, 1991; Bleeke and Ernst, 1995; Anand, 1999; Hagedoorn and Sadowski, 1999; Arend, 2004). However, this previous work does not offer empirical evidence for a causal effect of previous alliances on acquisition performance. For example, if one observes superior coordination in acquisitions that follow alliances, it is difficult to separate causal and selection effects. Potential acquirers may simply be using the alliance to select the best candidates for acquisition. Such an effect will be consistent with perspectives on information asymmetries (Reuer and Koza, 2000) or real options (Kogut, 1991). Thus, improved performance cannot be attributed to the alliance per se. In Agarwal et al. (2005), we use an experimental methodology to search for causal effects, controlling for selection. This chapter summarizes our methodology and results.

Any causal effect may be due to two possible theoretical drivers. First, learning-by-doing arguments suggest the development of coordination routines (Nelson and Winter, 1982; Zollo et al., 2002), which can have either positive or negative effects on post-acquisition coordination, depending on the appropriateness of these routines for application to the post-acquisition stage. Second, social contact achieved through exposure and communication in a pre-acquisition alliance can help align goals and facilitate the development of trust and empathy (Allport, 1954; Gulati, 1995; Brewer and Brown, 1998; Marks and Mirvis, 1998). Our experiment tests for each of these effects independently.

Prior resource interdependence

How do interactions between alliance partners that take place before an acquisition effect interactions after the acquisition? Both these sets of interactions involve mutual interdependence (Teece, 1986; Singh and Montgomery, 1987; Parkhe, 1991; Harrison et al., 1991). Both alliances and acquisitions provide firms with the opportunity to synergistically combine their resources. These combinations are difficult to achieve through market mechanisms or internal development, and can potentially lead to substantial value creation. Firms learn to cooperate within the alliance arrangement to achieve their joint objectives (Anand and Khanna, 2000). This learning can be embodied in the form of routinized interactions.

The routines formed during the alliance stage can play an important role in determining the extent of post-acquisition coordination. Since routines are often 'sticky', for example, they are difficult to change once formed; they are likely to carry over to the post-acquisition stage. The effect of these routines on post-acquisition coordination can be positive or negative depending on how appropriate these routines are for the post-acquisition stage (Gick and Holyoak, 1987; Cohen and Bacdayan, 1994). The appropriateness of the alliance routines to the acquisition stage depends on the similarity or dissimilarity of the alliance and acquisition environments.

Alliances and acquisitions are similar in the sense that both involve creating value through a combination of resources. Synergistic value creation is generally a core objective of both of these governance modes. Given this fundamental similarity, one may expect that the routines to achieve this goal of synergistic value creation in the alliance stage would also be appropriate for the post-acquisition stage. On the other hand, there is an important difference between these governance modes. There is an element of competition within an alliance that may not be appropriate after the acquisition. Alliance partners may cooperate in order to achieve synergistic value creation, but also compete for the fruits of this cooperation. Alliance partners may also attempt to free-ride by minimizing their contributions to the alliance while maximizing their benefits from it. In contrast to alliances, acquisitions lead to the eventual disappearance of interfirm boundaries, unified ownership and the convergence of the goals of the two firms. Consequently, relative to alliances, post-acquisition interactions are less likely to involve competition. Thus, to the extent that alliances routinize competition or free-riding, pre-acquisition alliances can impede post-acquisition performance.

In sum, depending on the relative similarity and differences between the governance modes represented in acquisitions vs. alliances, the routines formed in the alliance may or may not be effective at increasing coordination post-acquisition. We thus derive competing hypotheses on the effect of pre-acquisition alliances on post-acquisition performance.

Prior social contact

In addition to resource interdependence described above, alliances also permit social contact between partners (March and Simon, 1958; Gulati,

1995). Such contact can lead to communication, familiarity and empathy, which in turn can lead to superior coordination.

Alliances represent an opportunity for firms to work together, communicate more openly than otherwise possible, and develop a nuanced understanding of each other's cultures, values and mindsets (Marks and Mirvis, 1998). Communication regarding mutual orientation and positions on issues can help achieve coordination through timely conflict resolution and a close correspondence between expected and actual behaviours. Sharing of common goals helps in identifying the best course and reduces surprises by helping to form more accurate expectations. The role of communication between acquiring and acquired firms in achieving post-acquisition coordination has been noted previously (Shanley, 1988; Napier, 1989; Schweiger and DeNisi, 1991; Larsson and Finkelstein, 1999).

Contact among groups has long been shown to reduce tension among them in social psychology (Allport, 1954; Pettigrew, 1971; Brewer and Brown, 1998). For example, laboratory studies show the positive impact of discussion on the development of intergroup cooperation and a reduction in in-group bias (Brown, 1988). Communication can help achieve cooperative seeking of common objectives (Johnson et al., 1984). Communication also helps in acquiring new and more accurate information about other groups, which can help reject negative impressions held about other groups (Pettigrew, 1971). As a result, we expect that prior social contact in the alliance stage between transacting parties will have a positive effect on post-acquisition coordination.

Empirical analysis

We use experimental methodology to examine the post-acquisition coordination achieved by firms as a function of whether or not they engaged in alliances prior to the acquisition. Further, we distinguish between prior resource interdependence and prior social contact due to alliance participation, and their effects on post-acquisition coordination. The goal of our experiment is to isolate these individual effects, while controlling for selection effects and also obtaining clear dependent measures of post-acquisition coordination. Experiments have been used for many generations in psychology, sociology and management (Anand et al., 2003 provide a review of the relevant literature, including the advantages and limitations of the methodology). To the best of our knowledge, we are the first in our related research (Agarwal et al., 2005) and in this chapter to use experiments to investigate issues related to alliances and acquisitions.

Experimental design and procedure

For details regarding the experimental design and procedure, we refer interested readers to Agarwal et al. (2005). Briefly, our experimental design translates into an assurance game (Sen 1967; also called a stag-hunt game), where individuals want to cooperate if and only if they expect others to cooperate. As recommended by Smith (1982), we used the *induced valuation* methodology that involves paying participants in cash based on the profits they earn in the experiments.

The 213 participants for our experiment consisted of executive and regular MBA students at a major business school. Participants were randomly assigned in groups of three, and our experimental process adhered to the institutional review board requirements that participation be informed and voluntary. In a set of detailed instructions, participants were informed that they would simulate the role of managers who were responsible for allocating resources towards enhancing their own division's production, or joint production (combined activities) with other divisions/firms (which could be conceptualized as joint production, R&D, technology transfer or marketing). Participants interacted with each other in groups of three with the aid of a computerized interface. Two participants simulated the role of a divisional manager in the same firm, and the third represented a manager of the independent, to be acquired, firm.

In our experiment, we investigate a reduced form of interorganizational routine; that of coordination in a resource allocation setting. In the alliance stage, participants learn how much they need to contribute in order for the alliance to be successful. This routine can transfer in the post-acquisition stage, but need not. Of course, interorganizational routines in the field are substantially more complicated than this. However, to the extent that we observe transfers in this simple routine, one might imagine similar transfers in more complex settings as well.

The main task facing the managers is the allocation of the resources they control to either individual or combined production activities. Participants have a choice of allocating any amount (from zero to all) of the resources they control towards production in their own division/firm, which generates private profits, or towards combined activities, described as firm (or alliance) production. To capture synergistic gains from these combined activities, their success requires a minimum (threshold) amount of resources. The project is successful if the threshold level is met, providing each party with additional profits. If the threshold level is not met, the project is deemed unsuccessful, and all contributed resources are lost. The design of the experiment ensures that the threshold requires more resources than are controlled by any one manager, thus adhering to the principle that successful combined activities require the participation of multiple divisions and/or firms.

Our experimental design manipulates pre-acquisition status to test if post-acquisition coordination is enhanced by the existence of any pre-acquisition alliance activity. We also distinguish between the competing causes of post-acquisition coordination: prior resource interdependence and prior social contact. Figure 9.1 represents our 2×2 design which manipulates the pre-acquisition relationship between the two divisions of the first firm and the

		Prior Social Contact	
		Yes	No
Prior Resource Interdependence	Yes	Complete Alliance	Silent Treatment
	No	Discussion Only	Outright Acquisition

Figure 9.1: Pre-acquisition treatments

second (independent) firm based on the two dimensions of prior resource interdependence and prior social contact. The diagonal cells represent situations most often observed in the real world. The first cell, *Complete Alliance*, allows for complete interaction between the two divisions of the first firm and the second firm; both prior resource interdependence and prior social contact are permitted during the alliance stage. The diagonally-opposite case, *Outright Acquisition*, represents the condition in which the target firm has had neither prior resource interdependence nor prior social contact with the two divisions of the first firm. The non-diagonal cells represent different types of interactions not typically found in the field, thus enabling us to distinguish between the competing causes suggested for outcome differences. In the *Silent Treatment* cell, the two divisions and the second firm have prior resource interdependence; however, only the two divisions of the firm engage in prior social contact (via communication). In the *Discussion Only* cell, the opposite is true; while the second firm can benefit from prior social contact, there is no prior resource interdependence.

The first manipulation (prior resource interdependence) is implemented based on whether the second firm is engaged in an alliance in the pre-acquisition quarters. During the first three quarters, either the two divisions of the first firm only (in the cells where there is no prior resource interdependence) or the two divisions and the outside firm (in the cells where there is prior resource interdependence) engage in the resource allocation decision. The second manipulation (prior social contact) is implemented via a chat box. In the treatments without prior social contact, only the two divisions within the firm can discuss the situation and their decisions. This is the equivalent of inter-office communication. In the treatments with prior social contact, the second firm can observe and participate in these discussions.

After three quarters spent in the pre-acquisition stage, the participants are informed that the first firm has acquired the second firm. While the tasks remain the same, new parameters are introduced to represent payoffs consistent with the post-acquisition setting; in particular, the second firm now represents a division that engages in profit sharing with the other two divisions. Since all groups experience an acquisition, including those that have had unsuccessful pre-acquisition alliances, we eliminate the selection endogeneity present in field data. In the post-acquisition stage, the experience is the same for all participants in all four treatments.

Participants engage in multiple rounds of interaction (described as financial quarters). We avoid endgame effects by implementing a finite game with unknown end setting, with a probability of 0.8 that the game will continue for another round. Thus, participants are not told the exact number of quarters that they will play; instead they are informed that after each quarter there is an 80 per cent chance that the game will progress to the next quarter (and a 20 per cent chance that it will end). The continuation probabilities are indeed as described; no deception is used in this experiment.

Results

Our key measure of post-acquisition coordination is *Success*: whether the collective resource allocations of the divisions is greater than or equal to the threshold amount required for synergistic profits from combined activities. It is coded as 1 if the threshold value is met in the particular quarter, and is 0 otherwise. In Agarwal et al. (2005), we extend our examination to a number of other dependent variables as well. The main explanatory variables of interest are *Prior resource interdependence* – which takes the value of 1 if the treatment allows for the second firm to make decisions in the pre-acquisition stage (resource interdependence) – and *Prior social contact* – which takes the value of 1 if the treatment allows for the second firm to engage in communication in the pre-acquisition stage (social contact). Among the controls, we include *Quarter* – which denotes the quarter in which the decision is being made.

We present summary statistics regarding the average success rates in the first and all quarters in Table 9.1. In the first quarter after acquisition, the success rates for a *complete alliance* are 60 per cent, and across all quarters, the success rates increase to 83 per cent. In contrast, while *outright acquisitions* start off with a 50 per cent success rate in the first quarter, the success rates across all quarters end up being similar to the complete alliances at 84 per cent. Among the off-diagonal cells, the *silent treatment* cell (prior resource interdependence without prior social contact) starts off at the same success rate as outright acquisitions, but the success rate across all quarters is only 70 per cent, below that of outright acquisitions. In the *discussion only* treatment, the success rate in the first quarter is the highest at 75 per cent, and while the difference attenuates, remains the highest across all quarters at 88 per cent.

The formal analysis of success reveals that controlling for selection effects, prior resource interdependence has an adverse effect on success. This is consistent with negative transfer of routines from alliances to acquisitions. On the other hand, prior social contact has a beneficial impact on success. Finally, it is worth noting that repeated interactions in the post-acquisition setting have a beneficial effect on coordination. Consistent with the summary statistics in Table 9.1a and Table 9.1b, the effect of quarter is positive and significant for success.

Table 9.1a: Average success rates in first quarter after acquisition

	Prior social contact	No prior social contact
Prior resource interdependence	0.60 (0.50)	0.50 (0.51)
No prior resource interdependence	0.75 (0.45)	0.50 (0.51)

Standard deviation in parentheses

Table 9.1b: Average success rates in all quarters after acquisition

	Prior social contact	No prior social contact
Prior resource interdependence	0.83 (0.38)	0.70 (0.46)
No prior resource interdependence	0.88 (0.33)	0.84 (0.37)

Standard deviation in parentheses

Discussion and conclusions

This research project addresses a simple question: are there any benefits from engaging in alliance activity with a firm prior to its acquisition, and if so, why? Existing research provides important clues, yet does not answer this question completely. Many alternative mechanisms have been proposed (Reich and Mankin, 1984; Doz et al., 1986; Haspeslagh and Jemison, 1991; Kogut, 1991; Balakrishnan and Koza, 1993; Bleeke and Ernst, 1995; Hagedoorn and Sadowski, 1999; Chang and Rosenzweig, 2001), and observational evidence is unable to distinguish between competing causes of coordination differences that are observed. Further, the observational data examined suffer from selection effects; only successful alliances are transformed into acquisitions. In this chapter, we use an experimental approach to provide some clarity in an otherwise complex and interrelated set of explanations.

Controlling for selection effects, we find that prior resource interdependence in an alliance setting reduces rather than enhances post-acquisition coordination. Our principal explanation of this result relies on the interactive routines between the managers that are developed in the mixed-motive environment of an alliance. Our results indicate that even in simple task settings, it is more difficult to replace routines once formed than it is to create appropriate new routines. The effect of prior social contact, however, is unambiguously positive, as predicted by existing theory. When managers communicate before the acquisition, they have the opportunity to share individual positions and can develop a mechanism for understanding each other's positions. This leads to greater post-acquisition coordination.

These results complement those of previous studies and help to refine previous findings. Previous research indicates that interfirm learning may help in coordination, but that competitive or confrontational routines might hurt in alliances (Das and Teng, 2000; Zollo et al., 2002). Further, some previous work (Cohen and Bacdayan, 1994; Haleblian and Finkelstein, 1999) has noted the problems of applying an inappropriate past routine to new situations, though in a different context than ours. Our research adds to these findings by showing that confrontational routines that develop in an alliance setting may have adverse transfer effects when the alliance partners decide to dissolve the interorganizational boundaries.

This research enhances our understanding of acquisition integration, and suggests the mechanisms that may drive successful integration. Our study illustrates that negative routines develop even in simple settings – in contrast with the complex settings of the field, the only change in our experimental task between pre- and post-acquisition was in the incentive structure or the profit-sharing rule (representing a shift from an alliance to acquisition setting). Thus, it apprises managers to weigh the positive and negative effects of sequential strategies when they design their corporate development efforts. Specifically, it points out that in pre-acquisition alliances, managers should mitigate the formation of competitive routines, and that managers should try to communicate widely and openly both before and after the acquisition.

Notes

1. Rajshree Agarwal, College of Business Administration, University of Illinois at Urbana Champaign, 350 Wohlers Hall, 1206 S. 6th St., Champaign, IL 61820, Tel: (217) 265-,5513, Fax: 217-244-7969, Email: agarwalr@uiuc.edu
2. Jaideep Anand, Fisher College of Business, 836 Fisher Hall 2100 Neil Avenue, Columbus, OH 43210, E-mail: anand_18@cob.osu.edu
3. Rachel Croson, The Wharton School, 567 Jon M. Huntsman Hall, University of Pennsylvania, Philadelphia, PA 19104-6340, Tel: (215) 898-3025, Fax: (215) 898-3664 Email: crosonr@wharton.upenn.edu

References

Agarwal, R., Anand, J. and Croson, R. (2005) 'Do Pre-Acquisition Alliances Help in Post-Acquisition Coordination: an Experimental Approach', working paper.
Allport, G. W. (1954) *The Nature of Prejudice*, Cambridge, MA: Addison-Wesley.
Anand, B. and Khanna, T. (2000) 'Do Firms Learn to Create Value? The Case of Alliances', *Strategic Management Journal*, March.
Anand, J. (1999) 'How Many Matches are Made in Heaven?' *Financial Times*, Mastering Strategy Series, 25 October.
Anand, J., Croson, R. and Agarwal, R. (2003) 'Using Experiments in Strategy Research', mimeo, University of Illinois.
Arend, R. J. (2004) 'Conditions for Assymetric Information Solutions when Alliances Provide Acquisition Options and Due Diligence', *Journal of Economics*, 82(3): 281–312.
Balakrishnan, S. and Koza, M. P. (1993) 'Information Asymmetry, Adverse Selection, and Joint Ventures', *Journal of Economic Behavior and Organization*, 20: 99–117.

Bleeke, J. and Ernst, D. (1995) 'Is Your Strategic Alliance Really a Sale?', *Harvard Business Review*, January/February: 97–105.

Brewer, M. B. and Brown, R. J. (1998) 'Intergroup Relations', in D. Gilbert, S. T. Fiske and G. Lindzey (eds), *Handbook of Social Psychology* (4th edn) Boston: McGraw-Hill, 554–94.

Brown, R. (1988) *Group Processes: Dynamics Within and Between Groups*, Oxford: Blackwell.

Chang, S.-J. and Rosenzweig, M. (2001) 'The Choice of Entry Mode in Sequential Foreign Direct Investment', *Strategic Management Journal*, 22: 747–76.

Cohen, M. P. and Bacdayan (1994) 'Organizational Routines are Stored as Procedural Memory: Evidence from a Laboratory Study', *Organization Science*, 5(4): 554–68.

Das, T. K. and Teng, B.-S. (2000) 'Instabilities of Strategic Alliances: an Internal Tensions Perspective', *Organization Science*, 11: 77–101.

Doz, Y. L., Hamel, G. and Prahalad, C. K. (1986) 'Strategic Partnerships: Success or Surrender? The Challenge of Competitive Collaboration', presented at the 1986 AIB annual meeting, London, UK.

Gick, M. L. and Holyoak, K. J. (1987) 'The Cognitive Basis of Knowledge Transfer', in S. M. Cormier and J. D. Hagman (eds), *Transfer of Learning: Contemporary Research and Applications*, San Diego, CA: Academic Press, 9–46.

Gulati, R. (1995) 'Familiarity Breeds Trust? The Implications of Repeated Ties', *Academy of Management Journal*, 38: 85–112.

Hagedoorn, J. and Sadowski, B. (1999) 'Transition from Strategic Technology Alliances', *Journal of Management Studies*, 36(1): 87–107.

Haleblian, J. and Finkelstein, S. (1999) 'The Influence of Organizational Acquisition Experience on Acquisition Performace: a Behavioral Perspective', *Administrative Science Quarterly*, 44(1): 29–57.

Harrison, J., Hitt, M. et al. (1991) 'Synergies and Post-Acquisition Performance: Differences versus Similarities in Resource Allocation', *Journal of Management*, 17(1): 173–90.

Haspeslagh, P. C. and Jemison, D. B. (1991) *Managing Acquisitions: Creating Value through Corporate Renewal*, New York: Free Press.

Johnson, D. W., Johnson, R. T. and Maruyama, G. (1984) 'Goal Interdependence and Interpersonal Attraction in Heterogeneous Classrooms: a Meta-analysis', in N. Miller and M. Brewer (eds), *Groups in Contact: the Psychology of Desegregation*, Orlando, FL: Academic Press, 187–212.

Kogut, B. A. (1991) 'Joint Ventures and the Option to Expand and Acquire', *Management Science*, 37(1): 9–24.

Larsson R. and Finkelstein, S. (1999) 'Integrating Strategic, Organizational and Human Resource Perspectives on Mergers and Acquisitions: a Case Survey of Synergy Realization', *Organization Science*, 10(1): 1–26.

March, J. G. and Simon, H. A. (1958) *Organizations*, New York: Wiley.

Marks, M. L. and Mirvis, P. H. (1998) *Joining Forces*, San Francisco: Jossey-Bass.

Napier, N. K. (1989) 'Mergers and Acquisitions, Human Resource Issues and Outcomes: a Review and Suggested Typology', *Journal of Management Studies*, 26: 271–89.

Nelson, R. R. and Winter, S. G. (1982) *An Evolutionary Theory of Economic Change*, Cambridge, MA: Bellknap Press of Harvard University Press.

Parkhe, A. (1991) 'Interfirm Diversity, Organizational Learning, and Longevity in Global Strategic Alliances', *Journal of International Business Studies*, 22(4): 579–601.

Pettigrew, T. F. (1971) *Racially Separate or Together?*, New York: McGraw-Hill.

Reich, R. B. and Mankin, E. D. (1984) 'Joint Ventures with Japan Give Away Our Future', *Harvard Business Review*, March–April: 78–86.

Reuer, J. J. and Koza, M. P. (2000) 'On Lemons and Indigestability: Resource Assembly through Joint Ventures', *Strategic Management Journal*, 21(2): 195–8.

Schweiger, D. M. and DeNisi, A. S. (1991) 'Communication with Employees Following a Merger: a Longitudinal Field Experiment', *Academy of Management Journal*, 34(1): 110–35.

Sen, A. (1967) 'Isolation, Assurance, and the Social Rate of Discount', *Quarterly Journal of Economics*, 81: 112–24.

Shanley, M. T. (1988) 'Reconciling the Rock and the Hard Place: Management Control versus Human Resource Accommodation in Acquisition Integration', unpublished paper, Graduate School of Business, University of Chicago.

Singh, H. and Montgomery, C. A. (1987) 'Corporate Acquisitions and Economic Performance', *Strategic Management Journal*, 8(4): 377–86.

Smith, V. (1982) 'Microeconomic Systems as an Experimental Science', *American Economic Review*, 72(5): 923–55.

Teece, D. J. (1986) 'Profiting from Technological Innovation: Implications for Integration, Collaboration, Licensing and Public Policy', *Research Policy*, 15: 285–305.

Zollo, M., Reuer, J. J. and Singh, H. (2002) 'Interorganizational Routines and Performance in Strategic Alliances', *Organization Science*, 13: 701–13.

10
Interorganizational Governance Trajectories: Towards a Better Understanding of the Connections Between Partner Selection, Negotiation and Contracting

Paul W. L. Vlaar,[1] Frans A. J. Van Den Bosch[2] and Henk W. Volberda[3]

Introduction

Interorganizational relationships consist of several stages, such as a search and selection stage, a negotiation stage, and a contracting stage (e.g. Jap and Ganesan, 2000; Reuer, 1999, 2000). Each of these stages corresponds with distinct governance decisions, which collectively enable partners to achieve coordination and control during the life-cycle of their relationships. Hitherto, however, little research has examined the use of multiple mechanisms to structure exchange relationships (Jap and Ganesan, 2000), and studies on sequences of successive governance decisions are still rare in the literature (Long et al., 2002; Narayandas and Rangan, 2004). This has led to a significant gap in our understanding of interorganizational governance. This chapter therefore focuses on the following research question: *How are interorganizational relationships governed during different stages of cooperation, and how are the governance decisions in these stages related?*

By investigating this question, the chapter offers several contributions to the interorganizational governance literature. First, the results suggest that interorganizational governance should no longer be depicted as a discrete event, but as a process consisting of multiple, and possibly interrelated, decisions. Our findings illustrate that partners in interorganizational relationships do not align discrete governance decisions with firm and transaction characteristics (as proposed by, among others, adherents to transaction cost economics, agency theory and the resource-based view), but with series of governance decisions so as to achieve optimal performance over the entire lifetime of their relationships. The chapter underscores the importance of distinct phases of collaboration as elements of value creation, thereby offering a broader, more encompassing perspective on interorganizational governance than currently available (Cardinal, 2001; Narayandas and Rangan, 2004). Second, we divert the primary focus in governance research from the studying of contracts to inquiries into other means of coordination and control. Where examinations of the contractual aspects of interorganizational relationships have proliferated, inquiries into decisions concerning, among others, advance payment of suppliers, the use of standard-form contracts, and partner search and selection processes, are much scarcer.

To explore whether and to what extent these and other governance decisions are related to each other, we introduce the concept of *governance trajectories*. Subsequently, we report findings from an analysis of 911 buyer–supplier relationships involving IT suppliers and small- and medium-sized buyers. The results reveal that managers deploy a range of governance mechanisms that influence each other, and that are themselves influenced by distinct sets of antecedent variables, indicating that attempts to coordinate and control interorganizational activities are more diverse and multifaceted than often presented in the literature.

Towards a more comprehensive approach to interorganizational governance

Managers govern interorganizational relationships by directing the behaviour and performance of participants towards the production of actions desirable to the relationship and to themselves. By pursuing partial control over a partner's resources and behaviour, the occurrence of problems arising from goal divergence and asymmetrical objectives is limited (Blumberg, 2001), while coordination costs, resulting from the complexity and uncertainty involved in managing a cooperative relationship, are minimized (Park and Ungson, 2001). Governance is thus aimed at control and coordination, and it contemporaneously affects value creation and value appropriation.

Hitherto, interorganizational governance has frequently been depicted as a one-shot event, in which only a few options are available for coordinating and controlling the activities and behaviour of the partner. Whereas most research focuses on contractual aspects, governance can be achieved in more discriminating ways. Managers use distinct governance mechanisms to achieve similar functions (Miller et al., 2004), but also to address a complex array of problems and contingencies (Cardinal, 2001; Kirsch, 1997; Long et al., 2002). They implement portfolios of control modes to capitalize on a wide array of opportunities for achieving efficiency and effectiveness during the life-cycle of their relationships (Cardinal et al., 2004). In line with this, a large number of governance mechanisms has been proposed to help circumvent, mitigate or alleviate coordination and control problems, and to ensure that tasks are conducted in a way that is consistent with organizational goals (Heide, 1994; Kirsch, 1997). Consequently, research efforts should be redirected from examining singular governance forms to evaluating more complex governance systems (Long et al., 2002).

In this chapter, we therefore propose the concept of *governance trajectories*, which we define as *sequences of interrelated decisions that are made to influence the behaviour of participants in interorganizational relationships during successive stages of the cooperative life-cycle*. We presume that the governance decisions that are embedded in these trajectories are related to each other and that they jointly warrant value creation (Reuer, 1999). We discern three cooperative stages in which governance efforts are known to be ubiquitous: a partner selection stage, a negotiation stage, and a contracting stage. A review of the literature, as reflected in subsequent paragraphs, suggests that these stages at least involve decisions on: (1) the selection of a familiar or an unfamiliar partner; (2) exhaustiveness of selection efforts; (3) advance payments; (4) exhaustiveness of negotiations; (5) the use of standard contracts; and (6) contract completeness. Although the message of this chapter could have been conveyed by illuminating other governance decisions as well, we chose to focus on these mechanisms, as they feature prominently in the literature, and because we could obtain data on them for a large sample of interorganizational relationships. In the following paragraphs, we describe these six governance decisions. We show that they have different sets of antecedents and that they depend on some of the governance decisions by which they are preceded (see Figure 10.1).

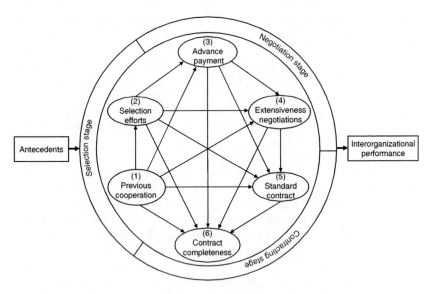

Figure 10.1: Conceptual framework of governance trajectories: antecedents, governance decisions and interorganizational performance

Partner selection stage

Partner selection refers to the identification of potential exchange partners and assessments of their quality and intentions (Buskens et al., 2003; Gulati, 1995). It serves to proactively solve potential governance problems and to guarantee complementarity of allying firms (Wathne and Heide, 2004). In this stage, focal organizations have to decide whether it is desirable and possible to work with a familiar partner or not. Furthermore, a decision has to be made as to the amount of effort that is invested in selecting a partner (Buskens et al., 2003). Concerning the first decision, it is recognized that organizations show a propensity to initiate relationships with familiar partners (Gulati, 1995; Kale et al., 2002), as these: have had the opportunity to build up interorganizational trust and reputation (Gulati, 1995); experience less uncertainty regarding their partner's reliability, intentions, interests, resources and capabilities (Li and Rowley, 2002); frequently intend to maintain a profitable relationship during longer time horizons (Ryall and Sampson, 2004); and do not require exhaustive evaluations (Li and Rowley, 2002). A second major decision in this stage concerns the *extent* to which search and selection efforts are undertaken. Extensive partner selection efforts reputedly assist in assessing the overall viability of interorganizational relationships (Geringer, 1991), and in reducing the occurrence of problems and conflicts of interests stemming from cultural, organizational, resource and strategic misfits.

Negotiation stage

In the negotiation stage, organizations at least have to make decisions on whether a supplier or another partner has to be paid in advance, and on what the appropriate length or exhaustiveness of negotiations should be. Concerning the first decision, the alliance literature is replete with articles on the choice between equity and non-equity relationships. However, other types of cooperation also entail decisions on equity transfer. Buyers and suppliers, for example, jointly decide whether advance payments for products and services are made. Such payments minimize the risk of hold-up experienced by suppliers (Helm and Kloyer, 2004), but they also pose additional risks to buyers, possibly influencing their use of other governance decisions. Next to advance payments, parties have to decide on the extent to which they want to negotiate. This governance decision concerns the length and intensity of formal bargaining processes (Ariño and Ring, 2004), and it differs conceptually from search and selection efforts and from contractual issues. Search and selection efforts, for example, might improve one's ability to negotiate. Furthermore, partners may be reluctant to lay down certain outcomes of their negotiations, as this might lead to high transaction costs or hold-up problems.

Contracting stage

In the contracting stage, decisions have to be made as to whether standard contracts are being used and to what extent complete contracting is sought. Regarding the first decision, standard contracts lower the efforts required to specify or compose contracts; enable fast interaction with a broad range of partners; reduce the strain on interpretive practices; and minimize the risk of inconsistent interpretations of contract clauses. However, they also preclude active buyer involvement and flexibility, and they are reputed to reflect the contract-issuing organizations' requirements, possibly leading to dissatisfaction on the part of partners (Korobkin, 2003). The resulting predicament indicates that decisions on the application of standard contracts are very significant. The second decision in this stage concerns the degree of contract completeness, which is a frequently used proxy for the extent to which partners attempt to coordinate and control interorganizational activities and outcomes (e.g. Anand and Khanna, 2000). Although higher levels of contract completeness facilitate coordination and control, they also entail higher transaction costs and reduced flexibility. Such dilemmas heighten the salience of decisions on contract completeness.

Interrelationships between governance decisions

Although each of the six foregoing governance decisions (see Figure 10.1) have been studied in isolation, relatively little is known about the relationships between them. Argyres and Liebeskind (1999) introduce the notion of governance inseparability to describe situations where there are interdependencies between governance decisions. Heide (1994) and Leiblein (2003) add that firms' past and current governance decisions constrain and enable the range and types of governance mechanisms that can be adopted in subsequent exchanges. In this respect, Avadikyan et al. (2001: 1448) suggest that the life of an interorganizational relationship should be considered as 'a succession of [value] allocation and creation problems and the events taking place within a given phase have strong impacts on the following periods'. Although these and other researchers have presumed that there are potential interdependencies across individual governance decisions, it is unclear what the nature of these interdependencies is (Heide, 2003).

Authors have, for example, demonstrated that the selection of a familiar partner influences contract completeness, as the need to reduce opportunistic behaviour is probably lower (Gulati, 1995), and the ability to contract may be higher (Poppo and Zenger, 2002). It appears that combinations of governance mechanisms generate positive synergy or negative tensions (Cardinal, 2001), making examinations of how governance decisions relate to each other highly pertinent (Heide, 1994; Reuer, 2000). We investigate whether each of the six governance decisions identified in this chapter at least possesses one direct link with another decision, which would substantiate our claim that studying series of governance decisions instead of discrete decisions is valuable.

We are also interested in differences between the antecedents of the six governance choices. When each of the governance mechanisms that we discerned has the same set of antecedents, results from the analysis on one governance decision can serve as a basis for inferences on other governance decisions. However, when different governance strategies are found to be appropriate under different conditions, this would demonstrate the efficacy of the concept of governance trajectories.

Method and results

Following Jap and Ganesan (2000), we examine data that have been collected at one point in time, and we classify variables along different stages of a relationship. To assess whether the concept of governance trajectories holds, we analyse survey data from a large sample of Dutch buyer–supplier relationships involving IT transactions, which were obtained from a data set called *The External Management of Automation* (MAT95) (Batenburg and Raub, 1995).[4] We perform ordinary logistic regression and logistic regression analyses to predict the application of each of the six governance mechanisms distinguished before. Although our measurements are generally consistent with other research based on the same data (see Batenburg et al., 2003; Buskens, 2002), we shift the analytic focus from the application of singular governance mechanisms towards series of governance decisions. Our analysis differs from these studies, because they either involve a smaller number of governance mechanisms (Buskens, 2002), or because they reduce the governance mechanisms that we distinguish to one additive measure (Batenburg et al., 2003). Consistent with recent work (Reuer and Zollo, 2005), and in line with recommendations from Colombo (2003) and Madhok (2002), we include both firm-level and transaction- or relation-level factors as explanatory variables of governance choices (see Table 10.1). The effects of most of these variables on various governance decisions are intuitively straightforward; they influence the need for and ability to coordinate and control.

Our analyses indicate that each of the six governance decisions is influenced by different sets of antecedents. Familiar partners are selected because partners might benefit from relation-specific investments, which they have made in earlier transactions with the same supplier (see also Zollo et al., 2002). Furthermore, cooperation with a familiar partner is more likely in situations characterized by higher measurability, higher importance of reputation, and larger numbers of alternative options, suggesting that buyers revert to suppliers they know when assessments of product or service quality are more difficult, or when products are highly standardized. The positive

Table 10.1: Results from regression analyses

Antecedents	Selection stage		Negotiation stage		Contracting stage	
	Familiarity partner	Selection efforts	Advance payment	Negotiation efforts	Standard contract	Contract complexity
Financial volume		+	+	+	−	+
Complexity				+	−	+
Asset-specificity	−	+		+		
Measurability	+	−				+
Size buyer				+	−	
Size supplier					+	+
Legal expertise						+
Other relationships		+				
IT expertise						
Importance reputation	+	+		+		+
Alternative options	+					−
Perceived dependence	+		+	+	−	
First user group	−					−
Age supplier	+	−	−	−		
Age of respondent				−		

association with perceived dependence suggests that organizations are occasionally forced to work with partners, possibly due to lock-in effects or the relative absence of alternatives (Klein Woolthuis et al., 2005). Finally, cooperation with a familiar partner becomes less likely when a buyer belongs to the first user group in its industry, or when a supplier is relatively young. These findings suggest that the selection of *familiar partners* is not only determined by a focal organization's ability to discern capable and reliable partners, or the routinized and standardized selection of partners (Li and Rowley, 2002). It also depends on the availability of familiar partners, and the difficulty on the part of a focal organization to break away from a familiar partner, as indicated by investments in relation-specific assets performed during earlier interactions, and the perceived degree of dependence on familiar partners.

Consistent with previous work on partner selection (Buskens, 2002; Buskens et al., 2003), *selection efforts* are influenced by a different set of antecedents, including the financial volume associated with a transaction, the importance a buyer attributes to the reputation of the supplier, and the prevalence of other relationships between a buyer and external organizations. These variables have a significant positive association with selection efforts. Investments in relation-specific assets tend to increase the exhaustiveness of firms' selection efforts. Measurability has a negative effect, which is congruent with the notion that selection efforts are being driven by uncertainty (Beckman et al., 2004). Finally, a supplier's age also shows a negative influence, which can be explained by the fact that older suppliers have better-known accomplishment records, and because they are perceived to be less risky business partners.

Advance payment of suppliers is influenced by the financial volume involved in a relationship and the perceived dependence of buyers on suppliers. Both variables exhibit positive relationships with ex ante payment. In contrast, the supplier's age has a significant negative influence on the likelihood that a supplier receives advance payments. This indicates that suppliers primarily demand advance payments from their buyers when the financial volume associated with a relationship carries significant costs and/or risks if not passed on to the buyer. Considering *negotiation efforts*, financial volume, complexity, asset-specificity, size of the supplier, importance of reputation, and perceived dependence are found to have a significant positive influence. In contrast, age of the supplier and age of the respondent exhibit a significant negative relationship to negotiation exhaustiveness.

Antecedents of the use of *standard contracts* consist of financial volume, complexity of the deal, size of the buyer, and perceived dependence. These are all found to have a negative association with the use of standard contracts. Size of the supplier has a positive influence on the use of standard contracts. Larger suppliers possess more resources and experience for developing standard contracts, and they have better opportunities for leveraging standard contracts over a larger number of transactions. Given that standard contracts are generally beneficial to suppliers (Korobkin, 2003), our finding that larger buyers show stronger resistance to the application of standard contracts is not surprising. Finally, *contract completeness* is positively affected by financial volume, complexity, measurability, the importance of reputation, legal expertise, and size of the supplier. The existence of alternative options and membership of a first user group exhibit a negative association with contract completeness.

We now extend previous work by researchers using the same database (Batenburg et al., 2003; Buskens, 2002), by assessing whether previous governance decisions influence subsequent governance decisions (see Figure 10.2). Hierarchical regression analyses reveal that the decision to cooperate with a familiar partner has a negative effect on selection efforts, negotiation exhaustiveness and contract completeness. The latter corroborates findings from Anand and Khanna (2000), who suggest that contracts between familiar organizations are systematically different from the ones in de novo pairings. It also supports the observation from Klein Woolthuis et al. (2005) that some firms do not fear opportunism during negotiations and contracting, because of their experiences with the other party. Selection

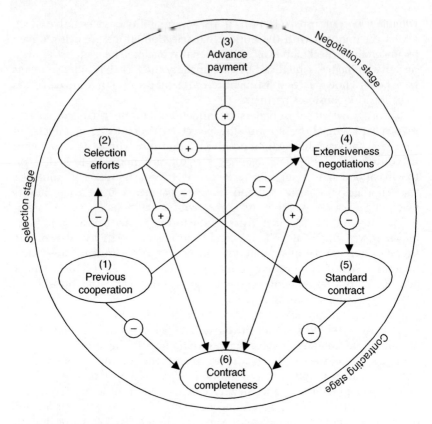

Figure 10.2: Relationships between governance decisions

efforts, in turn, positively influence the extent of negotiations and contract completeness, while they exhibit a negative relationship with the use of standard contracts. This suggests that searching, screening and selecting suppliers and products helps to assess the reliability and level of competence of potential suppliers (Blumberg, 2001), thereby reducing the risk of a transaction, and possibly reducing the need for formalization. Advance payment does not appear to be influenced by other governance decisions, but it does itself influence the degree of contract completeness.

Finally, the exhaustiveness of negotiations reduces the use of standard contracts and propagates contract completeness. In conclusion, it appears that each of the governance decisions discerned here at least influences one other governance decision within the same governance trajectory. Moreover, the six governance decisions are all associated with different sets of organization-level and relational-level antecedents, supporting our conceptualization of governance trajectories.

Discussion

In this chapter, we argued that interorganizational governance research frequently focuses on explaining singular governance decisions. However, in practice, managers deploy various governance mechanisms for the purpose of coordinating and controlling interorganizational activities and outcomes during the life-cycle of their relationships. This provoked the question as to how interorganizational relationships are governed during various stages of cooperation. In response to this question, we introduced the concept of governance trajectories, which was proposed to consist of *sequences of interrelated decisions that are made to influence the behaviour of participants in interorganizational relationships during successive stages of the cooperative life-cycle.*

Results from our analysis of 911 interorganizational relationships support our conceptualization of governance trajectories, showing that interorganizational governance should no longer be depicted as a discrete event, but as a process consisting of multiple, and possibly interrelated, decisions. Partners in interorganizational relationships align firm and transaction characteristics with series of governance decisions so as to achieve optimal performance over the entire lifetime of their relationships. The chapter thereby shifts the attention from discrete governance choices to a broader, more encompassing perspective on interorganizational governance than currently available (Cardinal, 2001; Narayandas and Rangan, 2004). It also diverts the primary focus in governance research from the studying of contracts to inquiries into other means of coordination and control, such as advance payment of suppliers, the use of standard-form contracts, and partner search and selection processes.

Managerial implications predominantly concern managers' awareness of the effects of governance decisions made in earlier stages of cooperation on decisions and outcomes in later stages. It appears that managers may use the interdependencies between these governance decisions deliberately (see also Heide, 2003). They may invest more in partner selection, for instance, to increase their ability to negotiate with potential partners, and to enable the development of tailor-made contracts. Furthermore, managers are advised to take multiple governance mechanisms, task-characteristics and contextual attributes into account when deciding on how to govern their relationships.

Future research could be directed at extending and refining the model presented here. A promising opportunity consists of including renegotiations and extensions of scope during the execution and implementation stage of collaboration in the model. This could reveal which firm and transaction characteristics and which of the governance decisions described in this chapter can predict whether renegotiations and redefinitions of scope are likely to occur.

Notes

1. Paul W. L. Vlaar, RSM Erasmus University, Department of Strategy and Business Environment, Burg. Oudlaan 50, Room T07-48, P.O. Box 1738, 3000 DR Rotterdam The Netherlands, E-mail: pvlaar@fbk.eur.nl
2. Frans A. J. Van Den Bosch, RSM Erasmus University, Professor of Management Interfaces between Organizations and Business Environment, Room T07-57,Tel: +31 10 408 1955, E-mail: f.bosch@rsm.nl
3. Henk Volberda, RSM Erasmus University, Full Professor, Room T07-59 Tel: +31 10 408 2761, E-mail: h.volberda@rsm.nl
4. The data set *The External Management of Automation* has been collected as part of the NWO-pioneer programme 'The Management of Matches' (PGS 50-370) and is available from the Steinmetz-Archive (study number P1512). For more details on the data-collection procedure, we refer to Batenburg (1997) and Batenburg et al. (2003).

References

Anand, B. and Khanna, T. (2000) 'The Structure of Licensing Contracts', *Journal of Industrial Economics*, 48: 103–35.

Argyres, N. S. and Liebeskind, J. P. (1999) 'Contractual Commitments, Bargaining Power, and Governance Inseparability: Incorporating History in Transaction Cost Theory', *Academy of Management Review*, 24(1): 49–63.

Ariño, A. and Ring, P. S. (2004) 'The Role of Justice Theory in Explaining Alliance Negotiations', Working Paper No. 534, IESE Business School.

Avadikyan, A., Llerena, P., Matt, M., Rozan, A. and Wolff, S. (2001) 'Organizational Rules, Codification and Knowledge Creation in Inter-organization Cooperative Agreements', *Research Policy*, 30: 1443–58.

Batenburg, R. S. (1997) 'The External Management of Automation: Fieldwork, Response, and Non-Response', Utrecht University, ISCORE Paper No. 59.

Batenburg, R. S. and Raub, W. (1995) 'The External Management of Automation' (data set), Utrecht University.

Batenburg, R. S., Raub, W. and Snijders, C. (2003) 'Contacts and Contracts: Dyadic Embeddedness and the Contractual Behavior of Firms', in V. Buskens et al. (eds), *Research in the Sociology of Organizations*, 20, Oxford: JAI Press: 135–88.

Beckman, C. M., Haunschild, P. R. and Phillips, D. J. (2004) 'Friend or Strangers? Firm-specific Uncertainty, Market Uncertainty, and Network Partner Selection', *Organization Science*, 15(3): 259–75.

Blumberg, B. (2001) 'Cooperation Contracts between Embedded Firms', *Organization Studies*, 22: 825–52.

Buskens, V. W. (2002) *Social Networks and Trust*, Boston: Kluwer.

Buskens, V. W., Batenburg, R. S. and Weesie, J. (2003) 'Embedded Partner Selection in Relations between Firms', in V. Buskens et al. (eds), *Research in the Sociology of Organizations*, 20, Oxford: JAI Press: 107–33.

Cardinal, L. B. (2001) 'Technological Innovation in the Pharmaceutical Industry: the Use of Organizational Control in Managing Research and Development', *Organization Science*, 12(1): 19–36.

Cardinal, L. B., Sitkin, S. B. and Long, C. P. (2004) 'Balancing and Rebalancing in the Creation and Evolution of Organizational Control', *Organization Science*, 15(4): 411–31.

Colombo, M. G. (2003) 'Alliance Form: a Test of the Contractual and Competence Perspectives', *Strategic Management Journal*, 24: 1209–30.

Geringer, J. M. (1991) 'Strategic Determinants of Partner Selection Criteria in International Joint Ventures', *Journal of International Business Studies*, 22(1): 41–62.

Gulati, R. (1995) 'Does Familiarity Breed Trust? The Implications of Repeated Ties for Contractual Choice in Alliances', *Academy of Management Journal*, 38: 85–112.

Heide, J. B. (1994) 'Interorganizational Governance in Marketing Channels', *Journal of Marketing*, 58(1): 71–85.

Heide, J. B. (2003) 'Plural Governance in Industrial Purchasing', *Journal of Marketing*, 67: 18–29.

Helm, R. and Kloyer, M. (2004) 'Controlling Contractual Exchange Risks in R&D Interfirm Cooperation: an Empirical Study', *Research Policy*, 33: 1103–22.

Jap, S. D. and Ganesan, S. (2000) 'Control Mechanisms and the Relationship Life Cycle: Implications for Safeguarding Specific Investments and Developing Commitment', *Journal of Marketing Research*, 37: 227–45.

Kale, P., Dyer, J. H. and Singh, H. (2002) 'Alliance Capability, Stock Market Response, and Long-term Alliance Success: the Role of the Alliance Function', *Strategic Management Journal*, 23: 747–67.

Kirsch, L. J. (1997) 'Portfolios of Control Modes and IS Project Management', *Information Systems Research*, 8: 215–39.

Klein Woolthuis, R., Hillebrand, B. and Nooteboom, B. (2005) 'Trust, Contract and Relationship Development', *Organization Studies*, 26: 813–40.

Korobkin, R. (2003) 'Bounded Rationality, Standard Form Contracts, and Unconscionability', *University of Chicago Law Review*, 70: 1203–95.

Leiblein, M. J. (2003) 'The Choice of Organizational Governance Form and Performance: Predictions from Transaction Costs, Resource-based, and Real Options Theories', *Journal of Management*, 29(6): 937–61.

Li, S. X. and Rowley, T. J. (2002) 'Inertia and Evaluation Mechanisms in Interorganizational Partner Selection: Syndicate Formation among US Investment Banks', *Academy of Management Journal*, 45(6): 1104–19.

Long, C. P., Burton, R. M. and Cardinal, L. B. (2002) 'Three Controls are Better than One: a Computational Model of Complex Control Systems', *Computational and Mathematical Organizational Theory*, 8(3): 197–220.

Madhok, A. (2002) 'Reassessing the Fundamentals and Beyond: Ronald Coase, the Transaction Cost and Resource-based Theories of the Firm and the Institutional Structure of Production', *Strategic Management Journal*, 23: 535–50.

Miller, S., Wilson, D. and Hickson, D. (2004) 'Beyond Planning Strategies for Successfully Implementing Strategic Decisions', *Long Range Planning*, 37: 201–18.

Narayandas, D. and Rangan, V. K. (2004) 'Building and Sustaining Buyer–Seller Relationships in Mature Industrial Markets', *Journal of Marketing*, 68: 63–77.

Park, S. H. and Ungson, G. R. (2001) 'Interfirm Rivalry and Managerial Complexity: a Conceptual Framework of Alliance Failure', *Organization Science*, 12(1): 37–53.

Poppo, L. and Zenger, T. (2002) 'Do Formal Contracts and Relational Governance Function as Substitutes or Complements?', *Strategic Management Journal*, 23: 707–25.

Reuer, J. J. (1999) 'Collaborative Strategy: the Logic of Alliances', *Mastering Strategy*, 4 Oct.: 12–13.

Reuer, J. J. (2000) 'Parent Firm Performance across International Joint Venture Lifecycle Stages', *Journal of International Business Studies*, 31(1): 1–20.

Reuer, J. J. and Zollo, M. (2005) 'Termination Outcomes of Research Alliances', *Research Policy*, 34: 101–15.

Ryall, M. D. and Sampson, R. C. (2004) 'Do Prior Alliances Influence Contract Structure? Evidence from Technology Alliance Contracts', The Bradley Policy Research Center, Working Paper No. FR 03-11.

Wathne, K. H. and Heide, J. B. (2004) 'Relationship Governance in a Supply Chain Network', *Journal of Marketing*, 68: 73–89.

Zollo, M., Reuer, J. and Singh, H. (2002) 'Interorganizational Routines and Performance in Strategic Alliances', *Organization Science*, 13: 701–13.

11

Strategic Alliance Governance: an Extended Real Options Perspective

Ilya R. P. Cuypers[1] and Xavier Martin[2]

Introduction

Amidst increasingly global competition, the decision about how to expand abroad has become one of the most strategic a firm has to make. Firms expanding abroad face highly uncertain and changeable conditions; the factors that determine the success of foreign investments are diverse and vary as new information becomes available. It has long been established that joint ventures (JVs) can be a means of addressing this uncertainty (Aharoni, 1966). This feature, as well as the fact that JV governance decisions such as equity shares can be adjusted over time, has encouraged scholars to study international JVs from a real option (RO) perspective (Kogut, 1991).

While both scholars and practitioners have received the concept of RO with considerable enthusiasm, questions have recently been raised about boundary conditions for applying RO theory (Adner and Levinthal, 2004). While this applies to RO theory in general, implications for JV research have received insufficient attention. Therefore, in this chapter we will discuss under which conditions RO theory accurately describes an important facet of alliance governance: the choice of equity share by foreign partners in JVs. The distribution of equity among partners is one of the most critical governance decisions because it affects the distribution of ultimate costs, benefits and control of a joint venture (Kobrin, 1987; Hennart, 1993).

We start with a short overview of RO theory. Next, we examine in more detail the RO literature that looks at JVs, and the role of uncertainty. We then develop arguments about conditions under which RO logic is applicable. We argue that RO logic applies when uncertainty is exogenous but not when uncertainty resolves endogenously, and describe some evidence to that effect. We then outline several theoretical perspectives that can be used to study JVs and relate each of these to RO theory. We conclude that the boundary conditions elaborated in this chapter make RO theory more precise for studying the ownership structure of JVs, and draw further implications for alliance research and practice.

Real options

Soon after the analysis of financial options was formalized, it was realized that an analogy exists between corporate investments and financial options (Myers, 1977). Namely, a firm's investments and capabilities can be seen as options for future strategic choices. Options on non-financial assets are referred to as 'real options' and represent contingent investment commitments that secure future decision rights (Trigeorgis, 1993).

Insights and techniques carried over from financial option theory have shown that the traditional Net Present Value (NPV) valuation approach does not fully capture the value of an investment. However, this does not mean that the traditional NPV approach should be put aside. Instead it should be expanded to take into account management's flexibility to adapt to unexpected developments (Trigeorgis, 1995). Such flexibility is valuable because it can limit investors' downside losses to their initial investment while increasing the upside potential (Trigeorgis, 1995). Thus, an expanded NPV approach should incorporate both a passive NPV component and a dynamic option value component (Pindyck, 1988).

Furthermore, the two different value components usually have to be captured in different ways requiring different sizes of investment. More specifically, the passive NPV component requires a large investment in order to capture as much cash flow as possible while the dynamic option component can be captured with a smaller investment (Chi and McGuire, 1996).

Joint ventures as options to acquire

We define joint ventures as equity-based collaborative arrangements whereby two or more organizations each contribute resources, including equity, for the joint pursuit of economic goals. Kogut (1991) first argued that JVs are used as real options. He pointed out that firms can use a JV to capture the upside potential of a JV by buying out the partner in a later stage when favourable information becomes available, meanwhile limiting their downside risk to the initial investment (Kogut, 1991). This option to acquire can be explicit, but this is not a necessity. Even when there is no ex ante contractual specification of which party holds the acquisition right and of the strike price, it remains possible for the parties involved to negotiate the acquisition and sale of their shares subsequently. Thus a JV has at least an embedded implicit call option to acquire a partner's stake (Chi, 2000).

Following Kogut (1991), numerous scholars have looked at JVs from an RO perspective (e.g. Chi and McGuire 1996; Reuer, 2000, 2002; Reuer and Leiblein, 2000). These studies show that two aspects of JVs are of particular interest – namely, the distribution of initial ownership shares in JVs and their subsequent stability.

Firstly, option considerations will affect the initial distribution of equity stakes depending on which value component each investor seeks to capture.

An investor who seeks the static NPV part will take a share as large as possible, so (s)he can fully capture the future cash flows; in the extreme, this will lead to an outright acquisition or greenfield investment rather than to a JV. By contrast, an investor who wants to capture the dynamic RO part will seek a smaller share of the JV. This was modelled in detail by Chi and McGuire (1996) and further discussed by Reuer (2002).

Secondly, the holder of a (call) option will hold on to the option until it either expires, meaning that the joint activity ceases, or a positive signal occurs, i.e. the value of the underlying asset exceeds the strike price at which the firm can increase its equity share. This discrete investment logic distinguishes an RO from other path-dependent and incremental investment processes (Adner and Levinthal, 2004). Kogut (1991) looked at the timing of the exercise of call options, when one JV partner buys out the other. He found that the timing of exercising is determined by positive product market signals, while negative signals do not affect the stability of the JV. This asymmetry of the effects of positive and negative signals, combined with the discrete nature of changes in ownership structure, is consistent with JVs being real options. Miller and Folta (2002) argued that the optimal time to exercise a real call option depends on the possibility of pre-emption, the current dividends and the nature of the option (simple or compound, proprietary or shared). Empirically, they found that the value of the underlying asset, the level of uncertainty, and the number of parties in the JV all influence the timing of striking the call option in a JV.

In summary, studies looking at the initial equity distribution in JVs and at its subsequent stability support the interpretation that JVs are real call options.

Real option theory and uncertainty

Although there are five drivers of option value, one of these, uncertainty, has been far more prominent throughout the RO literature because of its natural appeal to business scholars.[3] In the RO literature, two broad streams of research can be distinguished (Reuer, 2002): a first stream in which formal models are used to address theoretically how flexibility can create value and what the costs and benefits are of investing in different types of (real) options, and a second stream in which investment decisions are examined empirically to see whether they are consistent with RO theory. These streams address uncertainty in different but potentially complementary ways. Therefore, we will provide a brief overview of both streams, focusing on the role of uncertainty in JVs.

In the first stream, many theoretical models focus solely on one or two sources of uncertainty. For instance, Chi (2000) and Chi and McGuire (1996) looked at how market uncertainty and uncertainty about the partner in a JV can affect the value of the venture. Others focused on exchange rate uncertainty (Huchzermeier and Cohen, 1996) and demand uncertainty (Bollen,

1999). A number of authors have emphasized that RO theory applies to uncertainty outside the control of the firm (i.e. exogenous uncertainty). For instance, Miller and Folta (2002) argued that the value of a call option increases as the level of exogenous uncertainty increases. However, the value of a call option will not increase when the firm can control the uncertainty, as is the case for responding to the threat of pre-emption by rivals.

In the second empirical stream, Kogut (1991) found support of JVs being used as call options to make subsequent acquisitions when there is market uncertainty. Folta and Miller (2002) found that uncertainty, measured as the variability in stock-market sub-field indices, influences the timing of striking options in JVs. Nonetheless, a number of studies found results which are inconsistent with RO predictions. For instance, Folta (1998) found that multiple sources of uncertainty influence the propensity to take an RO position by making a minority investment (as opposed to making a full acquisition). However, such a relationship was only found for exogenous technological uncertainty when it comes to forming a JV as a call option. Furthermore, Reuer and Leiblein (2000) did not find evidence that entering into multiple JVs reduces the downside risk for firms, as RO theory would predict. In fact they found that international JVs were associated with higher, rather than lower, levels of downside risk for two of their three measures of downside risk. Finally, Reuer and Tong (2005) found that the likelihood that a firm has an explicit call option to acquire equity in an international JV increases as property rights- and diversification-related uncertainty increase, but not as cultural uncertainty increases.

In summary, differing sources and conceptualizations of uncertainty have been used in the RO literature. These different conceptualizations, combined with a lack of studies contrasting different sources of uncertainty, may explain the inconsistent results in the empirical RO literature pertaining to JVs. Therefore, there is a need for studies that contrast and differentiate between different types of uncertainty. One such critical distinction is whether or not uncertainty is exogenous to the actions of the firm. We elaborate on this in the next section.

The boundaries of real option theory

Recently, a debate about the boundaries of RO logic has emerged. Concerns have been raised about the gap between theoretical and empirical studies (Reuer, 2002) and about consistency in the use of RO concepts (e.g. Adner and Levinthal, 2004). In an ongoing research project (Cuypers and Martin, 2005), we seek to refine and expand conceptually and empirically the boundaries of RO theory, with application to ownership levels in JVs. We build on the distinction between forms of uncertainty which resolve endogenously and exogenously (Roberts and Weitzman, 1981). Exogenous uncertainty is uncertainty of which the resolution is unaffected by the actions of the firm, while endogenous uncertainty is resolved (at least partially) by the actions of the firm itself over time.

We theorize that only exogenous uncertainty will have the impact suggested by RO theory: it will encourage firms to make investments with a greater RO component, and therefore to take smaller stakes in JVs. Conversely, in the case of endogenous uncertainty, we argue that investors will have different investment incentives and that option valuation models will break down. Under exogenous uncertainty, a firm can only wait for the uncertainty to resolve itself, and therefore an RO stance is appropriate. However, under endogenous uncertainty, firms have an incentive to invest ahead so as to learn more, and each partner may move the JV's value accordingly. Therefore, we predict that RO logic will not apply.

Using a sample of 6472 Sino-foreign JVs established between 1979 and 1996, we find, as predicted by RO theory, a negative relationship between the initial equity share taken by the foreign partner and three sources of exogenous uncertainty: economic conditions, local institutions, and exchange rate fluctuations. Conversely, we find no such relationship with two sources of endogenous uncertainty: cultural distance and partner uncertainty associated with R&D activities.[4] Indeed, proper null-hypothesis tests show conclusively that these endogenous sources of uncertainty have no significant effect on the distribution of equity shares among partners.

In summary, we theorize and find empirically that initial alliance governance decisions, as represented by equity stakes upon entering into international JVs, conform to RO predictions when uncertainty is exogenous but not when uncertainty is endogenous. These results advance our understanding of the boundary conditions for applying RO theory, help explain apparent inconsistencies in past research findings, and have substantive implications for researchers and practitioners alike when it comes to knowing when, and how, to apply RO theory.

Other theoretical perspectives

Specifying more precisely the boundary conditions to the use of RO theory, as we do in Cuypers and Martin (2005), raises the question of what other theory can be used to complement RO theory, especially in the case where (some) uncertainty is endogenous. Next, we briefly discuss three alternative approaches that have been used to look at governance decisions, including the distribution of JV equity shares.

Transaction costs economics (TCE)

Transactions are arrayed on a continuum between markets and hierarchy; the optimal degree of integration (control) reflects the trade-off between cheating costs due to opportunism by arm's length parties, and shirking costs that tend to arise when the parties are brought into the same organization

(Williamson, 1985; Hennart, 1993). Behavioural uncertainty figures in TCE as an endogenous factor that can be addressed via governance decisions. Exogenous uncertainty figures in TCE theory as a conditional factor, that exacerbates other conditions (especially asset specificity) which increase ex-ante and ex-post costs of contracting (Williamson, 1985).[5] However, the few TCE studies of JV equity shares proper have yielded mixed results regarding uncertainty – especially exogenous uncertainty.

Gatignon and Anderson (1988) looked at the choice between full owner-ship and shared ownership, and at the ownership level in case of shared ownership. They argued that higher levels of control, through equity owner-ship, are preferred in case of higher asset specificity – especially in combin-ation with external (exogenous) uncertainty. While R&D and advertising intensity, marking asset specificity, were indeed associated with a preference for full ownership, the interactions between them and external uncertainty were insignificant. The authors were generally unsuccessful in explaining intermediate levels of ownership when ownership is shared. Henisz (2000), conversely, found that the effect of (exogenous) political hazards on the choice of majority (as opposed to minority) equity ownership by a foreign investor is contingent on transaction-specific contractual hazards; the indic-ators of contractual hazards/asset specificity, measured similarly to Gatignon and Anderson (1988) and suggesting latent behavioural uncertainty, had mixed direct effects.

Chi and Roehl (1997) distinguished between control and ownership level in JVs. They argued that cheating cost can be reduced by means of more control – measured by the number of key managerial positions held in the venture; shirking costs can be reduced by giving away more of the venture's payoff – measured by the level of equity ownership. Shirking costs depend on how measurable and how important a party's effort is to the overall success of the venture. They found positive relationships between the foreign partner's equity share and the amount of discretionary training provided by that partner; the proportion of JV output distributed by that partner; and the dissimilarity between the local firm's business and the venture. This suggests that the initial ownership distribution serves to align incentives when one party's expected contribution is important to the overall performance of the venture yet is hard to measure, rather than to increase control and thereby reduce the costs of making specific investments. While Chi and Roehl (1997) thus elaborated the role of endogenous uncertainty, they did not address exogenous uncertainty.

Agency theory

The ownership structure of companies affects agency costs, i.e. ineffi-ciencies resulting from the differing objectives of different parties (Jensen and Meckling, 1976). Potential agency costs arise for the foreign partner because the local partner has to bear the full costs of its efforts on behalf of the JV, while only receiving a share of the benefits proportionate to its ownership stake. By taking a smaller share in the venture, the foreign partner can reduce these agency costs (Nakamura and Yeung, 1994). Thus uncertainty about agent behaviour is endogenous. However, the foreign partner also has to protect the property rights of its resources, in particular intangible assets, to avoid spillovers to potential competitors. Nakamura and Yeung (1994) argued that the probability of such spillovers decreases non-linearly as the foreign partner's ownership share increases. They found empirical evidence whereby JV ownership is a trade-off between agency costs and the costs of possible spillovers. They also reported ownership differences across industries, but attributed these to their reliance on intangible assets – which is endogenous – rather than exogenous industry conditions.

Bargaining perspective

Ownership of a JV is the result of negotiations in which relative power plays a crucial role (Fagre and Wells, 1982). It is often assumed in these models that partners prefer full ownership to gain more control and greater payoffs from the venture; preferably, the preferred ownership structure predicted by other theories should serve as the starting point and the bargaining power of the venture's parties then be used to explain deviations from this preference (Blodgett, 1991).

Bargaining power, and thereby the equity distribution, seems to be influenced by numerous factors (Kobrin, 1987). Fagre and Wells (1982) found a partner's level of ownership to be positively related to the amount of technology that it contributes, its advertising intensity, and its provision of market access; and negatively related with its having more competitors. Blodgett (1991) found that partners which contribute technology tend to obtain higher initial ownership, especially when the other party only contributes local knowledge and marketing. Government restrictions also matter – though the exogeneity of this factor is not addressed in the bargaining perspective, which naturally tends to focus on firm-level determinants of bargaining power. In general, research from the bargaining perspective has paid attention to the potential manipulation of JV conditions to either party's advantage (i.e. endogenous behavioural uncertainty), but not to exogenous sources of uncertainty.

Placing real option theory in context

In summary, TCE and agency theory focus primarily on behavioural uncertainty, which is endogenous. When exogenous environmental uncertainty is introduced, it is supposed to have an interactive rather than a direct effect. Both theories have contributed substantially to the analysis of endogenous uncertainty as it affects JV equity share – but not yielded strong generalizable results regarding exogenous uncertainty. Thus, TCE and agency theory hold promise as complements to RO theory, with RO theory shedding light on exogenous uncertainty (Cuypers and Martin, 2005) while the other theories shed light on endogenous uncertainty.

Studies from a bargaining perspective have provided limited insight into exogenous uncertainty. That perspective, too, may be complementary with RO theory insofar as RO theory can be used to predict the base ownership level from which bargaining power may explain deviations. With respect to exogenous uncertainty, which we know to influence equity shares too, RO theory has shown itself to be a most promising starting point (Folta, 1998; Cuypers and Martin, 2005).

Conclusion

We have proposed that the way to improve the predictive power of RO theory is to focus on exogenous uncertainty, which fits squarely within the purview of the theory. Our current research confirms this, and also establishes that RO theory has less to say about endogenous uncertainty. Conversely, our brief review of alternative theories suggests that they may have much to say about endogenous sources of uncertainty, but less about exogenous uncertainty (see Table 11.1).

Upon elaborating the boundary conditions for RO theory, we argue that RO predictions regarding JV equity shares are not conflicting or redundant relative to the other theoretical perspectives we reviewed. Rather, TCE, agency theory and bargaining models are complementary to RO theory. We

Table 11.1: Comparison of four perspectives on equity share distribution in JVs

	Real option theory	*Transaction cost theory*	*Agency theory*	*Bargaining perspective*
Unit of analysis	Option, i.e. an investment sequence	Transaction	Principal and agent	Firm dyad (or firm-government dyad)
Focus	Investment value maximization via downside risk minimization	Transaction cost minimization	Agency costs minimization and effort maximization	Maximization of the share of benefits (relative to the partner)
Exogenous uncertainty	Direct effect	Conditional effect	(Conditional effect)	(Ignored)
Endogenous (behavioural) uncertainty	No effect	Direct and/or conditional effect	Direct effect	Direct effect

conclude that RO theory remains a powerful perspective to study investments under (exogenous) uncertainty in general, and JVs in particular – all the more so, in fact, as its boundary conditions are properly understood. In this chapter, we have highlighted the need for – and rewards from – a precise conceptualization of uncertainty. For managers, there is a fundamental difference between endogenous uncertainty, which they can influence (perhaps even manipulate), and exogenous uncertainty; the former calls for strategies of strong, proactive commitment while the latter requires patience and sophistication in exploiting (real) option opportunities. For researchers, this same distinction invites more explicit and elaborate argumentation as to what theory, or combination of theories, is suitable given the sources of uncertainty on hand. We showed this with respect to RO theory. Similar empirical tests of the other theoretical perspectives that we reviewed might yield additional insights about their respective boundaries. The study of strategic alliances stands to gain from such efforts, but also represents a particularly promising venue for such efforts. While we have mostly discussed initial JV ownership in this chapter, other questions of strategic alliance governance – including their stability, evolution and performance – also deserve attention in future research.

Notes

1. Ilya R. P. Cuypers, Tilburg University, Department of Organization and Strategy, P.O. Box 90153, 5000 LE Tilburg, The Netherlands, Tel.: +31 13 466 8765 Fax: +31 13 466 8354, E-mail: I.R.P.Cuypers@uvt.nl
2. Xavier Martin, Tilburg University, Department of Organization and Strategy, P.O. Box 90153, 5000 LE Tilburg, The Netherlands, Tel: +31 13 466 8098, Fax: +31 13 466 8354, E-mail: x.martin@uvt.nl
3. The five drivers of option value are value of the underlying asset, strike price, time to maturity, risk-free interest rate and volatility of the underlying asset. We refer to the latter as uncertainty. The concept of uncertainty used in options research is actually closer to what Knight (1921) refers to as risk, in that financial option valuation models assume that it is possible to specify the probability distribution of the future value of an asset (hence its volatility). We will nevertheless use the term 'uncertainty' as this is the one used in most of the RO literature, especially that regarding alliances.
4. In a separate, knowledge-based literature, authors have argued that JVs are a better mechanism than contractual alliances for transferring (tacit) knowledge *between* partners (e.g. Martin and Salomon, 2003; Colombo, 2003). The knowledge transfer literature has not examined extensively the distribution of equity shares. Still, it suggests that JVs may facilitate learning *about* partners too – which reinforces our point that endogenous uncertainty can be handled proactively in JVs.
5. Williamson (1985: 59) emphasizes the conditional effect of exogenous uncertainty as follows: 'The influence of [exogenous] uncertainty on economic organizations is conditional. Specifically, an increase in parametric uncertainty is a matter of little consequence for transactions that are nonspecific.'

References

Adner, R. and Levinthal, A. (2004) 'What is Not a Real Option: Considering Boundaries for the Application of Real Options to Business Strategy', *Academy of Management Review*, 29(1): 74–85.

Aharoni, Y. (1966) *The Foreign Investment Decision Process*, Boston, MA: Harvard University Press.

Blodgett, L. L. (1991) 'Partner Contributions as Predictors of Equity Share in International Joint Ventures', *Journal of International Business Studies*, 22(1): 63–78.

Bollen, N. P. B. (1999) 'Real Options and Product Life Cycles', *Management Science*, 45(5): 670–84.

Chi, T. L. (2000) 'Option to Acquire or Divest a Joint Venture', *Strategic Management Journal*, 21(6): 665–87.

Chi, T. L. and McGuire, D. J. (1996) 'Collaborative Ventures and Value of Learning: Integrating the Transaction Costs and Strategic Option Perspectives on the Choice of Market Entry Modes', *Journal of International Business Studies*, 27(2): 285–307.

Chi, T. L. and Roehl, T. W. (1997) 'The Structuring of Interfirm Exchanges in Business Know-How: Evidence from International Collaborative Ventures', *Managerial and Decision Economics*, 18: 279–94.

Colombo, M. G. (2003) 'Alliance Form: a Test of the Contractual and Competence Perspectives', *Strategic Management Journal*, 24(12): 1209–29.

Cuypers, I. R. P. and Martin, X. (2005) 'What Makes and What Does Not Make a Real Option? A Study of International Joint Ventures'. Working paper, Tilburg University. Presented at the Annual Meeting of the Academy of International Business, Quebec City, July 2005.

Fagre, N. and Wells, L. T. (1982) 'Bargaining Power of Multinationals and Host Governments', *Journal of International Business Studies*, 13(2): 9–23.

Folta, T. B. (1998) 'Governance and Uncertainty: the Trade-off between Administrative Control and Commitment', *Strategic Management Journal*, 19(11): 1007–28.

Folta, T. B. and Miller, K. D. (2002) 'Real Options in Equity Partnerships', *Strategic Management Journal*, 23(1): 77–88.

Gatignon, H. and Anderson, E. (1988) 'The Multinational Corporation's Degree of Control over Foreign Subsidiaries: an Empirical Test of Transaction Cost Explanations', *Journal of Economics, Law and Organization*, 4: 305–36.

Henisz, W. J. (2000) 'The Institutional Environment for Multinational Investment', *Journal of Law, Economics and Organization*, 16(2): 334–64.

Hennart, J. F. (1993) 'Explaining the Swollen Middle – Why Most Transactions are a Mix of Market and Hierarchy', *Organization Science*, 4(4): 529–47.

Huchzermeier, A. and Cohen, M. A. (1996) 'Valuing Operational Flexibility Under Exchange Rate Risk', *Operations Research*, 44(1): 100–13.

Jensen, M. C. and Meckling, W. H. (1976) 'Theory of Firm – Managerial Behavior, Agency Costs and Ownership Structure', *Journal of Financial Economics*, 3(4): 305–60.

Knight, F. H. (1921) *Risk, Uncertainty and Profit*, Chicago: University of Chicago Press.

Kobrin, S. J. (1987) 'Testing the Bargaining Hypothesis in the Manufacturing Sector in Developing Countries', *International Organization*, 41(4): 609–68.

Kogut, B. (1991) 'Joint Ventures and the Option to Expand and Acquire', *Management Science*, 37(1): 19–33.

Martin, X. and Salomon, R. (2003) 'Knowledge Transfer Capacity and its Implications for the Theory of the Multinational Corporation', *Journal of International Business Studies*, 34(4): 356–73.

Miller, K. D. and Folta, T. B. (2002) 'Option Value and Entry Timing', *Strategic Management Journal*, 23(7): 655–65.

Myers, S. C. (1977) 'Determinants of Corporate Borrowing', *Journal of Financial Economics*, 5(2): 147–75.

Nakamura, M. and Yeung, B. (1994) 'On the Determinants of Foreign Ownership Shares: Evidence from US Firms' Joint Ventures in Japan', *Managerial and Decision Economics*, 15(2): 95–106.

Pindyck, R. S. (1988) 'Irreversible Commitment, Capacity Choice, and the Value of the Firm', *American Economic Review*, 78: 967–85.

Reuer, J. J. (2000) 'Parent Firm Performance across International Joint Venture Life-cycle Stages', *Journal of International Business Studies*, 29: 263–79.

Reuer, J. J. (2002) 'How Real are Real Options? The Case of International Joint Ventures', in M. A. Hitt, R. Amit and R. D. Nixon (eds), *Creating Value: Winners in the New Business Environment*, Oxford: Blackwell Publishing.

Reuer, J. J. and Leiblein, M. J. (2000) 'Downside Risk Implications of Multinationality and International Joint Ventures', *Academy of Management Journal*, 43(2): 203–14.

Reuer J. J. and Tong, T. W. (2005) 'Real Options in International Joint Ventures', *Journal of Management*, 31(3): 403–23.

Roberts, K. and Weitzman, M. L. (1981) 'Funding Criteria for Research, Development, and Exploration Projects', *Econometrica*, 49: 1261–87.

Trigeorgis, L. (1993) 'Real Options and Interactions with Financial Flexibility', *Financial Management*, 22(3): 202–24.

Trigeorgis, L. (1995) 'Real Options: an Overview', in L. Trigeorgis (ed.), *Real Options in Capital Investment: Models, Strategies, and Applications*, Westport, Connecticut: Praeger.

Williamson, O. (1985) *The Economic Institutions of Capitalism*, New York: Free Press.

12
The Uncertainty-Governance Choice Puzzle Revisited: Theoretical Perspectives on Alliance Governance Decisions

Franziska Koenig[1] and Thomas Mellewigt[2]

Introduction

The concept of uncertainty has long been discussed as an important driver of managerial decisions. One stream of research particularly focuses on how governance structures reflect the effort to efficiently cope with uncertainty. Thereby different theoretical explanations can be found. The most prominent theoretical perspective on firms' governance decisions, transaction cost theory, suggests extending the level of ownership and vertical integration to conduct efficient control on sources of uncertainty (Williamson, 1991). In contrast, strategic management theory, and more recently papers based on real options theory, promote the notion of maintaining flexibility under uncertainty, and suggest limiting investments into the firm's vertical and horizontal scope until uncertainty is resolved (Folta, 1998; Folta and Leiblein, 1994; Harrigan, 1985). Notwithstanding its broad attention, the relationship between uncertainty and the firm's governance choice still represents a sort of theoretical and empirical puzzle (Leiblein, 2003; Sutcliffe and Zaheer, 1998). Moreover, empirical research provides in part contradicting results on how uncertainty affects the governance choice of the firm (Balakrishnan and Wernerfelt, 1986; Harrigan, 1985; Majumdar and Ramaswamy, 1994; Russo, 1992; Sutcliffe and Zaheer, 1998; Walker and Weber, 1987). The theoretical and empirical puzzle might exist for three reasons:

- Uncertainty is a multi-dimensional construct, and theories may therefore focus on different types of uncertainty, which differently affect firm performance, requiring different 'governance responses'. Yet, these relationships have not been clearly disentangled.

- Second, there are different roles of governance structures under uncertainty, such as control, coordination or flexibility – which are not being sufficiently considered (Leiblein and Macher, 2005).
- Third, differences in empirical findings might be ascribed to the influence of third variables.

Thus, there is a need to more precisely disentangle uncertainty-governance relationships in different theoretical perspectives. Focusing on the first argument elucidated above, our chapter contributes to a more thorough understanding of different uncertainty concepts by examining them along several dimensions. Recent articles have already indicated pitfalls in viewing uncertainty as one-dimensional construct (Carson et al., 2005; Leiblein, 2003; Santoro and McGill, 2005; Sutcliffe and Zaheer, 1998). Our chapter aims at advancing the idea of multiple uncertainty-governance choice links by providing a classification of uncertainty types, uncertainty effects, and governance mechanisms, which sheds light on the theoretical and empirical puzzle we have found. More specifically, we contribute to governance research in providing a more comprehensive, multi-theoretical overview, including a stronger differentiation of uncertainty-governance choice links. By more precisely describing the theoretical uncertainty concepts and suggested response (governance) mechanisms, our concept helps to determine each theory's boundaries in explaining the firm's governance choice under uncertainty. Second, our categorization enlightens managerial governance decisions by identifying how different types of uncertainty can be efficiently addressed. Such a more systematic approach is particularly valuable for managing strategic alliances, which have to cope with different types of uncertainty simultaneously (Das and Teng, 1998; Santoro and McGill, 2005). Although for this reason a larger number of market- and hierarchy-based governance mechanisms are available, there is a particular challenge in combining them to achieve an efficiently working governance design addressing different uncertainty effects.

Prior research

While early work on uncertainty did not distinguish between different forms of uncertainty (Burns and Stalker, 1961; Williamson, 1975), within more recent research it has been acknowledged that uncertainty may influence managerial decisions via different dimensions. For example, Williamson (1985) differentiated between *primary, secondary* and *behavioural uncertainty*: whereas primary uncertainty describes a lack of knowledge about states of nature, secondary uncertainty refers to the unpredictability of other economic actors' actions, such as competitors. Both are described as innocent and non-strategic forms of *environmental uncertainty*. In contrast, behavioural uncertainty refers to the deliberate non-disclosure of information or its misrepresentation by exchange partners and plays a vital role within the transaction cost framework. This and similar uncertainty classifications have been applied, distinguishing between environmental types of uncertainty affecting all firms equally and more relationship-specific forms of uncertainty (Das and Teng, 1998; John and Weitz, 1988). However, only a few empirical studies explicitly discussed different effects of these uncertainty types on governance decisions (Anderson, 1985; Henisz, 2004; Santoro and McGill, 2005; Sutcliffe and Zaheer, 1998).

Within the strategic management literature, other classification approaches can be found, referring to uncertainty as perceptual construct (Duncan, 1972; Miles and Snow, 1978). A comprehensive approach is offered by Milliken (1987), who highlighted three dimensions of uncertainty: *State uncertainty* refers to a lack of knowledge and predictability concerning environmental changes. *Effect uncertainty* reflects the inability to precisely predict the impact of uncertainty on the organization's performance. *Response uncertainty* describes problems in identifying and assessing possible options to respond to uncertainty. Within the governance literature, there are only a few papers which explicitly address different perceptual dimensions of uncertainty (Carson et al., 2005; Klein et al., 1990); although within most theoretical approaches, uncertainty is conceptualized as perceptual construct (while building on assumptions of bounded rationality; see theoretical reviews below).

The different categorization approaches in consensus apply the notion that different uncertainty types have different effects on managerial decisions; whereby some of these approaches have found empirical support. Despite these efforts to define more differentiated uncertainty constructs, we still lack a unified perspective on the relationship between uncertainty and the governance choice of firms. In terms of Milliken's (1987) three-dimensional uncertainty definition, most of the existing uncertainty classifications in the governance choice literature distinguish different uncertainty types on the state dimension of uncertainty.[3] Moreover, most of them apply a single-theoretical fundament. It results in overlapping uncertainty definitions across different theoretical approaches (Schilling and Steensma, 2002), while different and in part even contradictory responses (governance decisions) are linked to the same type of uncertainty.[4] There are only few efforts to integrate multi-theoretical predictions (Folta, 1998; Folta and Leiblein, 1994; Santoro and McGill, 2005), resulting in the theoretical and empirical puzzle we have already discussed.

The categorization approach we develop within this chapter,

(a) aims at reconciling different theoretical perspectives, focusing on transaction cost theory, the resource-based view, and real options theory;
(b) while simultaneously providing a more precise view on the underlying decision-making mechanisms. By applying Milliken's (1987) three-dimensional uncertainty definition, the different theoretical

uncertainty-governance choice concepts are categorized along the following questions:

- What *type* of uncertainty is addressed (state dimension)?
- Which *effects* of uncertainty are highlighted (effect dimension)?
- Which *response* (governance) mechanisms are suggested (response dimension)?

Transaction cost economics (TCE)

Basically, TCE assumes governance decisions reflect the need to make transaction-specific investments under uncertainty. Uncertainty thereby raises the potential for an opportunistic misappropriation of quasi-rents (uncertainty effect), which can be gained from transaction-specific investments (Klein et al., 1990). TCE suggests integrating transactions into the hierarchy in order to reduce the potential for opportunistic threats, by using hierarchical fiat and control mechanisms (uncertainty response). Within empirical research, this argumentation has been widely investigated with regard to two basic uncertainty types: environmental and behavioural uncertainty. *Environmental uncertainty* refers to the frequency of environmental changes that – due to bounded rationality – cannot be completely anticipated ex ante and force the renegotiation of contracts ex post. *Behavioural uncertainty* is specific to a particular exchange relationship and refers to opportunistic partner behaviour, such as moral hazard or hold-up (Das and Teng, 1998; Williamson, 1985). However, the empirical results for the TCE proposition on the effect of uncertainty are mixed (David and Han, 2004). In general, the results better support the proposition for behavioural uncertainty (Coles and Hesterly, 1998; Henisz, 2004; John and Weitz, 1988; Oxley, 1999; Schilling and Steensma, 2002), whereas the application of environmental uncertainty achieved less supportive results (Henisz, 2004; Poppo and Zenger, 2002; Robertson and Gatignon, 1998; Sutcliffe and Zaheer, 1998). One reason might be that the theoretically proposed *contingency effect of uncertainty* on the main effect of asset specificity has been insufficiently considered in empirical work (Coles and Hesterly, 1998; David and Han, 2004; Masten et al., 1991). Second, there might be a need to further improve the operationalization of uncertainty. For example, Klein et al. (1990), who distinguished between the two environmental uncertainty dimensions *diversity* and *volatility*, found contrary effects on the dependent variable channel integration. Third, although within the TCE both environmental changes and behavioural uncertainty play a central role, we do not yet understand sufficiently their relative importance and interaction effects. Moreover, there even might be a gap between theory and its empirical foundation.[5] Most studies investigated the direct effect of one of the two uncertainty types, while there are few contributions which explicitly investigate different as well as the interaction effects of both uncertainty types (Carson et al., 2005; Henisz, 2004; Robertson and Gatignon, 1998; Poppo and Zenger, 2002; Sutcliffe and Zaheer, 1998). Most of the latter contributions provided evidence, however, that behavioural and environmental uncertainty lead to different responses (governance decisions). While disentangling these uncertainty types with regard to their potential effects and their interaction, we might better understand those different responses. Behavioural uncertainty is related to concerns about the misappropriation of rents (direct effect), which increase the level of transaction costs for creating sufficient contractual control mechanisms (response). Environmental uncertainty raises the need to renegotiate contracts ex post (direct effect), creating a *potential* for misappropriation problems. Hence, the existence of environmental uncertainty may amplify the effect of behavioural uncertainty on the governance choice but does not *directly* affect the preference for hierarchical governance (Carson et al., 2005; Slater and Spencer, 2000). The effect of environmental uncertainty on the preference for hierarchy may therefore be dependent on the level of behavioural uncertainty. However, it seems that this interaction between environmental and behavioural uncertainty has been often neglected in the empirical literature, whereby a certain level of behavioural uncertainty might be taken as given, when measuring direct effects of environmental uncertainty on the preference for hierarchical governance structures. But in Williamson's argumentation, environmental uncertainty is rather a starting point for the explanation of the existence of firms; and even more, Williamson clearly argues that under autonomous types of disturbances (environmental uncertainty), market governance forms are more efficient in adaptation (Williamson, 1991). Because the resolution of external disturbances remains exogenous to the governance choice, market governance is more efficient as it provides autonomy to flexibly adapt to changes. With an increase in relationship-specific investments, behavioural uncertainty additionally affects the governance decision by driving the level of vertical integration. Behavioural uncertainty is conceptualized as being endogenously resolvable with hierarchical fiat and control. Overall, TCE-based literature paid more attention to the effects of behavioural uncertainty (Slater and Spencer, 2000), while the simultaneous need to autonomously adapt to environmental changes has been rather neglected.

Resource-based view (RBV)

Uncertainty plays a central role within the RBV, appearing in two different (perceptual) concepts. First, environmental uncertainty leads to information asymmetry (uncertainty effect) in the strategic factor market. Second, information asymmetry can also result from causal ambiguity, being the product of certain resource characteristics, such as tacitness, complexity and specificity (Reed and DeFillippi, 1990). Such information asymmetries are reflected in different expectations about the potential value of resources, which affect the resource accumulation strategies of firms (Barney, 1986;

Peteraf, 1993). We found different conceptualizations of how uncertainty influences governance decisions, whereby most studies concentrated on the effects from causal ambiguity. First, early RBV work highlighted the positive upside effects of uncertainty. It can be exploited by developing and integrating causally ambiguous resources within the firm, requiring an increasing level of *firm scope and ownership* (uncertainty response), which raises imitation barriers (Kogut and Zander, 1992; Reed and DeFillippi, 1990). For example, Leiblein and Miller (2003) showed that the motivation to exploit firm-specific production competencies in other markets significantly affected the decision to vertically integrate. A second and more dominant stream of research, drawing on the competence-based perspective, pointed to potential downside losses from the transfer of causally ambiguous resources, such as tacit knowledge, within and between firms (Conner and Prahalad, 1996; Simonin, 1999). This ambiguity is thereby conceptualized as endogenously resolvable, assuming that governance structures differ in their competencies and costs in addressing different levels of ambiguity. Following a similar discriminating alignment perspective to TCE, studies promote hierarchical *colocation* structures being suitable to efficiently address very complex (ambiguous) knowledge transfer problems, whereas market-based governance forms are efficient in resolving less complex problems (Leiblein and Macher, 2005; Nickerson and Zenger, 2004). A third group of studies, which apply the TCE logic to provide a further potential explanation of the *response* to causal ambiguity, points to problems of unintended knowledge transfer between exchange partners. Such problems are particularly virulent when tacit, ambiguous knowledge cannot be effectively protected by formal contracts and might therefore be opportunistically appropriated by the exchange partner (Colombo, 2003; Oxley, 1999). Hence, as we locate this third area of research to the interface between TCE and RBV research, we conclude this chapter with determining two basic uncertainty types in the RBV, each related to two potential effects and response mechanisms (see Table 12.1).

Real options theory (ROT)

The ROT perspective has recently been applied in order to provide alternative governance choice explanations to TCE, particularly related to uncertainty (Folta, 1998). The central construct is environmental uncertainty, here in terms of the volatile nature of the firm's environment.[6] ROT proposes that the value of holding an option on an asset increases with the volatility of the underlying asset's value. This concept includes the notion of copying with two uncertainty effects: first, the creation of options allows exploiting upside opportunities by hedging on the potential for 'positive shocks'; second, options simultaneously limit the exposure to downside risks in terms of sunk costs under negative shocks. Such costs may result from

Table 12.1: Summary of theoretical concepts

Theory	Uncertainty Type			Uncertainty Effects		Response to Uncertainty		Condition for Uncertainty Governance Choice Relationship	Selected References
	Uncertainty Definition	State Dimension*	Direct Effects	Effects on Firm Performance	Effect Dimension*	Response Dimension* (Uncertainty Resolution)	Governance Mechanisms		
		Volatility + Unpredictability	Inflexibility	Administrative costs		Exogenous	Autonomous adaptability (Flexibility)	Asset Specificity is low	• Williamson, 1991 • Hagedom et al., 2005
		Volatility + Unpredictability	Rent misappropriation by partner						• Coles and Hesterly, 1998 • Heide and John, 1990
TCE	Environmental changes	Volatility + Unpredictability	Behavioural uncertainty (ex-post contractual renegotiation needs)--> Rent misappropriation (indirect effect)	Transaction costs	Downside loss	Endogenous	Flat, control	Asset Specificity is high	• Carson et al., 2005 • Heniz, 2004 • Schilling and Steensma, 2002
	Behavioural uncertainty	Unpredictability	Rent misappropriation by partner						• Poppo and Zenger, 2002 • Robertson and Gatignon, 1998 • Sutcliffe and Zaheer, 1998

RBV	Environmental changes		Option value	Upside opportunity		Increase of firm scope and ownership Colocation		• Steensma and Corley, 2001
	Causal Ambiguity		Search cost / Option value	Downside loss / Upside opportunity	Endogenous	Increase of firm scope and ownership Colocation	n/a	• Jap, 1999 • Schilling and Steensma, 2002
	Unpredictability	Information asymmetry	Search cost	Downside loss				• Colombo, 2003 • Kogut and Zander, 2003 • Leiblein and Macher, 2005
ROT	Environmental changes	Increased exposure to positive shocks	(Growth) option value	Upside opportunity	Exogenous	(Sequential) increase of firm scope and ownership	Asset Specificity is high	• Miller and Folta, 2002 • Leiblein and Miller, 2003
	Volatility	Increased exposure to negative shocks	Administrative costs	Downside loss		Governance flexibility		• Folta, 1998 • Kale and Puranam, 2005 • Schilling and Steensma, 2002

* Three-dimensional uncertainty concept by Milliken (1987)

specific investments and a premature commitment to a particular investment path. Because vertical integration implies a stronger commitment to an
investment path, less hierarchical governance forms have often been conceptualized as option investments. They provide flexibility to adapt the underlying investment contingent upon the arrival of new information, while
economizing on administrative costs (Folta, 1998; Kogut, 1991). A second
stream of governance literature investigated more micro-level mechanisms
to create flexibility, such as the inclusion of particular contractual options
(Reuer and Tong, 2005). The theoretical conceptualization implies that the
resolution of uncertainty remains exogenous to the governance choice: while
options do not directly affect the level of uncertainty, they allow managing
the firm's exposure to upside opportunities and downside risks.

Theoretical integration and conclusions for future research

We have argued that the uncertainty-governance choice puzzle can be
solved by more precisely analysing different dimensions of uncertainty. Our
chapter therefore includes a focused review of three theoretical uncertainty-
governance choice concepts, wherein we try to disentangle the link between
uncertainty types, effects and suggested response (governance) mechanisms.
We conclude here with a first reconciliation of the different concepts. Our
review suggests that looking only at the type of uncertainty neglects the
more important differences between the theoretical explanations, which are
related to *uncertainty effects* and appropriate *response mechanisms*. Hence,
the disentangling of the theoretical concepts along the state, effect and
response dimension of uncertainty allows us now to systematically reveal
complementary and conflicting propositions on how uncertainty affects
the governance choice of firms, being briefly described in the following by
building pairs of theoretical combinations.

TCE and ROT

Both theories highlight the need to adapt to environmental changes
(uncertainty), which creates problems due to the specificity of investments.
Whereas TCE focuses on the misappropriation consequences from behavioural uncertainty, which result in a higher level of hierarchical integration,
ROT promotes the flexibility advantages of less integrated governance forms
to economize on administrative costs and to create option value. The literature suggests that a trade-off between the two concepts might be dependent
on the level of uncertainty (Folta and Leiblein, 1994), the influence of third
variables, such as the level of asset specificity (Folta, 1998; Leiblein and
Miller, 2003), the type of resources involved, whereby some resources require
more control than others (Das and Teng, 1998), or the level of trust (Sutcliffe
and Zaheer, 1998). Based on our multi-dimensional concept of uncertainty,
we suggest that the trade-off might also be influenced by how predictable

environmental changes are. Whereas TCE assumes incomplete contracts due to bounded rationality, the ROT applies stronger rationality assumptions and generally assumes firms are able to include all contingencies. The level of contractual completeness, being dependent on the perceived predictability of environmental changes, therefore might affect the relative importance of environmental versus behavioural uncertainty and thus the preference for hierarchical integration.

TCE and RBV

The complementarity of TCE's contractual perspective and the competence-based perspective, in particular with regard to the governance choice for knowledge-based resources, has been often highlighted. But despite their different perspectives, similar prescriptions on the appropriate governance form – that is, the preference of hierarchical governance forms when significant knowledge-based (or even tacit) resources are involved – have made it difficult to empirically discriminate between both theories (Colombo, 2003). One possibility to disentangle these different governance choice processes is to take a closer look at the underlying uncertainty concept. TCE highlights monitoring problems related to specific investments in knowledge-intensive resources and the resulting behavioural uncertainty. Hierarchical governance is recommended for an efficient *control* of potential misappropriation problems. In contrast, the competence perspective highlights the uncertainty in the form of causal ambiguity characterizing knowledge-based assets, which results in higher costs for transferring and integrating them into the firm. Here, hierarchical *colocation* structures are promoted to enable effective learning processes, which reduce such (search) costs (Nickerson and Zenger, 2004). An integration of both explanations suggests taking a more differentiated view – especially on alliance governance forms – with regard to the governance mechanisms used to address different uncertainty effects (Leiblein and Macher, 2005).

ROT and RBV

Both theories highlight the active exploitation of uncertainty, which is based on information asymmetries about the potential value of resources. While the RBV literature basically suggests integrating resources that are 'platforms on future developments' (Kogut and Zander, 1992: 385), the ROT may offer more nuanced propositions, suggesting to sequentially invest in options in order to limit the firm's exposure to downside shocks, while fully maintaining the access to potential upside gains. Considering the different theoretical uncertainty concepts, the level of chosen ownership may then depend on how exogenous or endogenous the source of information asymmetry is. If the source of information asymmetry is endogenous to the governance choice, such as in the case of causal ambiguity, firms prefer a high level of integration (equity). In contrast, information asymmetry based on volatile changes remains exogenous to the governance choice; hence firms prefer options on ownership (moderate level of integration, minority equity). Our classification concept, as summarized in Table 12.1, and the suggested points of integration may motivate further research to more precisely understand how firms efficiently address different uncertainty types and their effects. Such insights may also be useful to better explain the heterogeneity of alliance governance forms in the managerial practice, which we yet do not understand sufficiently.

Notes

1. Franziska Koenig, Freie Universität Berlin, Institute for Management, Garystraße 21, D-14195 Berlin, Tel: +49-611-5659937, E-mail:franziska. koenig@gmx.de
2. Thomas Mellewigt, Freie Universität Berlin, Institute for Management, Garystraße 21, D-14195 Berlin, Tel: +49-175-4009939, E-mail: tm@upb.de
3. Recent papers, which draw on real option theory, address the response dimension by distinguishing endogenous and exogenous forms of uncertainty resolution (Cuypers and Martin, 2005). However, these types of uncertainty have not been conceptualized as perceptual constructs.
4. For example, while several theories apply the concept of environmental uncertainty, they focus on different uncertainty *effects* and therefore suggest different response mechanisms.
5. This might result from the historical development of the framework. Early TCE literature did not clearly define the uncertainty construct. Only later, Williamson specified different types of uncertainty (primary, secondary and behavioural) (Williamson, 1985) and emphasized behavioural uncertainty as being the main driver of firms' governance decisions.
6. Based on strong rationality assumptions, this uncertainty construct is closer to Knight's description of risk (Knight, 1921), as there is no ambiguity surrounding volatile changes.

References

Anderson, E. (1985) 'The Salesperson as Outside Agent or Employee: a Transaction-cost Analysis', *Marketing Science*, 4(3): 234–54.

Balakrishnan, S. and Wernerfelt, B. (1986) 'Technical Change, Competition, and Vertical Integration', *Strategic Management Journal*, 7(4): 347–59.

Barney, J. B. (1986) 'Strategic Factor Markets: Expectations, Luck, and Business Strategy', *Management Science* 32(10): 1231–41.

Burns, T. and Stalker, G. M. (1961) *The Management of Innovation*, London: Tavistock.

Carson, S. J., Madhok, A. and Wu, T. (2005) 'Uncertainty, Opportunism and Governance: the Effects of Volatility and Ambiguity on Formal and Relational Contracting', forthcoming in: *Academy of Management Journal*.

Coles, J. W. and Hesterly, W. S. (1998) 'The Impact of Firm-specific Assets and the Interaction of Uncertainty: an Examination of Make or Buy Decisions in Public and Private Hospitals', *Journal of Economic Behavior and Organization*, 36: 383–409.

Colombo, M. G. (2003) 'Alliance Form: a Test of the Contractual and Competence Perspectives', *Strategic Management Journal*, 24(12): 1209–29.

Conner, K. R. and Prahalad, C. K. (1996) 'A Resource-based Theory of the Firm: Knowledge versus Opportunism', *Organization Science*, 7: 477–501.

Cuypers, I. and Martin, X. (2005) 'What Makes and What Does Not Make a Real Option? A Study of International Joint Ventures', Working paper, Tilburg University.

Das, T. K. and Teng, B. S. (1998) 'Resource and Risk Management in the Strategic Alliance Making Process', *Journal of Management*, 24(1): 21–42.

David, R. J. and Han, S.-K. (2004) 'A Systematic Assessment of the Empirical Support for Transaction Cost Economics', *Strategic Management Journal*, 25(1): 39–58.

Duncan, R. B. (1972) 'Characteristics of Organizational Environments and Perceived Environmental Uncertainty', *Administrative Science Quarterly*, 17: 313–27.

Folta, T. B. (1998) 'Governance and Uncertainty: the Trade-off Between Administrative Control and Commitment', *Strategic Management Journal*, 19: 1007–28.

Folta, T. B. and Leiblein, M. J. (1994) 'Technology Acquisition and the Choice of Governance by Established Firms: Insights from Option Theory in a Multinomial Logit Model', *Academy of Management Best Paper Proceedings*.

Hagedoorn, J., Cloodt, D. and van Kranenburg, H. (2005) 'Intellectual Property Rights and the Governance of International R&D Partnerships', *Journal of International Business Studies*, 36(2): 175–86.

Harrigan, K. R. (1985) 'Vertical Integration and Corporate Strategy', *Academy of Management Review*, 28(2): 397–425.

Heide, J. B. and John, G. J. (1990) 'Alliances in Industrial Purchasing: the Determinants of Joint Action in Buyer-Supplier Relationships', *Journal of Marketing Research*, 27(1): 24–36.

Henisz, W. J. (2004) 'The Institutional Environment for Multinational Investment', *Journal of Law, Economics and Organization*, 16(2): 334–64.

Jap, S. D. (1999) ' "Pie-expansion" Efforts: Collaboration Processes in Buyer-Supplier Relationships', *Journal of Marketing Research*, 36(4): 461–75.

John, G. and Weitz, B. A. (1988) 'Forward Integration into Distribution: an Empirical Test of Transaction Cost Analysis', *Journal of Law, Economics and Organization*, 4(2): 337–55.

Klein, S., Frazier, G. L. and Roth, V. J. (1990) 'A Transaction Cost-analysis Model of Channel Integration in International Markets', *Journal of Marketing Research*, 27(2): 196–208.

Knight, F. H. (1921) *Risk, Uncertainty and Profit*, Boston, MA: Houghton-Mifflin.

Kogut, B. (1991) 'Joint Ventures and the Option to Expand and Acquire', *Management Science*, 37(1): 19–33.

Kogut, B. and Zander, U. (1992) 'Knowledge of the Firm, Combinative Capabilities, and the Replication of Technology', *Organization Science*, 3(3): 383–97.

Kogut, B. and Zander, U. (1993) 'Knowledge of the Firm and the Evolutionary Theory of the Multinational Corporation', *Journal of International Business Studies*, 34(6): 516–29.

Leiblein, M. J. (2003) 'The Choice of Organizational Governance Form and Performance: Predictions from Transaction Cost, Resource-based, and Real Options Theories', *Journal of Management*, 29(6): 937–61.

Leiblein, M. J. and Macher, J. (2005) 'Alliance Organization and Technological Performance: Disaggregating the Cause and Consequences of Ownership and Colocation', Working paper.

Leiblein, M. J. and Miller, D. J. (2003) 'An Empirical Examination of Transaction- and Firm-level Influences on the Vertical Boundaries of the Firm', *Strategic Management Journal*, 24(9): 839–60.

Majumdar, S. K. and Ramaswamy, V. (1994) 'On the Role of Asset Specificity in the Channel Integration Decision', *Journal of Institutional and Theoretical Economics*, 150: 375–400.

Masten, S. E., Meehan, J. W. and Snyder, E. A. (1991) 'The Costs of Organization', *Journal of Law, Economics and Organization*, 7: 1–25.

Miles, R. E. and Snow, C. C. (1978) *Organizational Strategy, Structure, and Process*, New York: McGraw-Hill.

Miller, K. D. and Folta, T. B. (2002) 'Real Options in Equity Partnerships', *Strategic Management Journal*, 23(1): 77–89.

Milliken, E. J. (1987) 'Three Types of Perceived Uncertainty about the Environment: State, Effect, and Response Uncertainty', *Academy of Management Review*, 12(1): 133–43.

Nickerson, J. and Zenger, T. (2004) 'A Knowledge-based Theory of Governance Choice: the Problem Solving Approach', *Organization Science* 15(6): 617–32.

Oxley, J. E. (1999) 'Institutional Environment and the Mechanism of Governance: the Impact of Intellectual Property Protection on the Structure of Inter-firm Alliances', *Journal of Economic Behavior and Organization*, 38(3): 283–309.

Peteraf, M. A. (1993) 'The Cornerstones of Competitive Advantage: a Resource-based View', *Strategic Management Journal*, 14: 179–91.

Poppo, L. and Zenger, T. (2002) 'Do Formal Contracts and Relational Governance Function as Substitutes or Complements?', *Strategic Management Journal*, 23(8): 707–25.

Reed, R. and DeFillippi, R. (1990) 'Causal Ambiguity, Barriers to Imitation, and Sustainable Competitive Advantage', *Academy of Management Review*, 15(1): 88–102.

Reuer, J. J. and Tong, T. W. (2005) 'Real Options in International Joint Ventures', *Journal of Management*, 31(3): 403–23.

Robertson, T. S. and Gatignon, H. (1998) 'Technology Development Mode: a Transaction Cost Conceptualization', *Strategic Management Journal*, 19(6): 515–31.

Russo, M. V. (1992) 'Power Plays: Regulation, Diversification, and Backward Integration in the Electric Utility Industry', *Strategic Management Journal*, 13(1): 13–27.

Santoro, M. D. and McGill, J. P. (2005) 'The Effect of Uncertainty and Asset Co-specialization on Governance in Biotechnology Alliances', *Strategic Management Journal*, 26(13): 1261–9.

Schilling, M. A. and Steensma, H. K. (2002) 'Disentangling the Theories of Firm Boundaries: a Path Model and Empirical Test', *Organization Science*, 13(4): 387–401.

Simonin, B. L. (1991) 'Ambiguity and the Process of Knowledge Transfer in Strategic Alliances', *Strategic Management Journal*, 20: 595–623.

Slater, G. and Spencer, D. A. (2000) 'The Uncertain Foundations of Transaction Cost Economics', *Journal of Economic Issues*, 34(1): 61–87.

Steensma, H. K. and Corley, K. G. (2001) 'Organizational Context as a Moderator of Theories on Firm Boundaries for Technology Sourcing', *Academy of Management Journal*, 44(2): 271–91.

Sutcliffe, K. M. and Zaheer, A. (1998) 'Uncertainty in the Transaction Environment: an Empirical Test', *Strategic Management Journal*, 19: 1–23.

Walker, G. and Weber, D. (1987) 'Supplier Competition, Uncertainty and Make-or-Buy Decisions', *Academy of Management Journal*, 30: 589–96.

Williamson, O. E. (1975) *Markets and Hierarchies*, New York: Free Press.

Williamson, O. E. (1985) *The Economic Institutions of Capitalism*, New York: Free Press.

Williamson, O. E. (1991) 'Strategizing, Economizing, and Economic Organization', *Strategic Management Journal*, 12 (Winter Special Issue): 75–94.

13

A Time-Dependent Framework on Developing Perceptions of Relational Norms: the Role of Emotion and Uncertainty Reduction Factors

Laura Poppo[1] *and C. Jay Lambe*[2]

Introduction

A central problem of hybrid forms of market exchanges is coordinated adaptation – responding efficiently and effectively to unexpected changes and events. While various mechanisms exist to encourage adaptation, such as long-term contracts or incentive mechanisms based on expectations of repeat business, in this chapter we focus on relational norms – socially derived norms, such as flexibility, information exchange and solidarity, that govern and guide exchange partners to behave in a mutually beneficial and supportive fashion (MacNeil, 1980). Thus, as a social institution, relational governance specifies a precise way in which social relations support economic exchange, a line of inquiry that emerged soon after the publication of Williamson's seminal book in 1975 (see for example, MacNeil, 1980; Ouchi, 1980). While empirical work has confirmed the significant role of relational norms in easing market coordination by reducing transaction costs (e.g. Artz and Brush, 2000) and improving exchange performance (e.g. Poppo and Zenger, 2002), we have relatively less understanding of the factors that encourage its development. This lack of systematic inquiry is striking, especially as compared to the sizeable empirical literature on formal institutions (e.g. David and Han, 2004).

In this chapter, we develop a conceptual framework that argues that time is an important dimension that influences the processes and thus type of factors that influence perceptions of relational norms. We take such an approach because, on a broad level, received theory focuses on the importance of the passage of time in the development of relational norms in inter-organizational exchanges (MacNeil, 1980; Uzzi, 1997; Poppo and Zenger, 2002). That is, relational norms depend on repeated cooperative interactions to promote their development. Such path dependence exists because perceptions of relational norms, similar to that of trust, depends in large part on the accumulated firsthand knowledge of others and the interaction history of the two parties (e.g. Blau, 1964; Ring and Van de Ven, 1994; Lewicki and Bunker, 1996).

While we concur that time is an important determinant of relational norms, we argue that by focusing on dimensions of time, younger and older relationships, we can better understand time-dependent factors and processes that managers may use to assess their beliefs of the supplier, and thus factors that influence perceptions of relational norms.[3] This conceptual approach informs recent inquiry on the importance of developing trust and its normative conventions in order to increase the likelihood of an enduring relationship (Ariño and Torre, 1998) or to respond more effectively and efficiently to market-based time pressures (Lambe et al., 2000). In particular, we offer that for younger relationships, factors that reduce the level of uncertainty that the buyer has regarding the supplier's type (e.g. trustworthy or not), motives (e.g. cooperative or not), and competences (e.g. task-related abilities) can enhance perceptions of relational norms. In our model (see Figure 13.1) we specify four uncertainty reduction factors that inform buyers in their cognitive assessment of the supplier: the supplier's market reputation for fairness, the buyer's monitoring of the supplier, the supplier's pledge of continuance by making specialized investments, and trust.

Relatedly, our focus on comparing factors and processes across older and younger relationships informs an emerging literature on the benefits and risks of settled or stable beliefs, heuristics, in interorganizational relationships (McEvily et al., 2003; Nooteboom, 2002; Uzzi, 1997). This work ascribes relational factors, such as trust and its relational routines, as cognitive heuristics that in more established relationships set in place routines for decision-making and coordination. Once such heuristics are established, decision-making changes as heuristics constrain cognitive effort, such as attending to or screening the accuracy of the information and decision alternatives (Uzzi, 1997; McEvily et al., 2003). Similarly, parties may ignore contrary information. Therefore, it seems likely that relationship duration influences the degree to which perceptions of relational norms are informed by new information about an exchange counterpart's intentions and capabilities, or reliance on cognitive heuristics. Consistent with this logic, we argue that for older relationships the uncertainty-reduction factors that were once under active consideration for younger relations are no longer as salient – that is, the buyer is more inclined to resist cognitive processing of such factors because beliefs regarding the supplier type, competences and motives are more settled. As a result, the uncertainty reduction factors are less influential in determining perceptions of relational norms for older relationships.

We further argue that for older relationships, emotion becomes a central influence on perceptions of relational norms. In developing this logic we draw on recent work in social exchange theory that documents the

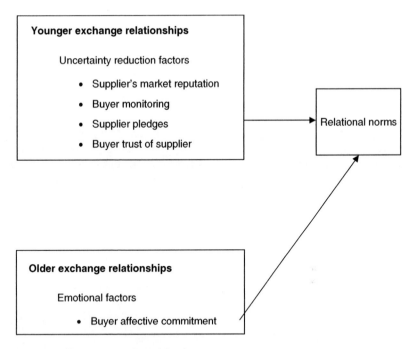

Figure 13.1: The conceptual model

important role that emotion has on promoting cohesive and committed behaviour (Lawler, 2001), such as that found in long-term attachments. We infer that since relational norms help promote cohesion and commitment in exchange, positive emotion is likely to influence perceptions of relational norms. Yet, we condition its influence: in younger relations, buyers are likely to discount the influence of such emotion on perceptions of relational norms since they lack cognitive-based assurances of the supplier's track record. Thus, buyers guard their emotion; that is, they try to withhold the influence of emotion until they have a credible basis for knowing that further development of long-term attachment and continuity through relational norms is desirable. Thus, during these earlier years cognitive beliefs based on observations and interaction with the supplier are more influential on perceptions of relational norms. Once beliefs become more settled regarding the supplier, however, emotion then influences perceptions of relational norms. Thus, the supplier guards the influence of this emotion until time has enabled a strong basis of interaction, cooperation and assurance of the supplier's type, motive and competences.

In this chapter, we further develop our logic for this orientation and then present some results based on a sample of buyer–supplier exchanges in the hotel industry in Norway. Our results demonstrate broad support for this conceptual approach.

A time-dependent perspective on factors that influence perceptions of relational norms

Models of relationship dynamics argue that a party's perception of relational norms is developed and maintained over time by accumulating actual experiences that indicate the kind of behaviour to expect from the other party (Ring and Van de Ven, 1994). We extend this logic by arguing that cognitive processing of such experiences changes over time and as such changes the factors that are likely to influence the development of relational norms. In the next two sections we explain how the influence of uncertainty reduction factors – the information gained through a supplier's market reputation, monitoring, supplier investments in specialized assets, and newly formed beliefs of trusts – have a stronger impact on the perceptions of relational norms in younger than in older relationships. We then argue that as beliefs become more settled over time, it provides a credible basis for unleashing the influence of emotion on perceptions of relational norms. Figure 13.1 illustrates our conceptual model.

Uncertainty reduction and relational norms in younger buyer–supplier relationships

A critical decision for buyers is to determine with whom to transact. By selecting a supplier with a positive market reputation, the buyer has some information on the likely direction of supplier's future behaviour. A market reputation may also promote beliefs of relational norms because it increases confidence that the parties will act in the future on a basis of shared expectations and conventions, such as those found in relational norms. This confidence is based on the assumption that the supplier will seek to preserve its market reputation for fair behaviour, and that unreciprocated actions would leak to the market and damage its reputation, which is a valuable, costly-to-develop exchange asset that sellers are motivated to protect.

We reason that a market reputation for fair behaviour has a greater influence on relational norms for younger relationships than older ones because buyers can readily use market information to formulate their beliefs. In older relationships, a market reputation is a less meaningful determinant of perceptions of relational norms because over time, buyer beliefs regarding the supplier have become settled. If settled to one's satisfaction, prior work has shown factors that were once under active consideration are no longer salient (Wilson, 1995). An emerging literature further offers that decision-making processes may be fundamentally altered for long-term trust-based relationships: heuristics, rather than a comprehensive rational search and evaluation, is likely to characterize decision-making (Uzzi, 1997; McEvily et al., 2003). Consistent with this logic, research further argues that settled beliefs are likely to be invariant to new information. In fact, parties are not likely to seek new information and, if provided, will resist contrary information (e.g. Fiske and Taylor, 1984) in favour of sustaining their beliefs (see McKnight et al., 1998: 484).

Received theory debates whether the second factor in our conceptual model, monitoring, has a positive and negative impact on relational norms. We contend that buyers may use behavioural monitoring to reduce uncertainties about the supplier – for example, can the supplier competently provide what they promised? Moreover, monitoring is likely to minimize supplier opportunistic behaviour as inspection will verify whether the supplier delivers what was promised. Thus, by deploying bureaucratic structures that provide written rules for monitoring the quality and quantity of the goods and services provided by the supplier, buyers can assess the supplier's competences and guard against opportunistic behaviour. Such formal structures produce a form of institutional trust or control between the two parties (Zucker, 1986: 55) and as such, function as a credible vehicle to assure the buyer that the supplier will deliver on what the buyer might perceive to be common understandings and expectations (Lewicki and Bunker, 1996: 120).

Others, however, argue that monitoring deters the evolution of trust and as such perceptions of relational norms. Since monitoring is inexplicably tied to perceptions of distrust of the other party, rational control may produce greater levels of opportunistic behaviour (Ghoshal and Moran, 1996: 24). Others argue further that institutional controls impose rigidity in response to conflict as opposed to the more flexible methods for conflict management found through relational norms (Sitkin and Bies, 1994).

Contrary to this logic, we argue that monitoring may actually facilitate perceptions of relational norms by providing a framework for its evolution. For simple transactions in which expectations are easy to specify, by observing their satisfactory fulfilment, the buyer gains confidence about the supplier's ability to deliver what is promised and to fulfil the terms of the agreement. Monitoring can further assist in the development of norms for complex exchanges as well. For some exchanges, common understanding and expectations require a transfer of knowledge that is highly specialized and idiosyncratic to the exchange. For such exchanges, it is difficult to clarify and develop joint expectations – thus monitoring enables a level of fine-grained coordination that fosters the development of joint norms.

Over time, however, we contend that the influence of monitoring on relational norms declines as beliefs regarding the supplier become more settled, making the effect of information gained from monitoring less meaningful or salient. Thus, monitoring has a greater net effect on relational norms in younger than older exchange relationships. We assume in our logic that monitoring is not institutionalized in a particular culture or industry context – if it is simply a collective symbolic action, then monitoring is not likely to impact perceptions of relational norms.

The third factor in our conceptual model is pledges: pledges are specific actions that not only demonstrate good faith intentions, but also bind the pledging party to the exchange relationship through irreversible, specialized investments (Williamson, 1985: 167). Because the specialized portion of an asset cannot be redeployed to alternative uses, the party risks a sizeable economic loss should exchange terminate prematurely. Since continuance is valued, the supplier may be more committed to developing relational norms, as the norms help promote exchange into the future (Poppo and Zenger, 2002).

We reason that pledges are a more influential determinant of relational norms in younger than in older relationships. As buyers in younger exchanges lack information on the supplier's intent and capabilities, pledges assure the buyer that the supplier has the required assets to adequately perform the service. In addition, since pledges signal cooperation and a desire for continuance, the buyer uses this information to infer that the supplier is also likely to desire relational norms, since those norms enhance both exchange performance and continuance. While pledges early in an exchange history help to initiate an expectation of reciprocity, they are unlikely to continue to have sizeable influence on beliefs of relational norms. Over time, the collective pattern or history of reciprocity becomes a key influence on relational norms (see, for example, Ring and Van de Ven, 1994).

The fourth factor in our conceptual model is the buyer's assessment of supplier trustworthiness. Trust is a desirable quality because once it exists it decreases exchange uncertainty through behaviour predictability (Lewicki and Bunker, 1996: 119). One important type of trustworthy knowledge is the partner's perceived benevolence: a trust that the supplier will not only sacrifice for the buyer, but also demonstrate concern, care and help (Mayer et al., 1995). We reason that buyers have greater confidence that benevolent suppliers will desire and reciprocate relational norms.

Our framework posits that relationship duration moderates the influence of benevolent trust on perceptions of relational norms. Most view trust as an important factor early in the relationship, and an essential precondition for the relationship to move to more committed stages of development (Ariño and Torre, 1998). Because of the central role trust plays in promoting exchange in the future, we reason that it is not settled, but under active consideration during the early years of exchange. This logic is consistent with models of relationship development that propose that buyers engage in trials and tests of their suppliers early in the exchange history to test their cooperation, and hence establish initial beliefs of trust (Ariño and Torre, 1998; Ring and Van de Ven, 1994). Over time, however, we advance that trust has less influence on beliefs of relational norms. Our logic is similar to that previously stated: settled beliefs imply resistance to cognitive processing.

Emotion and relational norms in older buyer–supplier exchanges

Social theorists argue that long-standing ties evolve as parties 'become friends with these people – business friends', or they treat one another as if 'they're . . . part of the company' or 'the family' (Uzzi, 1997: 42). As such, positive affect or emotion characterizes those ties because through frequent, long-term interaction, attachments are formed based upon reciprocated care and concern (McAllister, 1995). More recently, others contend that emotion may play a central role in creating long-term attachments (Lawler, 2001). Recent experiments support this inference. Repeated exchange with the same others generates positive emotions that, in turn, promote perceived cohesion and commitment behaviour (Lawler and Yoon, 1996, 1998).

In this study, we draw more formally on the concept of affective commitment to measure the emotional bond. Affective commitment refers to the level of positive feelings that one experiences as a result of the working relationship. It is a form of emotional attachment, which has been widely examined in organizational behaviour for its role in reducing withdrawal behaviour (e.g. lateness and turnover) and increasing extra-role behaviours (e.g. creativeness and innovation) in organizations (Mathieu and Dennis, 1990). Since relational norms provide a social process to facilitate timely and efficient adaptation of the economic exchange, parties can promote continuance of the exchange when uncertainties and economic challenges might otherwise threaten its future (MacNeil, 1980; Poppo and Zenger, 2002). Thus, relational norms provide a vehicle to better assure future interaction and continuance in the buyer–supplier relationship. Moreover, emotion may also increase attachment behaviour (Lawler, 2001), which provides the basis for relational beliefs.

Yet, consistent with the framework advanced so far, we reason that the influence of affective commitment on perceptions of relational norms depends on relationship duration. For younger relationships, positive feelings such as friendship and association may quickly develop from early positive experiences. The buyer, however, does not know how genuine the feeling is; whether the relationship can work through perceived incompatibilities; or whether the supplier has the necessary competences to build a mutually beneficial exchange relationship. Simply put, a rapid development of strong affection towards one another does not guarantee a mutually beneficial task orientation, thereby decreasing its influence on beliefs of relational norms.

In older relationships, the passage of time enables the friendship to be tried and tested in a number of task domains. As the buyer becomes more confident as to the supplier's task orientation and competency, this informs in a credible manner the emotional basis of the relationship. Invariably, such learning or uncertainty reduction has met with conflict from unmet expectations or unexpected events. Negative outcomes to such issues carry an emotional down, whereas strong positive work experiences and resolutions bring an emotional uplift (Lawler and Yoon, 1996). Thus, over time, the task-based track record and positive emotional reactions from success function to strengthen the influence of emotion, or affective commitment, on beliefs of relational norms. The rewards of positive feelings from successful joint work accentuate the desire to pursue greater levels of joint activity, and information credibly informs whether greater levels of joint work are warranted. So while settled, with respect to cognitive processing, relational beliefs are receptive to an emotional message of attachment for older exchange relationships.

Empirical context

We examine our conceptual model in the context of buyer–supplier relationships within the lodging industry.[4] Here, our unit of analysis is the exchange relationship between hotels and their major suppliers of goods and services in Norway. Since we examine the exchange relationship from the perspective of buyers, hotels were asked for their perceptions of their relationship with a frequently used supplier with respect to the relevant dimensions in this study. By sampling only buyer relationships with frequently used suppliers (on average, six buyer–supplier contacts per month), we were able to further limit extraneous variation by focusing on a sub-set of highly interactive relationships, namely those that have the interaction necessary to form relational norms.

We selected a systematic random sample of 280 hotels from a major database of corporate hotels in Norway. The database contains all hotels that submit annual accounts to the Norwegian Register of Business Enterprises. The hotels were contacted by phone and asked for their participation in the survey. Self-administered questionnaires were then sent to individuals who were identified over the phone as being knowledgeable about the exchange relationship in question. The resulting key informants were hotel directors, managers, or purchasing managers depending on the size of the hotel. Follow-up phone calls were made to encourage survey participation. A total of 150 questionnaires were returned, yielding a response rate of 53.6 per cent. Returned questionnaires containing substantial amounts of missing data were eliminated, resulting in 124 valid responses for the analysis.

Appendix 13.1 contains a summary of our measures, which are based on items that have been validated in prior published empirical papers. After determining that our variables have acceptable reliabilities and discriminate validity, we split our sample in two groups, younger and older exchange relationships, based on the median value of relationship tenure, 7 years. Since a median split of 7 does not at an intuitive level represent younger exchanges, we then did a sensitivity analysis to determine if the results were consistent using a split of 4 years. We find exactly the same pattern of significant results for both splits. Using multi-group analysis of our structural model, and including some relevant control variables, we then tested for differences for each factor coefficient across younger and older relationships. As assumed by our modelling technique, our theoretical constructs exhibited adequate cross-sample equivalence.

Consistent with our conceptual model illustrated in Figure 13.1, we find that the following significant effects – a supplier reputation for fairness, buyer performance monitoring, and benevolent trust – have a more positive and stronger effect on perceptions of relational norms in younger than in older buyer–supplier relationships. In fact, these factors have no significant effect on relational norms for older exchanges. Contrary to our conceptual model, however, no significant relationship between supplier pledges and perceptions of relational norms is found in either younger or older buyer–supplier relationships. Further analysis shows, however, that pledges have an indirect effect on relational norms through their positive effect on buyer benevolent trust. We further found that buyer affective commitment is positively and more strongly related to buyer beliefs of relational norms in older than in younger buyer–supplier relationships.

Discussion

Despite the well-documented benefits of relational norms, the dynamics underlying the formation of beliefs of relational norms in younger and older buyer–supplier exchanges are less understood. In this chapter we argue that the processes and thus factors that influence perceptions of relational norms change over time. Overall, our empirical findings support this approach. For younger relationships, factors that reduce uncertainty – monitoring of the supplier, supplier reputation for fairness, and buyer benevolent trust of supplier – have a greater influence on perceptions of relational norms in younger than in older relationships. We further find that while supplier pledges do not directly affect beliefs of relational norms in younger relationships, they have an indirect effect on relational norms through benevolent trust. For older relationships, these factors no longer influence relational beliefs, as beliefs about the supplier appear settled and resist such cognitive processing and updates. Alternatively, for those older relationships, we find that positive emotion, or affective commitment, engenders even greater perceptions of relational norms, validating the important influence of emotion in enduring buyer–supplier exchange relationships.

We reason that for younger exchange relationships, each factor helps to reduce uncertainty by providing different types and sources of information. For example, a market reputation enables the buyer to be more assured of the supplier's reliability and intent in the present exchange relationship. Perceptions of benevolent trust, which are based on the buyer's actual experience with the supplier, similarly foster greater confidence in the supplier. This information credibly assures the buyer that not only task-related obligations, but also relational expectations will be reciprocated. In doing so, the factors influence positively the perceptions of relational norms.

Our results regarding the effect of monitoring on beliefs of relational norms, however, are contrary to the logic of some, which show that monitoring signals distrust in exchange or impedes the development of flexibility in relational exchanges (Ghoshal and Moran, 1996: 23–4; Sitkin and Bies, 1994). Rather, consistent with the position of others (Zucker, 1986; Lewicki and Bunker, 1996), our results suggest that monitoring helps establish joint expectations by providing direct information on a number of task-related dimensions: the ability to verify the completion of obligations; to assess the supplier's competencies; and to clarify and develop joint expectations. Since the information required to implement and to fully understand an expectation is often tacit, complex and specialized, monitoring provides a critical vehicle in which to ascertain and to learn this knowledge. That mechanism is especially critical for younger relationships, since this expertise is necessarily both less visible and less understood than in older relationships.

As argued in our conceptual framework, none of those factors, which reduce uncertainty, affect the beliefs of relational norms in older buyer–supplier relationships. For older relationships those factors do not impact relational norms because the beliefs regarding the supplier are more settled, so buyers appear to ignore, discount or resist the sources of information. This finding is consistent with prior conceptualization: norms can function as a heuristic and thus economize on the kind of cognitive calculations that underlie risk-based decision-making (Uzzi, 1997: 44). Despite the economies and quality of decisions that relational beliefs may promote, however, theorists warn that such confidence in another's behaviour may prompt opportunities for malfeasance. Future work is needed to explore this issue.

For older relationships we find that increasing levels of affective commitment are associated with greater perceptions of relational norms. We infer that over time the friendship has been tried and tested though a range of task-related activities and conflicts. Thus, once credibly backed by such cognitive factors, positive affect deepens relational beliefs, presumably to promote the continuation, and performance of, not only joint activity, but also to deepen the fulfilment of basic social needs, such as belonging to one another. While for younger relationships positive feelings may develop quickly, their influence is necessarily weakened, because the buyer lacks sufficient information and experience with the supplier to adequately test the durability of the friendship. Thus, cognitive-based assurances that accrue over time appear necessary for emotion to influence beliefs of relational norms. That is, the influence of emotion is conditional upon a strong platform of time and experience with the supplier.

In sum, our framework endorses a time-based approach to understanding the processes, and thus factors that influence beliefs of relational norms. Further work is needed not only to replicate our empirical finding and results, but also to examine more fully situations in which a positive and dark side may stem from the use of long-term trading relations.

Appendix 13.1: Construct Measurement

Norm of Information Exchange
1. In this relationship, it is expected that any information that might help the other party will be provided to them.
2. Exchange of information in this relationship takes place frequently and informally, and not only according to a pre-specified agreement.
3. It is expected that we keep each other informed about events or changes that may affect the other party.

Norm of Flexibility
1. Flexibility in response to requests for changes is a characteristic of this relationship.
2. The parties expect to be able to make adjustments in the on-going relationship to cope with changing circumstances.
3. When some unexpected situation arises, the parties would rather work out a new deal than hold each other to the original terms.

Norm of Solidarity
1. Problems that arise in the course of this relationship are treated by the parties as joint rather than individual responsibilities.
2. The parties are committed to improvements that may benefit the relationship as a whole, and not only individual parties.
3. The parties in this relationship do not mind owing each other favours.

Supplier Reputation for Fairness
1. This supplier has a reputation for being concerned about customers.
2. This supplier has a good reputation in the market.
3. Most companies think that this supplier has a reputation for being fair.

Buyer Performance Monitoring
1. Prior to ordering, we check to see if the supplier can deliver the goods and services as promised.
2. We monitor to a great extent the quality of the supplier's goods and services.
3. After delivery, we examine our orders to see if they have accurately been filled.

Benevolent Trust
1. We have confidence that the supplier is willing to make sacrifices for us.
2. We have confidence that the supplier cares for us as a customer.
3. We have confidence that the supplier will go out on a limb for us.
4. We have confidence that the supplier will be benevolent and helpful.
5. When we share problems with the supplier, we know that it will respond with understanding.

Affective Commitment
1. We genuinely enjoy our relationship with this supplier.
2. We have positive feelings about working with this supplier.
3. We appreciate the way this supplier serves us.
4. We like being associated with this supplier.

Supplier Transaction Specific Investments
1. The supplier has made significant time and resource investments dedicated to gain knowledge about our business and methods of operation.
2. The supplier has made significant time and resource investments dedicated to build a relationship with us.
3. Our supplier has made significant investments that would be of little value outside of this relationship.

Appendix 13.1: (Continued)

Buyer Transaction Specific Investments
1. We have made significant time and resource investments dedicated to educate the supplier about our business and methods of operation.
2. We have made significant time and resource investments dedicated to build a relationship with this supplier.
3. We have made significant investments that would be of little value outside of this relationship.

Duration of buyer–supplier relationship
How many years' experience do you have in buying from this supplier:
__ years? (experience that is less than or equal to 6 months = 0.5).

Notes

1. Laura Poppo, Associate Professor of Management, Virginia Tech, 2100 Pamplin Hall, (0233), Blacksburg, VA 24061, Fax: 540-231-4553, 3076, E-mail: lpoppo@vt.edu
2. C. Jay Lambe, Assistant Professor of Marketing, Department of Marketing, Albers School of Business and Economics, Seattle University, Seattle, WA 98122, 206-296-2550, 2083 (fax), E-mail: jlambe@vt.edu
3. Another dimension of time that might shed light on relational dynamics is the quantity of the exchange parties' interactions with each other. For our model conceptualization, we assume frequent exchange interaction exists between the two parties; yet it is likely that interaction among the number of parties in both members' organizations is more constrained in younger relationships than older relationships. See Lambe et al. (2000: 213–14) for a review of these alternative dimensions.
4. We thank Kåre Sandvik for use of this data. Greater description of the empirical context can be found in Lambe, Poppo, Grzeskowiak, Brown and Sandvik, 'The Influence of Uncertainty Reduction and Emotion on Relational Norms in Younger and Older Buyer-Supplier Relations'.

References

Ariño, A. and Torre, J. (1998) 'Learning from Failure: Toward an Evolutional Model of Collaboration Ventures', *Organization Science*, 9: 306–25.

Artz, K. and Brush, T. (2000) 'Asset Specificity, Uncertainty, and Relational Governance: an Examination of Coordination Costs in Collaborative Strategic Alliances', *Journal of Economic Behavior and Organization*, 41: 337–62.

Blau, P. M. (1964) *Exchange and Power in Social Life*, New York: Wiley.

Brown, J. R., Dev, C. S. and Lee, D. J. (2000) 'Managing Marketing Channel Opportunism: the Efficacy of Alternative Governance Mechanisms', *Journal of Marketing*, 64 (April): 51–65.

David, R. and Han, S. K. (2004) 'A Systematic Assessment of the Empirical Support for Transaction Cost Economics', *Strategic Management Journal*, 25: 39–58.

Fiske, S. T. and Taylor, S. E. (1984) *Social Cognition*, Reading, MA: Addison-Wesley.

Ghoshal, S. and Moran, P. (1996) 'Bad for Practice: a Critique of the Transaction Cost Theory', *Academy of Management Review*, 21: 13–47.

Lambe, C. J., Spekman, R. E. and Hunt, S. D. (2000) 'Interimistic Relational Exchange: Conceptualization and Propositional Development', *Journal of the Academy of Marketing Science*, 28(2): 212–25.

Lawler, E. J. (2001) 'An Affect Theory of Social Exchange', *American Journal of Sociology*, 107(2): 321–52.

Lawler, E. J. and Yoon, J. (1996) 'Commitment in Exchange Relations: Test of a Theory of Relational Cohesion', *American Sociological Review*, 61: 89–108.

Lawler, E. J. and Yoon, J. (1998) 'Network Structure and Emotion in Exchange Relations', *American Sociological Review*, 63: 871–94.

Lewicki, R. and Bunker, B. B. (1996) 'Developing and Maintaining Trust in Work Relationships', in *Trust in Organizations: Frontiers of Theory and Research*, Thousand Oaks, CA: Sage Publications: 114–39.

MacNeil, I. R. (1980) *The New Social Contract: an Inquiry into Modern Contractual Relations*, New Haven, CT: Yale University Press.

Mathieu, J. E. and Dennis, D. M. (1990) 'A Review and Meta-analysis of the Antecedents, Correlates and Consequences of Organizational Commitment', *Psychological Bulletin*, 108: 171–94.

Mayer, R. C., Davis, J. H. and Schoorman, F. D. (1995) 'An Integrative Model of Organizational Trust', *Academy of Management Review*, 20: 709–34.

McAllister, D. J. (1995) 'Affect- and Cognition-Based Trust as Foundations for Interpersonal Cooperation in Organization', *Academy of Management Journal*, 38 (February): 24–59.

McEvily, Perrone, B. V. and Zaheer, A. (2003) 'Trust as an Organizing Principle', *Organization Science*, 14(1): 91–103.

McKnight, D. H., Cummings, L. L. and Chervany, N. L. (1998) 'Initial Trust Formation in New Organizational Relationships', *Academy of Management Review*, 23(3): 473–90.

Nooteboom, B. (2002) *Trust: Form Foundations, Functions Failures and Figures*, Northampton, MA: Edward Elgar.

Ouchi, W. G. (1980) 'Markets, Bureaucracies, and Clans', *Administrative Science Quarterly*, 25(1): 129–41.

Poppo, L. and Zenger, T. (2002) 'Do Formal Contracts and Relational Governance Function as Substitutes or Complements?' *Strategic Management Journal*, 23: 707–25.

Ring, P. S. and Van de Ven, A. H. (1994) 'Developmental Processes of Cooperative Interorganizational Relationships', *Academy of Management Review*, 19: 90–118.

Sitkin, S. B. and Bies, R. J. (1994) *The Legalistic Organization*, Thousand Oaks, CA: Sage.

Uzzi, B. (1997) 'Social Structure and Competition in Interfirm Networks: the Paradox of Embeddedness', *Administrative Science Quarterly*, 42: 35–67.

Williamson, O. E. (1985) *The Economic Institutions of Capitalism: Firms, Markets, Relational Contracting*, New York: Free Press.

Wilson, D. T. (1995) 'An Integrated Model of Buyer–Supplier Relationships', *Journal of the Academy of Marketing Science*, 23(4): 335–45.

Zucker, L. (1986) 'Production of Trust: Institutional Sources of Economic Structure, 1840–1920', *Research in Organizational Behavior*, 8: 53–111.

14
Matching Alliance Governance to Alliance Content

Glenn Hoetker[1] and Thomas Mellewigt[2]*

Introduction

Alliances allow firms to 'pool imperfectly tradable resources in order to gain greater efficiency in the use of existing resources as well as opportunities to create new resources' (Dussauge et al., 2000: 207). Successful alliances must accomplish two goals: coordinating the optimal combination of productive resources across parties and mitigating the risks of opportunistic behaviour (Mitchell et al., 2002; Nickerson and Zenger, 2004).

Work drawing primarily on transaction cost economics has argued that increases in exchange hazards will lead to the greater use of formal, contractual governance mechanisms (Williamson, 1991; Mayer and Argyres, 2004). At the same time, a parallel literature has argued for the role of more relational governance mechanisms based largely on trust and social identification, e.g. establishing teams, frequent direct managerial contact, shared decision-making and joint problem solving (Uzzi, 1997; Gulati, 1998). Recent work has shown that these approaches are not mutually exclusive (Poppo and Zenger, 2002; Hoetker, 2005). However, we understand little about when one approach is superior to the other.

In this chapter, we argue that the optimal configuration of controls in a relationship depends critically on the amount of property-based assets and knowledge-based assets involved. Property-based assets that are easily codifiable and transmitted will be more suited to formal/contractual controls. On the other hand, knowledge-based assets will be best suited to the use of relational governance mechanisms due to the inability to specify exact processes and outcomes in advance. Furthermore, we argue that a mismatch between the governance mechanism and the content of an alliance can harm the performance of a relationship.

By introducing this critical contingency, our findings contribute to transaction cost economics, the literature on relational governance, and recent work studying their interaction. We advance transaction cost economics by showing that considering the content of an alliance, rather than just the level of potential opportunism, allows more precise predictions about the appropriate level of formal, contractual governance for a transaction.

Additionally, we extend the literature on interfirm alliances along three related dimensions. First, we contribute to the nascent but strongly under-investigated empirical literature on the management of alliances (Sobrero and Schrader, 1998; Ireland et al., 2002). Second, we show that the most effective means of governing an alliance depends critically on the specific content of that alliance. Lastly, our findings suggest an optimal sequence of alliance activities between firms, initially focusing on property-based assets, including knowledge-based assets only once the foundation for relational governance mechanisms has developed.

Achieving cooperation and coordination in alliances

Successful alliances must accomplish two goals: mitigating the risks of opportunistic behaviour and coordinating the optimal combination of productive resources across parties (Nickerson and Zenger, 2004; Gulati et al., 2005). We consider potential opportunism first.

Opportunistic behaviour can arise from several sources. To the degree that one firm has made relationship-specific investments, it is vulnerable to the other firm attempting to extract additional rents through hold-up or other opportunistic behaviour (Williamson, 1985). A firm can misrepresent its capabilities or resources during the negotiating process prior to the alliance (Akerlof, 1970). During the alliance, a firm can shirk its contracted responsibilities by failing to live up to its promised contribution of resources (Klein, 1980) or applying the resources gained via the alliance to markets or products outside of the agreed-upon scope (Caves et al., 1983).

Coordination of the alliance members' activities is critical to achieving the collective goal(s) of the alliance (Loasby, 1996). Coordination addresses the pooling of resources, the division of labour across partners and the subsequent integration of the dispersed activities, all of which are critical to the generation of value in an alliance (Sobrero and Schrader, 1998; Mitchell et al., 2002). Accomplishing this coordination requires developing the appropriate linkages between different and interdependent task units (Alchian and Allen, 1977; Adler, 1995). This task is complicated by differences in each firm's structure and experiences (Lawrence and Lorsch, 1967) and the fact that individuals in each firm may not understand the interdependencies of their actions and those of others (Thompson, 1967).

Two common approaches to mitigate opportunism and achieve coordination in the context of alliances are the use of formal/contractual governance mechanisms and relational governance mechanisms (Martinez and Jarillo, 1989; Dekker, 2004). The approaches are not exclusive; both may occur to varying degrees within the same alliance (MacNeil, 2000; Mellewigt et al., 2004).

Formal/contractual governance mechanisms are generally understood to include 'depersonalized exchanges, a reliance on financial parameters, and the drafting and implementation of formal contracts' (Ferguson et al., 2005: 217).

Relational governance mechanisms, on the other hand, are generally understood to include people- or social-based mechanisms that enhance open communication and the sharing of information, trust, dependence and cooperation (Eisenhardt, 1985).[3]

Formal/contractual governance mechanisms

Formal/contractual governance mechanisms can play a vital role in enabling transactions that require investments in specific assets. By placing credibly enforceable limits on the actions of each party, contracts help *mitigate potential opportunism*, constraining the subsequent ability of one party to extract additional rents from the other by failing to perform as agreed (Williamson, 1985). Additionally, recent work has drawn attention to the role of formal/contractual governance mechanisms in *coordinating* the efforts of alliance partners (Gulati, 1995; Sobrero and Schrader, 1998; Ryall and Sampson, 2003). Mayer and Argyres (2004: 404) found that firms included clauses regarding delivery dates and information about system interactions to enable 'better information flow between the parties, so as to avoid coordination failures'. Such prior arrangements enable coordination by enhancing the predictability of each party's actions and structuring communication flows (Galbraith, 1977; Gulati et al., 2005).

Relational governance mechanisms

Relational governance mechanisms refer broadly to mechanisms based largely on trust and social identification (Martinez and Jarillo, 1989; Dyer and Singh, 1998). They represent the social or 'people-based' strategy for control and coordination (Eisenhardt, 1985). Examples include establishing teams, tasks forces and committees (Schrader, 1991; Grandori, 1997); direct managerial contact through trips, meetings and even the transfer of managers (Martinez and Jarillo, 1989); mechanisms for shared decision-making (Saxton, 1997: 446); and formal systems for conflict resolution relying on two-way communication and joint problem solving (Kale et al., 2000).

Each of these mechanisms helps mitigate *opportunism* by building trust and social identification through the interaction of personnel across firms. Through repeated interaction, managers in each firm learn about each other and develop personal ties (Macaulay, 1963; Shapiro et al., 1992). The exchange of extra effort voluntarily given and reciprocated builds trust (Uzzi, 1997), while first-hand knowledge of a partner's behaviour provides some information regarding their future actions (Granovetter, 1985).

Beyond their role in mitigating potential opportunism, relational governance mechanisms support *coordination* across partners. Repeated interaction of individuals from each firm can lead to the development of interfirm communication and coordination routines (Mitchell and Singh, 1996; Dyer and Singh, 1998), a common language for discussing technical and market issues (Buckley and Casson, 1976), and a shared representation of their task environment (Gulati et al., 2005).

In contrast to formal/contractual governance mechanisms, the identity of the parties (executives transferred, members of task forces) is critical for relational governance mechanisms. Different individuals will bring different knowledge and behaviours to these relationships and, once developed, the fruits of the relationships do not easily transfer to others (Haytko, 2004). Further, because of the critical role played by individuals and their relationships, relational governance mechanisms differ from formal/contractual mechanisms in that specific outcomes or behaviours cannot be stipulated in advance (Makhija and Ganesh, 1997).

The benefits of using relational governance mechanisms in strategic alliances come at considerable costs in terms of time and resource allocation (Larson, 1992; Das and Teng, 1998), because they depend on the repeated interaction of personnel across the firms, particularly in face-to-face meetings, multiple employees, often highly compensated, and engaged in meetings rather than their normal productive activities.

Matching governance to alliance content

Both formal/contractual governance mechanisms and relational governance mechanisms have been found to be successful in governing alliances (Poppo and Zenger, 2002). However, it is unclear when one type of mechanism would be more effective than the other. We argue that the appropriate mix of governance mechanisms depends on the type of assets involved in the alliance being governed. Drawing on Miller and Shamsie (1996) and Das and Teng (2000), we contrast two types of assets. *Knowledge-based assets* are a firm's intangible know-how and skills. Examples include marketing knowledge and customer service expertise. *Property-based assets* are legal properties owned by firms, including physical resources (buildings, infrastructure), financial capital, licences and rights of way, human resources, and the like.

We develop our predictions based on two key arguments. First, property-based assets and knowledge-based assets present different governance problems, which formal/contractual governance mechanisms and relational governance mechanisms address with different degrees of effectiveness. Second, the asset types pose different coordination problems, which formal/contractual and relational governance mechanisms differ in their ability to resolve.

Governing knowledge-based assets

The first governance issue posed by the exchange of knowledge-based assets is a variation of the well-known appropriability problem (Arrow, 1962). Once a party discloses knowledge to a potential buyer, that buyer is in a position to apply that knowledge without paying for it. Of course, a potential buyer will not agree to pay for the knowledge until it has the opportunity to evaluate it. In the governance context, it is unlikely that the parties will be able to negotiate a mutually acceptable contract in this situation (Teece, 1986).

It may be difficult to develop concrete performance criteria for knowledge that one party is to supply, particularly in light of the reluctance on the part of the asset owner to disclose detailed information about the knowledge, handicapping the parties' ability to develop formal/contractual governance mechanisms such as internal prices, economic efficiency calculations, or performance indices (Teece, 1988). The range of potential remedies also varies for property-based and knowledge-based assets. Firms can be forced to return property, but it is difficult to force a firm's employees to unlearn the knowledge once transferred (Arora et al., 2001: 118).

Knowledge-based assets are difficult to coordinate across firms because they tend to be embedded in the routines and culture of the originating firm, composed largely of tacit (hard to articulate) knowledge and couched in the firm's specialized technical language (Nelson and Winter, 1982). These all militate against their written specification (Arrow, 1974; Kogut and Zander, 1992). For all of these reasons, contractual governance mechanisms are likely to be a sub-optimal response to transactions involving extensive knowledge-based assets. Thus, we do not expect firms to vary their use of formal/contractual mechanisms according to the presence or absence of knowledge-based assets.[4]

Relational governance mechanisms provide a more flexible means of addressing this problem by allowing the parties to move forward with a less fully specified contract under the assumption that contingencies will be addressed in good faith and shirking will not occur (Cusumano, 1985). Relational governance mechanisms also help overcome the embedded and tacit nature of knowledge-based assets through the routines, common language and social cohesion developed by repeated interaction across partners. Because relational governance mechanisms offer advantages over contractual mechanisms in governing and coordinating the use of knowledge-based assets, we expect the use of relational governance mechanisms to increase when substantial knowledge-based assets are involved in an alliance.

Governance of property-based assets

We argue that formal/contractual governance mechanisms are generally superior to relational governance mechanisms for governing property-based assets. Formal/contractual governance mechanisms do not face the same obstacles when governing property-based assets as they do when governing knowledge-based assets. The advantages provided by relational governance mechanisms are less relevant and no longer justify the time-consuming, often costly, activities they require or the risk of poorer performance via diminished incentives.

Greater pre-agreement disclosure makes it easier for the parties to negotiate a mutually acceptable contract and to specify performance criteria that will form the basis of formal/contractual mechanisms such as economics efficiency calculations, internal prices, detailed business plans and performance indices. In the event of disagreement, the courts can refer to these criteria in judging the performance of each party. The court also has recourse to a wide range of remedies for property-based assets, since – unlike knowledge – firms can be forced to return property (Arora et al., 2001: 118).

Formal/contractual governance mechanisms are also capable of coordinating property-based assets. Coordination of a specific property, e.g. delivery of a generator or access to a network, is easier to specify in advance than the coordination of knowledge-based assets, with their attendant tacitness and embeddedness (Kogut and Zander, 1992). Business plans and service-level agreements can precisely enumerate the tasks to be accomplished and define specific procedures to be followed for property-based assets in a way that they cannot for knowledge-based assets.

Therefore, we expect firms to bring formal/contractual governance mechanisms to bear when considerable property-based assets are involved, since they provide effective and efficient governance and coordination of these assets. Since relational mechanisms are a less effective means of governing property-based assets, we do not expect the use of relational governance mechanisms to be affected by the presence or absence of property-based assets. A stronger prediction would be that firms would avoid using relational governance mechanisms in the presence of considerable property-based assets. However, we do not believe theory supports such a strong prediction.

We conclude by arguing that performance differences between alliances may be attributable to the matching of asset type with appropriate governance mechanisms (Yin and Zajac 2004). More specifically we argue that alliances that pursue a strategic fit between the assets involved in the alliance and the governance mechanisms used will enjoy greater alliance performance, while a mismatch, e.g. extensive use of relational governance mechanisms in the presence of considerable property-based assets, might harm performance.

Sample and methods

The research sample was alliances in the German telecommunications industry. According to Section 4 of the German telecommunications law, every company that wants to offer telecommunications services is required to notify the regulatory authority. Therefore, the register of the German regulatory authority for telecommunication and postal services was used as the starting data source for this study. This register is updated twice a year and is publicly available. Targeted respondents in this study were all telecommunications companies that owned a class 3 licence (i.e. a network licence allowing the company to build network infrastructure), or a class 4 licence (i.e. a service licence allowing the company to offer voice telephony to the public) according to Section 6 of the German telecommunications law. Most of the alliances covered multiple functions, with a majority including aspects of both infrastructure and marketing/customer service.

In total, 257 companies were identified that owned a class 3, a class 4, or both licences. Surveys were sent to the CEO of the respective company and completed by the CEO, the Director of Business Development or the Director of the Legal Department. Of the 257 questionnaires mailed, 83 questionnaires were obtained, representing a 32 per cent response rate. Our analysis takes place in two steps: modelling the amount of formal/contractual and relational governance mechanisms used in a relationship and modelling the performance of the alliance as a function of the mechanisms chosen. We addressed the potential problem of endogeneity regarding the choice of formal/contractual and relational governance mechanisms by calculating two-stage least squares.

Results and discussion

The results of our analysis show that when large amounts of knowledge-based assets are involved in an alliance, firms employ more relational governance mechanisms and these mechanisms have a positive impact on the overall performance of the alliance. When large amounts of property-based assets are involved, firms employ more formal/contractual mechanisms and actually find relational mechanisms prejudicial to the success of the alliance, reflecting its relative inefficiency as a means of governing purely property-based assets.

We have found evidence that the optimal choice of governance mechanisms in an alliance depends on the types of assets involved. Consideration of this contingency has direct implications for three elements of the literature on alliances that are not otherwise evident: their governance, their scope and content, and the optimal sequence of alliance activities between firms. On the subject of alliance governance, we believe our work has immediate relevance to two underlying literatures: transaction cost economics and the literature on relational governance. We find support for the central tenets of each, while also establishing important boundary conditions for their application. Furthermore, we advance transaction cost economics by showing that considering the content of an alliance, rather than just the level of potential opportunism, allows more precise predictions about the appropriate choice of governance mechanisms for a transaction.

Consistent with the literature on relational governance, we find that relational governance mechanisms play a critical role in helping firms exploit knowledge-based assets in alliances. However, their costs may be higher than has previously been appreciated. When the only assets being governed are amenable to contractual mechanisms, e.g. property-based assets, relational mechanisms may be unnecessarily burdensome. Indeed, they may actually be counter-productive due to high costs and over-socialization.

This research also extends recent work examining the interaction of relational and contractual governance. Consistent with prior work, we find that relational and contractual governance mechanisms often co-occur. However, our findings demonstrate that they are not interchangeable. Each has distinct limitations, making the optimal combination of governance mechanisms highly dependent on the content of the alliance, a contingency absent in both literature streams.

Our findings also inform the optimal scope and content of alliances. Both property-based and knowledge-based assets may contribute to the alliance's goals; further, bundling activities together offers governance advantages through raising the cost of opportunistic behaviour (de Figueiredo and Teece, 1996). Our work also implies an optimal sequence of alliance activities between two firms. Relational governance mechanisms effectively manage alliances rich in knowledge-based assets, but cannot be deployed simply at will. Consistent with recent studies (e.g. Gulati and Sytch, 2005), our results suggest that the move to the greater use of relational governance mechanisms over time is not inevitable, however.

Notes

* The authors gratefully acknowledge the helpful comments of Rajshree Agarwal, Anoop Madhok, Scott Masten, Joanne Oxley, Jeff Reuer, Sonali Shah, Antoinette Weibel and Charlie Williams, attendees at the 2004 meeting of the Academy of Management as well as attendees of the 'Strategic Alliances: Governance and Contracts' conference in Barcelona 2005 (IESE). Any remaining errors are the authors' responsibility. Both authors contributed equally to this research.

1. Glenn Hoetker, College of Business, University of Illinois at Urbana-Champaign, 305 Wohlers Hall, 1206 S. Sixth Street, Tel: (217) 265-4091, Fax: (217) 244-7969, E-mail: ghoetker@uiuc.edu
2. Thomas Mellewigt, Freie Universität Berlin, Institute for Management, Garystraße 21, D-14195 Berlin, Tel.: +49-175-4009939, E-mail: tm@upb.de
3. Ferguson et al. (2005: 220) note that terms including hard, explicit, formal and written have been associated with formal/contractual governance and relationalism, social, informal self-enforcing governance, and procedural governance coordination with relational governance.
4. We state our prediction in a strong form, while recognizing that contracts are not completely without utility in the presence of knowledge assets (see e.g. Lyons,

1994). In particular, to the degree that they contribute to the overall smooth operation of the alliance, they may create the cooperative environment necessary to elicit a willingness to share knowledge.

References

Adler, P. S. (1995) 'Interdepartmental Interdependence and Coordination: the Case of the Design/Manufacturing Interface', *Organization Science*, 6(2): 147–67.

Akerlof, G. A. (1970) 'The Market for "Lemons": Qualitative Uncertainty and the Market Mechanism', *Quarterly Journal of Economics*, 84: 488–500.

Alchian, A. A., and Allen, W. R. (1977) *Exchange and Production: Competition, Coordination, and Control*, 2nd edn, Belmont, CA: Wadsworth Publishing Co.

Arora, A., Fosfuri, A. and Gambardella, A. (2001) *Markets for Technology: the Economics of Innovation and Corporate Strategy*, Cambridge, MA: MIT Press.

Arrow, K. J. (1962) 'Economic Welfare and the Allocation of Resources for Invention', in R. R. Nelson (ed.), *The Rate and Direction of Inventive Activity: Economic and Social Factors*, Princeton: Princeton University Press.

Arrow, K. J. (1974) *The Limits of Organizations*, New York: Norton.

Buckley, P. and Casson, M. (1976) *The Future of Multinational Enterprise*, London: Macmillan.

Caves, R., Crookell, H. and Killing, J. P. (1983) 'The Imperfect Market for Technology Licenses', *Oxford Bulletin of Economics and Statistics*, 45(3): 249–67.

Cusumano, M. (1985) *The Japanese Automobile Industry: Technology and Management at Nissan and Toyota*, Cambridge, MA: Harvard University Press.

Das, T. K. and Teng, B. S. (1998) 'Between Trust and Control: Developing Confidence in Partner Cooperation in Alliances', *Academy of Management Review*, 23(3): 491–512.

Das, T. K. and Teng, B. S. (2000) 'A Resource-based Theory of Strategic Alliances', *Journal of Management*, 26(1): 31–61.

de Figueiredo, J. M. and Teece, D. J. (1996) 'Mitigating Procurement Hazards in the Context of Innovation', *Industrial and Corporate Change*, 5(2): 537–60.

Dekker, H. C. (2004) 'Control of Inter-organizational Relationships: Evidence on Appropriation Concerns and Coordination Requirements', *Accounting Organizations and Society*, 29(1): 27–49.

Dussauge, P., Garrette, B. and Mitchell, W. (2000) 'Learning from Competing Partners: Outcomes and Durations of Scale and Link Alliances in Europe, North America and Asia', *Strategic Management Journal*, 21(2): 99–126.

Dyer, J., and Singh, H. (1998) 'The Relational View: Cooperative Strategy and Sources of Interorganizational Competitive Advantage', *Academy of Management Review*, 23(4): 660–79.

Eisenhardt, K. M. (1985) 'Control: Organizational and Economic Approaches', *Management Science*, 31(2): 134–49.

Ferguson, R. J., Paulin, M. and Bergeron, J. (2005) 'Contractual Governance, Relational Governance, and the Performance of Interfirm Service Exchanges: the Influence of Boundary-spanner Closeness', *Journal of the Academy of Marketing Science*, 33(2): 217–34.

Galbraith, J. R. (1977) *Organization Design*, Reading, MA: Addison-Wesley.

Grandori, A. (1997) 'An Organizational Assessment of Interfirm Coordination Modes', *Organization Studies*, 18(6): 897–925.

Granovetter, M. (1985) 'Economic Action and Social Structure: the Problem of Embeddedness', *American Journal of Sociology*, 91(3): 481–510.

Gulati, R. (1995) 'Does Familiarity Breed Trust – the Implications of Repeated Ties for Contractual Choice in Alliances', *Academy of Management Journal*, 38(1): 85–112.

Gulati, R. (1998) 'Alliances and Networks', *Strategic Management Journal*, 19(4): 293–317.

Gulati, R., Lawrence, P. R. and Puranam, P. (2005) 'Adaptation in Vertical Relationships: Beyond Incentive Conflict', *Strategic Management Journal*, 26(5): 415–40.

Gulati, Ranjay and Sytch, Maxim (2005) 'Does Familiarity Breed Trust? Revisiting the Antecedents of Trust', Mimeo.

Haytko, D. L. (2004) 'Firm-to-Firm and Interpersonal Relationships: Perspectives from Advertising Agency Account Managers', *Journal of the Academy of Marketing Science*, 32(3): 312–28.

Hoetker, G. (2005) 'How Much You Know versus How Well I Know You: Selecting a Supplier for a Technically Innovative Component', *Strategic Management Journal*, 26(1): 75–96.

Ireland, R. D., Hitt, M. A. and Vaidyanath, D. (2002) 'Alliance Management as a Source of Competitive Advantage', *Journal of Management*, 28(3): 413–46.

Kale, P., Singh, H. and Perlmutter, H. (2000) 'Learning and Protection of Proprietary Assets in Strategic Alliances: Building Relational Capital', *Strategic Management Journal*, 21(3): 217–37.

Klein, B. (1980) 'Transaction Costs Determinants of "unfair" Contractual Arrangements', *American Economic Review*, 70(2): 56–62.

Kogut, B. and Zander, U. (1992) 'Knowledge of the Firm, Combinative Capabilities, and the Replication of Technology', *Organization Science*, 3(3): 383–97.

Larson, A. (1992) 'Network Dyads in Entrepreneurial Settings: a Study of the Governance of Exchange Relationships', *Administrative Science Quarterly*, 37(1): 76–104.

Lawrence, P. R. and Lorsch, J. W. (1967) *Organization and Environment: Managing Differentiation and Integration*, Boston: Division of Research, Graduate School of Business Administration, Harvard University.

Loasby, B. J. (1996) 'The Organization of Industry', in N. J. Foss and C. Knudsen (eds), *Towards a Competence Theory of the Firm*, London: Routledge, 38–53.

Lyons, Bruce R. (1994) 'Contracts and Specific Investment: an Empirical Test of Transaction Cost Theory', *Journal of Economics and Management Strategy*, 3(2): 257–78.

Macaulay, S. (1963) 'Non-contractual Relations in Business', *American Sociological Review*, 28: 55–70.

MacNeil, I. R. (2000) 'Relational Contract Theory: Challenges and Queries', *Northwestern University Law Review*, 94(3): 877–907.

Makhija, M. V. and Ganesh, U. (1997) 'The Relationship between Control and Partner Learning in Learning-related Joint Ventures', *Organization Science*, 8(5): 508–27.

Martinez, J. I. and Jarillo, J. C. (1989) 'The Evolution of Research on Coordination Mechanisms in Multinational Corporations', *Journal of International Business Studies*, 20(3): 489–514.

Mayer, K. J. and Argyres, N. S. (2004) 'Learning to Contract: Evidence from the Personal Computer Industry', *Organization Science*, 15(4): 394–410.

Mellewigt, Thomas, Madhok, Anoop and Weibel, Antoinette (2004) 'Trust and Formal Contracts in Interorganizational Relationships: Substitutes and Complements', Mimeo.

Miller, D. and Shamsie, J. (1996) 'The Resource-based View of the Firm in Two Environments: the Hollywood Film Studios from 1936 to 1965', *Academy of Management Journal*, 39(3): 519–43.

Mitchell, W., Dussauge, P. and Garrette, B. (2002) 'Alliances with Competitors: How to Combine and Protect Key Resources', *Journal of Creativity and Innovation Management*, 11(3): 1–21.

Mitchell, W. and Singh, K. (1996) 'Precarious Collaboration: Business Survival after Partners Shut Down or Form New Partnerships', *Strategic Management Journal*, 17(3): 95–115.

Nelson, R. R. and Winter, S. G. (1982) *An Evolutionary Theory of Economic Change*, Cambridge: Belknap Press of Harvard University Press.

Nickerson, J. A. and Zenger, T. R. (2004) 'A Knowledge-based Theory of the Firm: the Problem-solving Perspective', *Organization Science*, 15(6): 617–32.

Poppo, L. and Zenger, T. (2002) 'Do Formal Contracts and Relational Governance Function as Substitutes or Complements?' *Strategic Management Journal*, 23(8): 707–25.

Ryall, Michael D. and Sampson, Rachelle C. (2003) 'Do Prior Alliances Influence Contract Structure? Evidence from Technology Alliance Contracts', Simon School of Business Working Paper No. FR 03-1.

Saxton, T. (1997) 'The Effects of Partner and Relationship Characteristics on Alliance Outcomes', *Academy of Management Journal*, 40(2): 443–61.

Schrader, S. (1991) 'Informal Technology-transfer between Firms: Cooperation through Information Trading', *Research Policy*, 20(2): 153–70.

Shapiro, D. L., Sheppard, B. H. and Cherasking, L. (1992) 'In Theory: Business on a Handshake', *Negotiation Journal*, 8: 365–77.

Sobrero, M. and Schrader, S. (1998) 'Structuring Inter-firm Relationships: a Meta-analytic Approach', *Organization Studies*, 19(4): 585–615.

Teece, D. J. (1986) 'Profiting from Technological Innovation: Implications for Integration, Collaboration, Licensing and Public Policy', *Research Policy*, 15(6): 285–305.

Teece, D. J. (1988) 'Technological Change and the Nature of the Firm', in G. Dosi, C. Freeman, L. Soete and G. Silverberg (eds), *Technological Change and Economic Theory*, London: Pinter Publishers.

Thompson, J. D. (1967) *Organizations in Action: Social Science Bases of Administration*, New York: McGraw-Hill.

Uzzi, B. (1997) 'Social Structure and Competition in Interfirm Networks: the Paradox of Embeddedness', *Administrative Science Quarterly*, 42(1): 35–67.

Williamson, O. E. (1985) *The Economic Institutions of Capitalism*, New York: Free Press.

Williamson, O. E. (1991) 'Comparative Economic Organization: the Analysis of Discrete Structural Alternatives', *Administrative Science Quarterly*, 36(2): 269–96.

Yin, X. and Zajac, E. (2004) 'The Strategy/Governance Structure Fit Relationship: Theory and Evidence in Franchising Arrangements', *Strategic Management Journal*, 25: 365–83.

15

The Enforcement Space: a Perspective on Stability of Strategic Alliances

Silviya Svejenova,[1] *Mitchell P. Koza*[2] *and Arie Y. Lewin*[3]

Introduction

Achieving and maintaining cooperation in strategic alliances requires mechanisms that ensure partners refrain from post-contractual opportunism and deliver on commitments as time passes and new opportunities arise. Trust is often considered essential for interfirm cooperation, yet it remains unclear how far 'cooperation can come about independently of trust' (Gambetta, 1988: 213). This chapter advances an enforcement framework to clarify the role of trust in safeguarding interfirm collaboration and identifies other mechanisms that could generate reliability and predictability of partners' cooperative behaviour. Thus, we do not allege that trust is unwarranted or unlikely to emerge in a process of productive cooperation, only that its many roles may have been overstated.

Frequently used in studies of interfirm relationships, trust is a difficult concept to delineate because of its ubiquity in ordinary life and the diverse phenomena it denotes, and the 'complex integration of the psychological, sociological and economic dimensions in an irreducible whole experience' it provides (Parkhe, 1998: 227). For scope limitations, we cannot review the extensive literature on trust. Despite the numerous articles, journal special issues and books on it, however, trust remains an unresolved concern (Burt, 2001). Doubts are raised about the universality of its effects on business transactions (Casciaro, 2003) and non-trust explanations start appearing (Madhok and Tallman, 1998). Hence, there is a need for alternative approaches and more nuanced explanations of interfirm relationships' enforcement.

This chapter makes several contributions to the alliance literature. First, it goes beyond trust explanations and advances an enforcement framework, which allows for a more refined understanding of partnership stability. Second, in defining the enforcement framework, it brings together mechanisms identified by TCE and social embeddedness, along what we label as legal, social and ownership dimensions. Lastly, the framework allows us to distinguish when trust is a requisite for cooperation and when it may not be essential.

The chapter is structured as follows. First, we provide arguments for a more refined perspective on alliance stability. Next, we discuss separately the elements of the enforcement space: the legal, social and ownership dimensions. Then, we combine the three elements to introduce the enforcement space as a perspective on alliance stability, and discuss its implications. Finally, we provide some concluding comments and outline avenues for further research.

La bourse ou la vie: towards a cooperation-enforcement framework

Enforcement enables collaboration and ensures partners act consistently with expectations. Its mechanisms differ from deterrence mechanisms, which rely on avoidance and preclusion of certain behaviour (Das and Rahman, 2002). There is a lack of agreement in the literature on when trust is the enforcement mechanism and when other mechanisms create an enforcement environment with trust-like outcomes. It is unlikely, for example, that the Mafia families of nineteenth-century Sicily 'trusted' one another; it is more likely that the certainty of enforcement played a significant role in the alliance's stability. The focus (and over-reliance) on trust in the alliance literature obscures a more general treatment of the nature and role of enforcement mechanisms. It may also confound the most interesting sources of variation in bringing stability to a partnership.

Stability is important not per se but for the opportunity it brings to the alliance parties to achieve benefits and build reputations as partners (Reuer and Koza, 2000). Borys and Jemison (1989) discuss three mechanisms for the stability of alliances: shared norms and expectations of justice, adoption of common industry practices, and reliance on the legal system to enforce hybrid contracts. Stability is promoted by the parties' ability to reward altruistic behaviour and reciprocate penalties for competitive behaviour (Kogut, 1989), by 'a stable interorganizational organization that regulates them' (Leblebici and Salancik, 1982: 228), or by third parties that make the partnership 'public' (Burt and Knez, 1996).

An alliance partner can be trusted to behave appropriately because the partner is viewed as an altruist, fears retaliation in the courts, and is cognizant of reputation effects in different national, professional or other communities (Koza and Lewin, 2005).

Two main approaches provide alternative explanations of enforcement in interfirm partnerships: transaction cost economics (TCE) and social embeddedness. TCE (Williamson, 1993) focuses on formal governance arrangements such as contracts and equity. TCE assumes that uncertainties and coordination costs can be decreased by drawing up detailed contracts. Useful in setting out mutual expectations and obligations, detailed contracts per se are not sufficient. They require transparent laws and efficient adjudication in court.

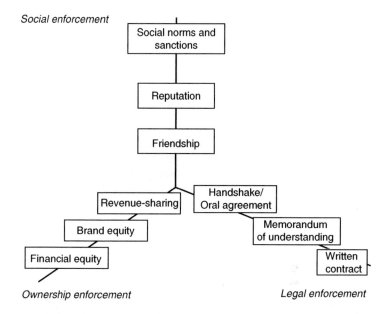

Figure 15.1: The enforcement space

Embeddedness (cf. Dacin et al., 1999 for a review) emphasizes the role of informal arrangements such as agreed expectations of cooperative behaviour in networks of relationships (Koza and Lewin, 2005). The exchange logic of embeddedness suggests that 'ongoing social ties shape actors' expectations and opportunities in ways that differ from the economic logic of market behavior' (Uzzi, 1996: 676). The key implication is that the nature and level of embeddedness have behavioural consequences because they constrain or enable the actions of individual actors and influence their dispositions. Embeddedness operates through a patterned social structure, which interprets signals and transfers beliefs, values and resources among firms (Uzzi, 1996).

Next we review in greater detail the structures and processes of several legal, social and ownership-based mechanisms for enforcement of desired behaviours in a partnership (see Figure 15.1). Here we assume these three dimensions are orthogonal in the enforcement space, although we note that exploring the potential for covariation of the dimensions would be interesting and important, given the diversity of institutional environments that strategic alliances may span.

Legal enforcement

Legal enforcement is manifested in the legal system's reliability, with its codification and transparency of laws (e.g. property, contract and commercial law) and realistic expectation for fair and speedy legal adjudication in courts. A partnership is embedded in the legal system when based on a complete contract that can be adjudicated within a reliable legal system. The agreement can be formal, informal, written, oral, or 'taken-for-granted' (Malhotra and Murnighan, 2002).

The legal dimension, or legal rationale in Weber's terms (Weber, 1947), may vary from relatively weak to strong. An *oral agreement* or 'handshake' is a good example of reliance on a weak form of legal enforcement. Although in principle enforceable in the law courts, documenting the existence and nature of rights and responsibilities of partners to an oral agreement may often prove elusive in practice. A *memorandum of understanding* (MOU) – typically a written document specifying partners' mutual expectations on the nature of collaboration – is more dependable from a legal point of view than an oral agreement. MOUs may include, but are not limited to, statements of alliance ambition, work sharing agreements, division of revenue, facilities' sharing, grievance adjudication procedures, governance, and termination time horizon, if any. Often reviewed by corporate counsel, MOUs typically aim to document a *managerial* point of view. Finally, *formal written contracts* are an example of a strong form of legal enforcement. These agreements are fully enforceable in courts and document mutually beneficial activities between relevant partners. They serve as routinized solutions to problems of agency, control and uncertainty by constraining individual and organizational behaviour (Malhotra and Murnighan, 2002).

Whether a contract succeeds in enforcing alliance cooperation depends on the ability of the parties to articulate their intent and act in ways that are consistent with their expressed intentions (Ring, 2002). Due to its relative inflexibility, a contract is best suited for cases where the behaviour is simple to describe and prescribe. A complete contract, attentive to all relevant contingencies, is difficult and costly to draw up and legally enforce. Particularly difficult are contracts involving learning or exploration relationships with higher levels of ambiguity. Further, the role of national and international courts has implications for contracts' enforceability. In the USA, for example, a uniform commercial code, contract law and legal protection for intellectual property leads to comparability and similarity of practices and expectations, and shared assumptions about how business is conducted.

The process of negotiating contractual safeguards, as well as their ex post contingent adaptability, is conducive to better cooperation (Reuer and Ariño, 2002). Furthermore, contracts can also be viewed as a source of flexibility, as less joint decision-making is mandated and more leeway is left to the partners. Their obligation is to abide by the terms of explicit contractual agreements while having the freedom to act on issues outside the contracts' scope (Das and Teng, 1996). The creative complexity and variety of alliance forms has outpaced the legal arena and the analytical tools used by anti-trust enforcement agencies to assess their legality (Mohr et al., 1994). Hence mechanisms other than contracts are used as complements to or substitutes for legal enforcement.

Social enforcement

Social embeddedness is another source of enforcement. Drawing on the sociological literature (e.g. Granovetter, 1985; Coleman, 1988; Burt, 1992), there are several mechanisms for social enforcement, such as friendship (enforcement by the strength of interpersonal bond), reputation (enforcement by an open network of third parties), and social norms and sanctions (enforcement by a closed, cohesive network, such as kinship relations).

If *friendship* is the only tie that binds alliance partners, without any common direct or indirect network of reference, the source of alliance stability is the partners' commitment to the relationship. As long as this commitment continues, it can provide certain safeguards for cooperation. However, if it fails or the persons responsible for the alliance are replaced by others without such commitment, this may threaten the cooperation and lead to alliance dissolution in the absence of other safeguards.

Reputation is an aggregate perception of multiple stakeholders about a firm or individual's salient characteristics and general esteem (Fombrun, 1996). Reputation is enhanced or damaged by third parties who generate and exchange gossip (Burt and Knez, 1996) or provide endorsement to young firms willing to enter partnerships but lacking favourable reputation due to liability of newness (Doz and Williamson, 2002; Gulati and Higgins, 2003). Reputation effects can influence behaviour in open networks through the informal exchange of information, which 'can create a reputational lock-in whereby good behavior is ensured through a concern for local reputation' (Gulati and Gargiulo, 1999: 1447). A dyad embedded in an open network is less restricted and bound by social norms, and more vulnerable to opportunism, than a dyad embedded in a closed network with strong sanctions for deviance.

Reputation as an enforcement mechanism is based on generating and carrying throughout an open information network on the reliability of partners, their competencies and needs (Gulati and Gargiulo, 1999). It is associated with strong reliance on third-party information in choosing both reliable and suitable alliance partners as a means to reduce the hazards of cooperation and raise the odds of success. Structural embeddedness is associated with constant signalling and updating of the network members' reputation (cf. Burt, 1992; Gulati, 1995; Uzzi, 1996). High structural embeddedness is found in professional service firms (Jones et al., 1998). In such networks, reputation effects are strong and serve to prevent opportunistic behaviour or diminish transaction costs by making opportunism costly (Gulati et al., 2000).

The nature of social enforcement changes when a partnership is embedded in a closed, dense network, where the power of *social norms and sanctions* drives behaviour. Members of closed social networks are much more strongly connected among themselves than to others. They share identity and behavioural expectations through social norms and sanctions, which in extreme cases can lead to exclusion. There are instances in which third-party signalling of a partner's reliability is of less relevance because firms have repeated exchanges with the same partners, and hence obtain information on the reliability and capability of the partner through direct observations and experiences. Relational rather than structural embeddedness accounts for the effects of such cohesive ties (Gulati and Gargiulo, 1999).

Relational embeddedness relates to the so-called *collectivist strategy* of highly inclusive and stable over time constellations of firms (Jones et al., 1998). Some examples are the highly integrated family-owned Korean *chaebols*; the looser, inward-oriented and steady Japanese *keiretsu* enterprise groups (Fligstein and Freeland, 1995); or the clans that thrive on shared values, beliefs and goals which are transferred and instilled through socialization processes (Ouchi, 1979). Those restrictive networks, however, may also take dysfunctional forms such as fiefs (Boisot and Child, 1996), illegal networks of price-fixing conspiracies (Baker and Faulkner, 1993), or the Mafia (Gambetta, 1988, 1993; Reed, 2001).

Ownership enforcement

A third source of enforcement is *ownership*. Ownership mechanisms differ in enforcement scope and reliability depending on their nature: revenue-sharing, brand equity, or financial equity are prototypes of ownership forms. *Revenue sharing agreements* typically do not involve equity participation of the partners in one another, or a joint venture child. A relatively weak form of enforcement, revenue sharing, gives a unilateral or multilateral claim on the revenue stream of an alliance business activity. *Brand equity* provides a more significant source of enforcement, especially in franchise or licensing relationships, and more so if the intellectual property of technology included is proprietary and difficult to imitate. In the hotel business, registered brand names are a potent source of control, and the threat of withdrawing permission to use the brand moderates the opportunistic behaviour of the firm's international partners (Contractor and Kundu, 1998: 333). Retaining strategic or de facto control over strategic assets such as brands can moderate local partners' opportunism. It is unlikely, for example, that a McDonald's franchise holder would benefit from joining the franchise, learning about the restaurant business, defecting, and setting up their own restaurant. In this case ownership of the brand gives the franchisor significant powers to deter opportunistic behaviour and ensure cooperation. Finally, *financial equity*, particularly partial equity in a strategic alliance partner or child, provides outright claims as residual claimant that, net of political expropriation, may provide the full range of managerial and legal means to ensure desired behaviour. Ceteris paribus, the greater the equity participation, the greater is the likelihood of cooperation.

The enforcement space

Korczynski (2000: 1) argues that 'it is through the dialogue between insights from economics and sociology that real advances in the analysis of trust can be made'. In addressing enforcement of an interfirm partnership, we define an enforcement space along legal, social and ownership dimensions. As shown in Figure 15.1, the three dimensions constitute an enforcement framework where the role of trust varies with different combinations of legal, social and ownership-based mechanisms. Although each dimension has important individual implications for cooperation enforcement, the three may act as complements rather than substitutes (Poppo and Zenger, 2002). There is a range of intermediary cases shaped by different combinations of enforcement mechanisms along the three dimensions. For example, within this framework, trust is a *requisite* enforcement mechanism when friends cooperate based on a handshake or an oral agreement, and share revenues. Trust is dispensable when there is assurance, i.e. 'expectations of benign behavior from an exchange partner based on knowledge of an incentive structure that encourages such behavior rather than exploitation' (Molm et al., 2000: 1403). For example, assurance rather than trust can enforce cooperation when a partnership is embedded in a closed, cohesive network, and based on a detailed contract and exchange of equity.

Social and legal embeddedness differs across countries due to different cultures, religions or legacies of the former colonial powers (Redding, 2005). Using the enforcement framework, we hypothesize that firms historically and spatially embedded in cultures with weak or underdeveloped institutions will tend to favour relations as safeguarding mechanisms, as opposed to contracts. In China, for example, 'Personal networks are ... particularly significant modes of economic transacting ... because of the weak institutional sanctions against reneging on commitments' (Boisot and Child, 1999: 247). However, these personal networks can be of little use to a foreign company without access to these networks or previous history of collaboration when considering the Chinese firm as a partner.

Concluding comments and avenues for further research

This chapter contributes to the alliance literature by challenging the universal role of trust in interfirm cooperation and proposing enforcement as a more balanced view on when trust matters. Three enforcement dimensions with different mechanisms were discussed: partners' social and legal embeddedness, and the existence of ownership relationship. Further empirical and theoretical work on non-trust mechanisms with trust-like properties and outcomes is necessary.

First, research could explore the impact of business and state elites as matchmakers of partnerships. Renown is the influence of businessmen and politicians in triggering, providing legitimacy to parties, and sustaining inter-firm alliances. Further attention is needed to these and other strategics that firms use to convey an image of reliable partners, for example entrepreneurial firms partnering with incumbents to enhance legitimacy and reputation (Doz and Williamson, 2002).

Second, an agenda on interorganizational partnerships should consider their dysfunctional consequences and negative effects (Whetten and Leung, 1979). A critical issue for further development is the notion and dynamics of failure in a strategic alliance (Park and Ungson, 2001). Research on dysfunctional outcomes of alliances and networks could improve understanding on how and why firms get locked into and sustain unproductive partnerships that could hinder opportunities to collaborate with other viable firms (Gulati et al., 2000).

Third, focus on the dynamics of nation-institutional configurations (Witt and Lewin, 2004) rather than on culture may be more meaningful in capturing differences along the enforcement dimensions. Importing and integrating insights from political-institutional approaches to sociology (Fligstein and Freeland, 1995) into the field of alliances could provide a more comprehensive view of interfirm collaborations. How do adjustments in nation-state institutional arrangements affect interfirm relationships and choices of alliance partners? How are differences in institutional contexts imprinted on management decisions about initiating and maintaining inter-national alliances? In particular, there is a need for studies of alliances established in developing countries, especially from the viewpoint of local partners, which has been largely neglected (Miller et al., 1996).

Interfirm relationships continue to be a vast and vibrant scholarly domain in need of further clarification and integration of disparate contributions. For future research to result in a better-informed perspective on stability in alli-ances, studies must incorporate approaches from comparative sociology and economic geography, which can provide a broader and better foundation than culture. Researchers must strive to separate trust from trust-like mech-anisms for initiating and maintaining a partnership, which would allow an explanation of how firms who are 'strangers' can initiate a potentially profitable relationship in the absence of a common relational history. They should aim for multi-level studies and co-evolutionary perspectives (Koza and Lewin, 1998, 2005; Volberda and Lewin, 2003). We hope this chapter is a step in this direction.

Notes

1. Silviya Svejenova, ESADE Business School, Av. de Pedralbes, 60-62, 08034, Barcelona, E-mail: silviya.svejenova@esade.edu
2. Mitchell P. Koza, Rutgers University School of Business – Camden, 227 Penn Street, Camden, NJ 08102-1656, USA. Tel: +1 (856) 225-6217, E-mail: mitchell. koza@camden.rutgers.edu

3. Arie Y. Lewin, Fuqua School of Business, Duke University,1 Towerview Drive, Durham, NC 27708, Tel: (919) 660-7832, Fax: (919) 681-6244, E-mail: ayl3@mail.duke.edu

References

Baker, W. E. and Faulkner, R. R. (1993) 'The Social Organization of Conspiracy: Illegal Networks in the Heavy Electrical Equipment Industry', *American Sociological Review*, 58: 839–60.

Boisot, M. and Child, J. (1996) 'From Fiefs to Clans and Network Capitalism: Explaining China's Emerging Economic Order', *Administrative Science Quarterly*, 41: 600–28.

Boisot, M. and Child, J. (1999) 'Organizations as Adaptive Systems in Complex Environments: the Case of China', *Organization Science*, 10(3): 237–52.

Borys, B. and Jemison, D. B. (1989) 'Hybrid Arrangements as Strategic Alliances: Theoretical Issues in Organizational Combinations', *Academy of Management Review*, 14(2): 234–49.

Burt, R. (1992) *Structural Holes*, Cambridge, MA: Harvard University Press.

Burt, R. (2001) 'Bandwidth and Echo: Trust, Information, and Gossip in Social Networks', in A. Casella and J. E. Rauch (eds), *Networks and Markets: Contributions from Economics and Sociology*, New York: Russell Sage Foundation.

Burt, R. and Knez, M. (1996) 'Trust and Third-party Gossip', in R. M. Kramer and T. R. Tyler (eds), *Trust in Organizations: Frontiers of Theory and Research*, Thousand Oaks, CA: Sage, 68–89.

Casciaro, T. (2003) 'Determinants of Governance Structure in Alliances: the Role of Strategic, Task and Partner Uncertainties', *Industrial and Corporate Change*, 12(6): 1223–51.

Coleman, J. S. (1988) 'Social Capital in the Creation of Human Capital', *American Journal of Sociology*, 94: S95–S120.

Contractor, F. J. and Kundu, S. K. (1998) 'Modal Choice in a World of Alliances: Analyzing Organizational Forms in the International Hotel Sector', *Journal of International Business Studies*, 29(2): 325–58.

Dacin, M. T., Ventresca, M. J. and Beal, B. D. (1999) 'The Embeddedness of Organizations: Dialogue and Directions', *Journal of Management*, 25: 317–56.

Das, T. K. and Rahman, N. (2002) 'Opportunism Dynamics in Strategic Alliances', in F. J. Contractor and P. Lorange (eds), *Cooperative Strategies and Alliances*, Oxford: Pergamon, 89–118.

Das, T. K. and Teng, B. S. (1996) 'Risk Types and Inter-firm Alliance Structures', *Journal of Management Studies*, 33(6): 827–43.

Doz, Y. L. and Williamson, P. (2002) 'Alliances as Entrepreneurship Accelerators', in F. J. Contractor and P. Lorange (eds), *Cooperative Strategies and Alliances*, Oxford: Pergamon, 773–97.

Fligstein, N. and Freeland, R. (1995) 'Theoretical and Comparative Perspectives on Corporate Organization', *Annual Review of Sociology*, 21: 21–43.

Fombrun, C. J. (1996) *Reputation: Realizing Value from the Corporate Image*, Boston, MA: Harvard Business School Press.

Gambetta, D. (ed.) (1988) *Trust: Making and Breaking Co-operative Relations*, Oxford: Basil Blackwell.

Gambetta, D. (1993) *The Sicilian Mafia: the Business of Private Protection*, Cambridge, MA: Harvard University Press.

Granovetter, M. S. (1985) 'Economic Action and Social Structure: the Problem of Embeddedness', *American Journal of Sociology*, 91: 481–510.

Gulati, R. (1995) 'Social Structure and Alliances Formation Patterns: a Longitudinal Analysis', *Administrative Science Quarterly*, 40: 619–52.

Gulati, R. and Gargiulo, M. (1999) 'Where do Interorganizational Networks Come From?' *American Journal of Sociology*, 104(5): 1439–93.

Gulati, R. and Higgins, M. (2003) 'Which Ties Matter When? The Contingent Effects of Interorganizational Partnerships on IPO success', *Strategic Management Journal*, 24: 127–44.

Gulati, R., Nohria, N. and Zaheer, A. (2000) 'Strategic Networks', *Strategic Management Journal*, 21: 203–15.

Jones, C., Hesterly, W. S. Fladmoe-Lindquist, K. and Borgatti, S. P. (1998) 'Professional Service Constellations: How Strategies and Capabilities Influence Collaborative Stability and Change', *Organization Science*, 9(3): 396–410.

Kogut, B. (1989) 'The Stability of Joint Ventures: Reciprocity and Competitive Rivalry', *Journal of Indusrial Economics*, 38: 183–98.

Korczynski, M. (2000) 'The Political Economy of Trust', *Journal of Management Studies*, 37(1): 1–21.

Koza, M. P. and Lewin, A. Y. (1998) 'The Co-evolution of Strategic Alliances', *Organization Science*, 9(3): 255–64.

Koza, M. P. and Lewin, A. Y. (eds) (2005) *Strategic Alliances and Firm Adaptation: a Coevolution Perspective*, Basingstoke: Palgrave Macmilan.

Leblebici, H. and Salancik, G. R. (1982) 'Stability in Interorganizational Exchanges: Rulemaking Processes of the Chicago Board of Trade', *Administrative Science Quarterly*, 27(2): 227–42.

Madhok, A. and Tallman, S. B. (1998) 'Resources, Transactions and Rents: Managing Value Through Interfirm Collaborative Relationships', *Organization Science*, 9(3): 326–39.

Malhotra, D. and Murnighan, J. K. (2002) 'The Effects of Contracts on Interpersonal Trust', *Administrative Science Quarterly*, 47: 534–59.

Miller, R. R., Glen, J. D., Jaspersen, F. Z. and Karmokolias, Y. (1996) 'International Joint Ventures in Developing Countries. Happy Marriages?', *International Finance Corporation, Discussion Paper*, no. 29.

Mohr, J. J., Gundlach, G. T. and Spekman, R. (1994) 'Legal Ramification of Strategic Alliances', *Marketing Management*, 3(2): 38–46.

Molm, L. D., Takahashi, N. and Peterson, G. (2000) 'Risk and Trust in Social Exchange: an Experimental Test of a Classical Proposition', *American Journal of Sociology*, 105(5): 1396–427.

Ouchi, W. (1979) 'A Conceptual Framework for the Design of Organizational Control Mechanisms', *Management Science*, 25(9): 833–49.

Park, S. H. and Ungson, G. R. (2001) 'Interfirm Rivalry and Managerial Complexity: a Conceptual Framework of Alliances Failure', *Organization Science*, 12(1): 37–53.

Parkhe, A. (1998) 'Understanding Trust in International Alliances', *Journal of World Business*, 33(3): 219–40.

Poppo, L. and Zenger, T. (2002) 'Do Formal Contracts and Relational Governance Function as Substitutes or Complements?' *Strategic Management Journal*, 23: 707–25.

Redding, G. (2005) 'The Thick Description and Comparison of Societal Systems of Capitalism', *Journal of International Business Studies*, 36(2): 123–55.

Reed, M. (2001) 'Organization, Trust and Control: a Realist Analysis', *Organization Studies*, 22(2): 201–28.

Reuer, J. J. and Ariño, A. (2002) 'Contractual Renegotiations in Strategic Alliances', *Journal of Management*, 28(1): 47–68.

Reuer, J. J. and Koza, M. P. (2000) 'Asymmetric Information and Joint Venture Performance: Theory and Evidence for Domestic and International Joint Ventures', *Strategic Management Journal*, 21(1): 81–8.

Ring, P. S. (2002) 'The Role of Contract in Strategic Alliances', in F. J. Contractor and P. Lorange (eds), *Cooperative Strategies and Alliances*, Oxford: Pergamon, 145–62.

Uzzi, B. (1996) 'The Sources and Consequences of Embeddedness for the Economic Performance of Organizations: the Network Effect', *American Sociological Review*, 61: 674–98.

Volberda, H. W. and Lewin, A. Y. (2003) 'Guest Editors' Introduction – Co-evolutionary Dynamics Within and Between Firms. From Evolution to Co-evolution', *Journal of Management Studies*, 40(8): 2105–30.

Weber, Max (1947) *The Theory of Social and Economic Organization*, translated by A. M. Henderson and Talcott Parsons, New York: Free Press.

Whetten, D. A. and Leung, T. K. (1979) 'The Instrumental Value of Interorganizational Relations: Antecedents and Consequences of Linkage Formation', *Academy of Management Journal*, 22(2): 325–44.

Williamson, O. (1993) 'Calculativeness, Trust, and Economic Organization', *Journal of Law and Economics*, 34: 453–502.

Witt, M. and Lewin, A. Y. (2004) 'Dynamics of Institutional Change: Institutional Stickiness and the Logic of Individual Action', working paper, INSEAD.

Part II

Contractual Foundations of Strategic Alliances

16
Revisiting Our Views of Contract and Contracting in the Context of Alliance Governance

Peter Smith Ring[1]

Introduction

Since the early 1930s an increasing number of scholars, from a variety of disciplines, have concerned themselves with questions related to the organization of economic activities. These inquiries have led to theories designed to provide explanations for the existence and nature of business firms, the nature of markets and the organization of industries, and of cooperative economic relationships between firms (Coase, 1937; Fama and Jensen, 1983; Hart and Moore, 1990; Posner, 1981; Williamson, 1985). The concept of contract is central to each of these theories.

In organizational studies, the concept of contract has been relied on as well, both in its formal manifestations as a means of governing economic exchanges (Poppo and Zenger, 2002), and its informal manifestations (Malhotra & Murnighan, 2002). A primary focus of contract based research in this area has been on issues related to so-called psychological contracts, and derives from early work by Kotter (1973), among others.

Needless to say, the contract branches of the law also provide significant insights into the meaning and nature of contract (MacNeil, 1974; Hillman, 1998). In addition, the concept of contract has also been explored by sociologists (Macaulay, 1963) and by philosophers (Held, 1990).

This significant body of research gives rise to the underlying premise of this chapter: researchers rarely define what they mean by contract; nor do they typically consider how different types of contract could affect the decisions of management. Less surprisingly, they have paid little attention to the purely legal aspects of contract. Finally, processes of contracting are rarely explored in the contexts of specific types of contracts. This chapter seeks to provide some insights into how these shortcomings might be remedied.

Economic exchanges undertaken by clairvoyant individuals who would faithfully live up to their contractual obligations would produce no real need for a contract. But most exchanges will involve uncertain futures, fallible memories and unreliable economic actors. As a consequence, contract-based exchanges involve a wide variety of contingencies that cannot be fully and adequately anticipated, various risks that cannot be dealt with efficiently, and all sorts of information that cannot be effectively communicated by the parties.

Just as there are a variety of perspectives regarding contract based in economics or psychology, so too are there a number of perspectives of contract based in law and in legal theory.[2] A primary divide exists between civil and common law legal systems (France versus the United Kingdom). Within the United States there are both case-based (common-law) and statutory sources of contract *law*. Within the common law tradition in the United States there are *theories* of contract, for example, that have been described as neo-classical and relational.

In general, for an agreement between two (or more) parties to be considered a legally enforceable contract, four elements must be present. Initially, the parties must be *competent*. For example, minors cannot be bound to a contract. The subject matter of the agreement must also be something that does not violate notions of public policy (for example, a contract that created conditions of unfair competition – if it violated anti-trust provisions – would not be upheld).

The more difficult elements of legally binding agreements arise out of efforts by the parties to (1) reach a meeting of the minds (mutual assent) and (2) define consideration. In large measure the problems that parties face in agreeing on terms and conditions and on consideration are those that give rise to the kinds of 'problems' economists and others worry about.

Summarily, discussions of contract as found in these literatures appear to be based around eight economic and psychological elements outlined in Table 16.1. Almost all of these economic and psychological dimensions of contract give rise to more than one set of assumptions. The differing assumptions relate to different kinds of 'contract' as economists use the term. These 'contracts' are addressed in the next few sections. These contracts have different purposes and the parties that rely on them are seeking to accomplish differing economic objectives.

Discrete contracts

One of the most widely cited types of contract is the *discrete* contract, a vehicle by which many 'simple' kinds of market exchanges are governed. Assets are non-specific and readily available; consequently the transactions tend to become 'standardized' and are usually self-liquidating. The utility (economic or legal) of a discrete contract is in memorializing a fundamentally clear-cut economic exchange in the event that one or more of the parties become incapacitated or dies.

The theory of discrete contract is based on assumptions that economic actors are boundedly rational, self-interested (opportunistic), and risk

Table 16.1: An expanded view of contracts and contracting processes

				Psychological and Economic Assumptions					
Rationality	Interest orientation	Asset specificity	Frequency	Uncertainty	Risk propensity	Ordering	Safeguards	Implied type of contract	Implied contracting process
≈	+	$k=0,p$	−	ß	Ñ	−	$(\varphi \geq 0), í$	Discrete	Arm's length bargaining
≈	+	$k>0,s,d$	≈	Θ, ß	Ñ	−	$\varphi > 0, í$	Neo-classical	Arm's length bargaining
≈	≈, Ω	$k \geq 0, p, s, d$	+	Θ, ß	Ñ, Ä	π	$\varphi \geq 0, í$	General clause	Recurrent
≈	+, ≈	$k>0,d,s$	−	ß	Ñ	−	$\varphi > 0, í, \Phi$	Incomplete long term	Recurrent
≈	+	$k \geq 0, s, d$	−	ß	Ñ	−	$\varphi > 0, í$	Comprehensive	Relational
+	+	$k>0,s,d$	−	Θ, ß	Ñ	π	$\varphi 0, í$	Contingent claims	Relational
τ	Ω	$k \geq 0$	+, −, ≈	Ω	Ñ, Ä	−	$\varphi = 0$	Bliss	Relational

Key:

Rationality: Maximizing (+); Bounded rationality (≈); Organic Rationality (≈); Absent (τ)

Interest orientation: Opportunism (+); Simple (≈); Obedience (−); Trust (Ω)

Asset specificity: physical (p); site (s); human (h); dedicated (d); non-specific (k = 0); idiosyncratic (k > 0)

Frequency: recurrent (+); occasional (≈); rare (−)

Uncertainty: behavioural (ß); state contingent (Θ)

Risk propensity: neutral (Ñ); adverse (Ä)

Ordering: public or private (_); exclusively private (π)

Safeguards: absent (φ = 0); present (φ > 0); incentives (í); specialized governance (Φ); trading regularities (ü)

neutral. Theory suggests that the resources the parties exchange are usually physical in nature and are assumed to be available under conditions approximating pure competition; thus the only form of uncertainty confronting the parties is behavioural (as a consequence of assuming self-interest).

In these kinds of exchanges the level of cooperation needed to conduct economic exchange is minimal. The assumed competitiveness of the market implies that price (and the information it provides about the assets being exchanged) is reasonably well understood (and, perhaps, non-negotiable).[3] This minimizes the need for extensive cooperation to produce a legally binding contract, and even if there are negotiations they should create few (if any) conflicts. The parties either find a zone of contract, or self-liquidate; for example, if the level of conflict escalates too much, the parties walk away from the deal and find someone willing to exchange the physical assets on more agreeable terms. Safeguards, to the extent that they exist, take the form of incentives, and if conflict arises ex post contract, the parties are likely to ignore the terms and conditions of the 'legal' agreement that produce conflict and resolve the matter 'informally' (see, Macaulay, 1963); or rely on public ordering.

In light of the foregoing, using the term 'discrete contract' to describe mechanisms governing most strategic alliances, in my view, would be totally inappropriate. It would be hard to define how such exchanges could either be strategic in nature or reflect the cooperative nature of an alliance. An exception might be found in technology licensing arrangements within more complicated umbrella contracts.

Neo-classical contracts

Neo-classical contracts take place in those cases in which economic actors are assumed to be both boundedly rational and opportunistic. These contracts will govern exchanges of mixed or idiosyncratic resources, but the parties will only need access to them occasionally. Unlike non-specific resources, information regarding these resources is not easily reflected by the price mechanism. Consequently, the parties must cooperate at a higher level if exchange is to occur. Ex ante contract conflicts will arise from attempts to agree upon production function competence and these levels of conflict will be significant with this kind of contract, ceteris paribus.

Because the resources cannot be easily redeployed, the parties in these kinds of transactions also have strong reasons to continue to cooperate with each other: these contracts tend to be long-term. If they were able to foresee the future more perfectly, or if they did not have to worry about each other acting opportunistically, the parties would worry less about conflict. These assumptions give rise to what many economists think of as a 'complex world'.

Assumptions that behavioural and state contingent uncertainty will create unforeseen problems, lead to assumptions that parties need to safeguard their investments. However, because they need to continue to cooperate in order to maximize the benefits flowing from the resources they have committed to the exchange, parties are assumed to resort to private ordering, employing incentives and, as last resort, third party governance mechanisms such as arbitrators to resolve their disputes. They are assumed to be concerned about their reputations and thus they try to balance holding each other to the letter of the law against maintaining high levels of goodwill.

It seems likely that parties employing neo-classical contract will focus more heavily on the potential for conflict ex post contract than ex ante, because of the assumption that small numbers of problems arise ex post, once a commitment of idiosyncratic resources has been made. In addition, the parties are also more likely to be concerned with controlling state contingent uncertainties (and the conflicts they give rise to) that will arise ex post because they will not be able to easily redeploy these resources. Thus, their environmental monitoring and their monitoring of each other's behaviour are likely to be much more intense; and, by themselves, may lead to additional conflict between the parties.

Because neo-classical contracts involve infrequent exchanges of idiosyncratic assets, it seems likely that their use in discussions of strategic alliances would be rare. An exception might be the case of long-term R&D alliances involving firms from very different kinds of industries such as fuel cell R&D efforts in which the likelihood of sustained cooperation once a commercially viable product was developed would be remote. They also might be an appropriate means of governing an equity joint venture; but in light of the fact that the kinds of assets they are assumed to involve are only physical or dedicated this seems less likely. Equity joint ventures frequently entail exchanges of both site-specific and human assets.

General clause contracts

The purpose of a general clause contract is to enable parties that can rely on some degree of trust to deal with an uncertain future, ex post contract. When economic actors need to transact non-specific resources on a recurrent basis, many researchers argue that they should rely on general clause contracts.[4] This form of economic contract ought to be highly relevant to the governance of some types of strategic alliances, particularly those where the parties are trying to accomplish complex, uncertain and (sometimes) risky business tasks such as basic R&D. Nonetheless, it is rarely mentioned by those who have studied alliance governance.

Because of the need to have more frequent access to the same kind of non-specific or idiosyncratic resources, researchers can assume that the parties operate on the basis of simple interest orientation (Williamson, 1985: 49). Economic actors are presumed to be somewhat more open in their dealings with each other, in part because they have a history and anticipate future dealings; i.e. they have previously and in the future will continue to cooperate with each other. In fact, in these kinds of contracts the parties generally promise that they will provide their partners with all information deemed relevant to their objectives and that they will not act in opportunistic ways, even when opportunities to do so arise. These are quite clearly conditions surrounding alliance formation.

General clause contracts are relied on by economic actors who are assumed to be risk neutral. But many of them are risk adverse. They will rely exclusively on private ordering (because of their interest orientations) and their contracts will contain a general clause that spells out a variety of approaches to dealing with the unexpected (in the form of a variety of safeguards and/or forms of specialized governance and trading regularities). Because they may rely on some level of trust, there is no need to fully spell out all the contingencies that they might expect to arise in the future. General clause contracts are likely to produce more conflict ex post contract than ex ante. Reliance on a general clause contract means that the parties can reach agreement in relatively short order, and with relatively little conflict, and leave all the action to ex post contract stages. They simply agree, comprehensively, to keep each other informed, to not act in opportunistic ways, and on the steps that they will take as they cope with conflicts as they arise.

If they are able to cooperate, the general clause provides the parties with opportunities to safeguard against conflict arising from this form of uncertainty by defining the conditions under which their equity objectives will be re-evaluated as the future becomes known. Reliance on private ordering in adjusting for the future as it becomes more apparent to the parties is an ex post contract approach to mitigating the likelihood that conflict will destroy an economic relationship.

Comprehensive or contingent claims contracts

In those cases in which the purpose of a contract is to govern an infrequent, short-term exchange of non-specific resources by opportunistic parties, there is an assumption that comprehensive or contingent claims contracts will be relied on by the parties. In comprehensive or contingent claims contracts, the parties (ex ante contract) seek to accomplish an identification of all possible sources of conflict and resolve them in advance of finalizing an agreement. This kind of contract is assumed to be possible by changing assumptions about the rationality of the economic actors from one in which bounded rationality is presumed to one in which a strong form of rationality is assumed (Williamson, 1985: 45): maximizing rationality of the type presumed in neo-classical economics. In the costless world of transacting created by neo-classical economists, this shift in assumptions is (somewhat) easily accepted.

In the world of real exchanges, however, contracting processes are not costless. Since the parties in contingent claims contracting are assumed to be opportunistic, their negotiations are designed, primarily, to deal with the effects of behavioural uncertainty and the varieties of conflict than can flow from these sources of uncertainty.

The strong form assumption regarding the rationality of the parties resolves uncertainty problems of the state contingent variety, although the negotiation is occasioned by efforts of the parties to define the conflict that might flow from all possible future states of nature as well as the likelihood estimates associated with each. The parties also focus their attention on identifying incentives that will safeguard their expectations regarding equity outcomes, and in defining the private ordering that they will employ ex post contract to resolve conflicts as they arise. These ex ante contract processes are more likely to produce greater conflict than either discrete or general clause contracting because of the attempt to minimize ex ante so much of the state contingent and behavioural uncertainty present in transactions. Given that parties to most strategic alliances understand that their purposes and what they are trying to accomplish require their continued cooperation, trying to resolve all problems associated with the economic exchanges underlying their alliances in advance unnecessarily protracts the start of an alliance. And since many alliances are a consequence of intense competitive pressures to be first to market with new products or first to a market, time is of the essence. Thus, it seems unlikely that theories of comprehensive or contingent claims contracts would have much utility in describing the governance mechanisms of alliances.

Contracting processes

It is one thing to talk about a contract. But contracts are products, sometimes only artefacts, of processes of 'negotiations' between two or more parties. Thus, is important to consider whether differences in contracts are associated with different contracting processes that produce them and the assumptions associated with those processes. In Table 16.1, I suggested that three contracting processes might be implied in the types of contracts that I have discussed above.

Arm's-length bargaining assumes that the parties are autonomous and are more likely than not to enjoy limited and non-unique relationships. Typically the subject matter of these bargaining processes entails one-time transfers of fairly well-defined property rights. Agents tend to negotiate on behalf of principals, and the agents are frequently (but not exclusively) lawyers. The hard bargaining is more likely to be positional than principled (Fisher and Ury, 1981), and is likely to focus on consideration and ensuring that a meeting of minds has occurred on issues considered to be critical to all of the parties. There are likely to be 'deal-breakers' that all of the parties bring to the table, and when they cannot be resolved the bargaining processes are likely to be terminated.

Given the assumptions associated with discrete and neo-classical contracts, the contracting processes that produce them are likely to resemble arm's-length bargaining. The infrequency of exchange would mitigate the need for making extensive investments in relationships. Because the assets that are the subject of these kinds of exchanges are either physical or dedicated, volume, price and quality issues are likely to become primary foci of the parties' bargaining. Since these are considerably somewhat 'objective' in nature, arm's-length bargaining is likely to produce relatively low levels of ex ante conflict, and thus an appropriate approach to contracting.

Parties relying on general clause contracts will engage in what Ring and Van de Ven (1992) describe as recurrent contracting processes. Because these parties may be able to rely on fragile trust (Ring, 1996), they may use the opportunity to 'write' new general clause contracts for each new deal, building in the 'learning' that they have accomplished in their prior relationships to describe a new set of safeguards. They may also use the occasion to engage in more risky kinds of deals because they may have developed a new-found sense of confidence in their competence and their behaviour. Recurrent contracting involves repeated exchanges of resources that have moderate degrees of transaction specificity. The terms that are important in defining the conditions under which the exchange will occur tend to be certain, but some contingencies may be left to resolution as the (uncertain) future evolves. In temporal terms, the duration of the agreements is relatively short term (typically less than 18 months). The parties see themselves, and each other, as autonomous, legally equal actors. However, they are already contemplating even greater levels of cooperation. They rely on recurrent contracting to explore how each of them deals with efforts to achieve outcomes other than efficiency. They also use recurrent contracting to experiment with various types of safeguards, and with alternative methods for resolving conflict. In cases in which the parties use recurrent contracting to govern economic exchanges, neo-classical contract law (MacNeil, 1974) provides the legal framework within which these predominantly market-based transactions will be governed.

In contrast, Ring and Van de Ven (1992) argue that relational contracting tends to involve longer-term investments. Temporally, these investments may be defined in fixed terms (for example, 5–10 years), but more often than not termination of the relationship depends on factors other than time. In cases in which they rely on relational contracting, the parties may be relying on groundwork laid by recurrent contracting processes related to the production and transfer of property rights. Parties relying on relational contracting processes also are likely to see each other as legally equal and autonomous parties. In contrast to recurrent contracting, however, they may view themselves as being more committed to long-term cooperation, and are thus willing to forgo some aspects of their autonomy.

The property, products or services cooperatively developed and exchanged in transactions governed by relational contracting entail highly specific investments in ventures that cannot be fully specified or controlled by the parties in advance of their execution. Thus, in economic terms the contracts produced by relational contracting processes are likely to be comprehensive or contingent claims contracts. As a consequence of the assumption of bounded rationality, the parties to these relational contracts are likely to be exposed to a broader variety of trading hazards than other economic actors. Disputes are resolved through internal mechanisms designed to preserve the relationship and ensure that both the efficiency and equity outcomes sought in the cooperative effort are realized.

Conclusions

In the foregoing discussion I have sought to identify kinds of contract, based in economic theory, relevant to discussions of alliance governance. I have also sought to identify contracting processes that would produce these kinds of contracts. If the purpose of a contract is merely to define governance, then its execution by the parties has accomplished that task. In discrete and neo-classical contracts this is likely to be the primary reason why the parties invest resources in producing a contract. Needless to say, many of the economic exchanges governed by these kinds of contract take place within a well-defined and relatively short time frame (in many instances as goods are exchanged for 'money').

Strategic alliances, on the other hand, are typically designed for the long(er) run and in many instances to accomplish tasks that entail a great deal of uncertainty at the time they are negotiated. Thus, the contracts that govern them ought to take account of these uncertainties; provide for means for governing conduct in the uncertain future; and provide institutional guarantors with relatively clear evidence of the intentions of the parties about these matters at the time that they reached a meeting of minds and agreed upon consideration.

Interestingly, such contracts can be very long and well defined (lots of clauses, contingencies, boiler plate, etc.) or be very short and yet, in both cases, be legally complete. For researchers, the former kinds of contracts are more likely to provide a wider set of variables that might explain associations between operational outcomes and provisions in a contract. Researchers appear to be less worried about the investments of time and money required to produce almost complete contingent claims contracts and their impact on economic outcomes, in part because it is very hard to measure these costs and/or to get reliable and valid data on them. Nonetheless, managers do have to worry about these things, particularly about the amount of time required to negotiate ex ante all possible (or almost all) ex post contingencies. In such circumstances, time is likely to be more critical than monetary costs because alliances are frequently employed in races to markets (for products and/or 'customers'). Thus, managers are likely to be predisposed to look for contracts that are short (i.e. easily written) and flexible (i.e. leave open lots of room for ex post contract adjustments to the contract that serve the accomplishment of the business purposes of the alliance). Of course, their lawyers may (and in many instances will) have a different point of view. Thus, the trade-offs between what managers need and what lawyers want are an essential variable in understanding the outcome that is called a 'contract'. These trade-offs may be a function of the contracting processes employed by the parties. If my assertion is correct, then alliance scholars need to become more involved in expanding our understanding of possible relationships between alliances, the types of 'contracts' that are associated with alliances, and the processes that are employed by the parties in producing those 'contracts'.

Notes

1. Peter Smith Ring, College of Business Administration, Loyola Marymount University, 1 LMU Drive, Los Angeles, CA 90045, E-mail: pring@lmu.edu
2. Williamson (1985: 161) does acknowledge, in passing, that 'the possibility of many pertinent contract laws goes unremarked'.
3. The meaning of numbers on a 'price tag' is more subject to 'cultural' than to legal variation.
4. A general clause contract is sometimes referred to as an *incomplete long-term contract* (Williamson, 1975: 91–4), although as reflected in Table 16.1 there are differences in assumptions.

References

Coase, R. H. (1937) 'The Nature of the Firm', *Economica*, 4: 386–405.
Commons, J. R. (1924) *Institutional Economics*, Madison, WI: University of Wisconsin Press.
Fama, E. and Jensen, M. (1983) 'Separation of Ownership and Control', *Journal of Law and Economics*, 26: 301–25.
Fisher, R. and Ury, W. (1981) *Getting to Yes*, New York: Penguin Books.
Hart, O. and Moore, J. (1990) 'Property Rights and the Nature of the Firm', *Journal of Political Economy*, 98: 1119–58.
Held, V. (1990) 'Mothering versus Contract', in Jane Mansbridge (ed.), *Beyond Self-Interest*, Chicago: University of Chicago Press, 287–304.
Hillman, R. A. (1998) *The Richness of Contract Law: an Analysis of Critique of Contemporary Theories of Contract Law*, Dordrecht: Kluwer Academic Publishers.
Kotter, J. P. (1973) 'The Psychological Contract: Managing the Joining Up Process', *California Management Review*, 15: 91–9.
Macaulay, S. (1963) 'Non-contractual Relations in Business', *American Sociological Review*, 28: 55–70.
MacNeil, I. R. (1974) 'The Many Futures of Contract', *Southern California Law Review*, 47: 691–816.
Malhotra, D and Murnighan, J. K. (2002) 'The Effects of Contracts on Interpersonal Trust', *Administrative Science Quarterly*, 47: 534–59
Poppo, L. and Zenger, T. (2002) 'Do Formal Contracts and Relational Governance Function as Substitutes or Complements?' *Strategic Management Journal*, 23: 707–25.
Posner, R. (1981) *The Economics of Justice*, Cambridge, MA: Harvard University Press.

Radner, R. (1992) 'Hierarchy: the Economics of Managing', *Journal of Economic Issues*, 30: 1382–415.

Ring, P. S. (1996) 'Fragile Trust and Resilient Trust and their Roles in Cooperative Interorganizational Relationships', *Business & Society*, 35(2): 148–75.

Ring, P. S. and Van de Ven, A. H. (1992) 'Structuring Cooperative Relationships between Organizations', *Strategic Management Journal*, 13: 483–98.

Williamson, O. E. (1975) *Markets and Hierarchies: Analysis and Antitrust Implications*, New York: Free Press.

Williamson, O. E. (1985) *The Economic Institutions of Capitalism*, New York: Free Press.

17
Designing Interorganizational Contracts: the Role of Detailed Task Descriptions

Kyle J. Mayer[1]

Introduction

Strategic alliances and other interorganizational arrangements are important mechanisms through which firms design, exchange and distribute a wide variety of products and services (e.g. Daft and Lewin, 1993). Many interorganizational relationships, however, have proven challenging to design and manage, as many of them have failed to live up to the expectations of the parties involved. Problems that have limited the effectiveness of alliances include misunderstandings of roles and responsibilities, opportunistic behaviour and changing market and technological conditions. One factor that plays a key role in the success of alliances and other interorganizational arrangements is the contract used to govern the interaction (e.g. Mayer and Argyres, 2004; Reuer and Ariño, 2002; Ryall and Sampson, 2005).

Too often contracts are viewed as merely legal documents that serve only to ensure the enforcement of an agreement through the threat of litigation (or arbitration). Contracts are much more than just tools to protect each party and ensure enforcement of an exchange (Macaulay, 1963; MacNeil, 1974, 1978); they serve as the blueprint for an alliance – i.e. they provide the over-riding structure and framework for managing the alliance. The prevailing view of contracts as a tool for enforcement has led away from the study of how contracts can be used in a more positive and constructive way to help develop a long, productive relationship – without sacrificing the legal protections that contracts provide. Contracts may help alliance partners develop close, trusting relationships by clearly defining roles and responsibilities and aligning the expectations of the exchange partners, which can help avoid conflicts during the execution of the interorganizational exchange (Mayer and Argyres, 2004).

This chapter will explore the factors that influence the use of more detailed contracts in interorganizational exchanges. I describe how contracts can be used to support interorganizational exchanges by applying transaction cost economics (Williamson, 1975, 1985), agency theory (Holmstrom, 1979;

Holmstrom and Milgrom, 1991) and the resource-based view of the firm (Peteraf, 1993; Wernerfelt, 1984, 1995) to issues of contract design. While the information technology (IT) service contracts that will be discussed shortly are not traditional alliances, they are very similar in function, but smaller in scope. I will discuss the findings from my empirical analysis and qualitative insights from discussions with managers. This chapter is fundamentally designed to help address the role of contracts in governing interorganizational relationships and to show that more detailed contracts can help facilitate relationship development.

Clearly specify roles and responsibilities

What scares many people about alliance contracts is the extensive involvement of lawyers in the process. The roles and responsibilities of each party, however, are often negotiated by managers and engineers, who know the specifics of the business processes and technology, rather than lawyers, who are experts on the law and protecting the firm's interests (Argyres et al., 2005). Thus the detailed involvement that can occur when firms take the time to carefully define their roles is most likely to be product related when it involves managers and engineers. The lawyers can deal with the parts of the contract that are more sensitive to legal interpretation – decision rights, risk, liability, etc. (Bamford et al., 2003).

Some of the biggest problems with alliances and other interorganizational exchanges involve Firm A doing something that Firm B didn't expect. Firm B must now decide whether this was a misunderstanding or if Firm A is intentionally deviating from the agreement. If not handled correctly, this can lead to unwillingness on the part of Firm B to fully participate in the alliance and dramatically reduce the odds of the alliance achieving the goals the two firms set when they entered it. While a detailed contract is not the answer to everything, there is often much to be gained from spending more time describing the tasks (the roles and responsibilities of each party) so that the interaction between the firms can flow as smoothly as possible – and most alliances involve close interaction between the firms.

While there are certainly problems with using overly detailed contracts (e.g. long and possibly contentious negotiations, working inflexibly to the letter of the agreement), a properly designed contract can facilitate productive interaction and help an alliance function more effectively. One factor in determining whether contracts will have an enabling or disruptive impact on the relationship between alliance partners is the complexity of the task the parties are to complete. For simple exchanges of standardized goods, the roles and expectations of each party are well understood. MacNeil (1974: 738) describes simple market contracting as 'sharp in by clear agreement; sharp out by clear performance'. The contract is primarily a legal confirmation that a customer has placed an order and a supplier has agreed to fulfil it. For more complex, interdependent exchanges such as alliances, the roles of each party are more ambiguous and disagreements can develop over who was supposed to do what.

In alliances, a contract can help by clearly defining the roles and responsibilities of each party and ensuring they have the same set of expectations – while still serving to protect the interests of each party (Mayer and Argyres, 2004). The key point to realize is that alliance contracts can simultaneously protect each firm while also creating a framework that maximizes the chances for a productive relationship to develop.

One key step in clarifying expectations is determining the amount of detail that needs to go into the description of the tasks to be completed in the contract. Sometimes tasks are sketched out in high-level terms with the intent that they will become clearer as the relationship evolves. In other cases, the parties make much greater effort to spell out the tasks to be performed by each party so as to avoid problems of misunderstanding and to protect themselves by minimizing the possibility of the alliance partner acting opportunistically.

There is an inherent trade-off in determining the level of task description that should go into an alliance contract. There is no universally appropriate level of detail for all alliances; the correct amount of detail depends on the circumstances of each alliance. The intent of this chapter is to explore theory-driven factors that influence when more or less detail would be preferred by drawing on two sets of factors. The first set of factors involves the prior relationship between the potential alliance partners, while the second set examines the characteristics of the tasks involved in the alliance.

The prior relationship

There is a lot of debate about how prior relationships will affect contract design. Sociologists and organization theorists have long argued, however, that it is not enough to look at transactions in isolation as business exchanges are strongly influenced by relationships and social context (e.g. Granovetter, 1985; Gulati, 1995, Uzzi, 1996). Economists and transaction cost researchers, while placing a different degree of emphasis on context, have more recently espoused similar arguments (e.g. Williamson, 1991; Baker et al., 1994; Argyres and Liebeskind, 1999). While consensus is growing as to the importance of context, debate continues regarding both the causal mechanisms and the subsequent implications of the context–contract link. For example, within the literature, two conflicting logics have been offered to explain the influence of prior relationships on contract design.

The first holds that the existence of a prior relationship will decrease reliance on contracts. The underlying reasoning is that as relationships evolve and trust develops, relational governance (relying on norms and values to manage the exchange) becomes viable. Since relational governance is argued to provide the same safeguarding benefits as contracts without many of the disadvantages (e.g. antagonistic enforcement, high costs of designing the contracts), parties will tend to substitute relational governance for formal contracts (Ring and Van de Ven, 1994; Dyer and Singh, 1998).

The alternative logic proposes that prior interaction produces learning/experience benefits that help the parties craft more effective contracts (Mayer and Argyres, 2004). By working together, the transacting parties gain valuable knowledge about the partner's capabilities and needs, and may lead to the development of a common language to define process, or the resolution of key uncertainties (e.g. technology direction, probable industry standards, internal priorities) (Zollo et al., 2002). Moving forward, such accumulated knowledge may enable the parties to codify roles and responsibilities more precisely in ways that help them avoid past mistakes. Given the potential for more efficient design as well as the ongoing 'roadmap' value of contracts, contracts may be expanded rather than phased out as a relationship develops (Poppo and Zenger, 2002).

In the context of strategic alliance contracts, the latter logic that suggests a prior relationship may lead to more detailed task descriptions seems more appropriate. Alliance contracts are not going to disappear. Given the complexity of most alliances, contracts are very important in helping firms align expectations and firms should learn to become better at contracting with specific alliance partners as they do more deals together. While the time to reach agreement should decrease as firms do repeated alliances together, it is also likely that the amount of detail used to describe the tasks may increase (assuming the alliances are in related areas and what is learned in one alliance can be applied – with some modification – to the next alliance).

Attributes of the transaction

There are several attributes of the transaction that will play a role in the level of detail used to describe each party's tasks, including the ability to measure quality and the degree to which the alliance requires interdependent work. In addition, one other attribute of the contract, the payment terms, will also play a key role in the need for task description in the contract.

Measurement costs

Measurement costs (i.e. difficulty in measuring output) create a moral hazard by generating noise in the relationship between effort and outcome (Alchian and Demsetz, 1972; Eisenhardt, 1985; Holmstrom, 1979). Projects vary in the cost of determining the quality of the work that was done after the project has been completed (Jones, 1987). Observation or a simple diagnostic test can easily assess the quality of some projects, while others involve output that is much more difficult to examine and thus its quality is much more costly and difficult to verify. For example, assessing the quality of upgrading a network;

designing a complex, integrated software application; or designing networks or applications to accommodate future expansion is difficult.

If the output of the task of either alliance partner is difficult to measure, the parties will need to determine how to ensure the job is done correctly. Quality issues are important because firms have an incentive to maintain their reputation in order to enhance their competitive position (Kreps, 1990; Rao and Ruekert, 1994; Shapiro, 1985). At first glance, it might seem that measurement costs would lead firms to craft more detailed task descriptions in alliance contracts, but this is actually not the case. Firms are unlikely to spend excessive amounts of time specifying detailed tasks when it is very difficult to see if they have been done correctly. It is much more likely that firms would turn to different parts of the contract to deal with situations where measurement of quality is difficult. For example, firms might use detailed monitoring clauses that give them the right to monitor the progress of the task as it unfolds and rely on one or more employees to ensure the alliance partner is making the appropriate investments in quality (Mayer et al., 2004).

The bottom line is that putting in additional task description is costly and firms will only do it when there is a clear benefit (Mayer, 2006). More clearly specified tasks help the firms determine what is to be done and help build trust by allowing them to show that they honour their agreements. The point of more detail is both to align expectations and to avoid opportunism. When quality is hard to measure, it fails to serve the latter function and the firms will turn to other mechanisms to ensure high quality.

Interdependence

While interdependence influences the formation of ties between firms (Gulati, 1995; Pfeffer and Nowak, 1976), it also influences contract design. Interdependencies among tasks within an alliance create challenges because each step must happen in a precise pattern so that resources are not idly waiting for a critical input. Interdependence, as used here, does not capture situations in which each firm must do its part in order for the final product to function properly. By interdependence I am referring to a situation of bilateral dependence in which each firm must wait for the other to complete one or more tasks before they can begin one or more of their tasks. Such a condition is consistent with what Thompson (1967) called reciprocal inter-dependence and with Gulati and Singh (1998: 785), who state that 'the primary concerns from interdependence are the administrative challenges of coordinating tasks between partners'.

This problem of bilateral dependence between the alliance partners is one that can be addressed by additional contract detail. When the costs of delay are high, firms will take steps to keep the project on track. A major cause of delay is misunderstandings that cause one firm to produce something that is not quite what the other firm needed, so it must be revised before the other firm can begin their next steps. Any delay can be costly, but when a delay causes resources to be idle, the costs can escalate quickly. Crafting more detailed task descriptions helps firms deal with interdependence by helping to align expectations (i.e. to ensure each party understands exactly what is expected of them) and minimize any incentive to shirk by clearly specifying what is required. In the absence of interdependence, delays may be less of a problem and thus efforts to add more detailed task descriptions may be less important.

Payment terms

The payment terms of the contract are managed carefully to align expectations and create strong incentives (e.g. Allen and Lueck, 1992, 1993; Corts and Singh, 2004; Kalnis and Mayer, 2004; Lafontaine, 1992). The payment structure is a critical part of the contract for any interorganizational exchange, whether it is a multi-million dollar alliance or a smaller interorganizational exchange. Two distinct payment terms can be identified that are often included in interorganizational contracts: a fixed fee or payment based on time and expenses incurred. A standard fixed fee contract calls for a firm to complete a specific task in exchange for a predetermined total price. The other archetype is a contract that does not specify a total amount due beforehand, but instead bases payment on the time and expenses incurred by the supplier – typically by specifying an hourly wage (plus expenses).

The payment terms are likely to have a major impact on the level of detail in the task descriptions. In order to quote a fixed fee, firms need to know exactly what is required so they can determine how much it will cost to make (Eswaran and Kotwal, 1985; Kalnins and Mayer, 2004). As they will be hurt by any cost overruns, they will want to ensure that the requirements are tightly nailed down up front by defining the task very clearly. A contract specifying payment based on one party's costs is very different (Banerjee and Duflo, 2000). Now the task can be left much more ambiguous because the costs of any additional effort can be easily absorbed into the alliance by charging the other party for the additional hours of work required. While there are many variations on these two payment mechanisms, they create very different incentives for the parties to include detailed task descriptions.

A study of contracting for information technology services

These ideas were supported in a study I conducted in the information technology (IT) services industry. One large Silicon Valley IT firm granted me access to their contracts with customers who had procured their IT service during the late 1980s and 1990s. Most of these exchanges were smaller than the typical strategic alliance, but they inform the use of contracts to govern complex exchange in an environment with a lot of change and uncertainty – very much like alliance contracts.

I found that the effect of a prior relationship on the level of task description in the current contract depended on how the prior relationship was measured. If I just used a count of prior ties, then I found no significant relationship between prior ties and task detail. The problem with this measure is that it fails to account for the fact that not all prior ties are equal and that the incremental value of successive ties is likely to decline over time. The core of the issue is how relationships develop. First, more significant interactions should contribute more to a relationship than smaller, less intense interactions. Ten jobs lasting only one day each might lead to some relationship development, but one job lasting two years is likely to require much more interaction and thus lead to the development of a much deeper relationship. Second, if two firms interact once and it goes well, that makes a sizeable difference in their decision to work together again – they have gained valuable information and experience they didn't have before. But after many interactions, however, the marginal value of another interaction on their relationship is likely to be much smaller – they already know each other quite well. Thus a functional form should be used that decreases the weight attached to subsequent interactions to reflect the fact that learning to work together and trust each other occurs more in the early stages of a relationship (i.e. the marginal value of successive interactions gets smaller). To incorporate information on the size of the prior relationship and the declining marginal value of interaction, I use the log of the size of prior projects (measured in dollars or days of interaction – the results are very similar). When I use these measures, then a greater prior interaction (i.e. more of a relationship between the firms) leads to more detailed task descriptions in the current contract. The firms involved highlighted the learning that had taken place and the fact that they knew better what to expect when describing the evolution of the contracts.

The results were more directly supportive of the role of measurement costs, interdependence and payment terms. When quality was difficult to measure, the contracts contained less detailed task descriptions. They saw little point in spending more time on these details in favour of closer monitoring and other mechanisms designed to ensure the supplier worked hard to create a quality product.

When the project required interdependence between the two parties, the task descriptions in the contract were much more detailed. Instances of tight interdependence were taken very seriously by the firms and they went to great lengths to ensure that they communicated what they needed and what they were going to provide. These negotiations sometimes took a bit longer, but they ended up with contracts that clearly spelled out the responsibilities of each party. It was particularly important in terms of interdependence that the main task description negotiators from the supplier and virtually all the customers were managers or engineers rather than lawyers. When managers negotiated with other managers, they felt a freedom to deal with the issues that needed to be addressed. When managers dealt with lawyers, they were more reluctant to bring up issues in formal contract negotiations because they did not want the lawyers to require excessive protections that would have hindered the working relationship of the managers and engineers from the two firms.

Finally, the results also showed that contracts that required a fixed fee contained significantly more task description than those that specified an hourly or daily wage. The firms intentionally used more open-ended hourly wage contracts when they did not want to go to the trouble of specifying all the details of the project – they wanted to remain flexible. Flexibility does have its limits, however. One manager complained to me that hourly wage contracts were a real problem for him because they were lowering his margins. He indicated that the customers were very effective at using the leverage of taking their business to competitors if the supplier did not provide them with a very low hourly wage in the contract. He believed that he had a better chance to increase margins with a fixed fee contract because the customers did not really know how much the job cost and he could take advantage of the fact that his engineers were some of the best in the industry and could typically complete jobs in fewer hours than most of the firm's competitors.

These results are one part of a broader view of how contracts can be used to support exchange. I have now written several papers on this topic involving a variety of contractual clauses, including task description (Argyres et al., 2005; Mayer, 2006), the extent of contingency planning (i.e. planning for things that might occur during the alliance) (Mayer and Bercovitz, 2005, 2006), early termination provisions (Mayer, 2005), extendability clauses (Mayer and Weber, 2005), and contract type (i.e. the payment structure) (Kalnins and Mayer, 2004). Several themes have emerged from this body of research.

First, contracts clearly matter for business in ways that are not limited to legal protections. Firms use contracts strategically to not only protect their interests, but to proactively manage exchanges and build relationships. A poorly specified contract that masks underlying misaligned expectations can destroy a relationship even if both parties are acting in good faith by creating the perception of opportunistic behaviour. While contracts can certainly be over-specified, insufficient attention has been paid to the positive role that contracts can play in managing interorganizational exchange. Second, not all contracts play such a product purpose. There is an interesting conflict in complex transactions. These transactions are the ones with the most uncertainty and thus the greatest likelihood of misaligned expectations, but these are also exchanges where it is difficult to specify everything in advance. Knowing what the key issues are and dealing with them and then allowing the lesser issues to flow from the foundational decisions seems to be a successful way of balancing these conflicting issues that arise in complex exchanges.

Third, exchanges of any size and complexity are affected by the prior relationship between the parties. While the attributes of the transaction (e.g. asset specificity, measurement cost, interdependence, appropriability) clearly matter, we also need to account for important rigidities (Mayer and Bercovitz, 2006), learning (Mayer and Argyres, 2004) and potentially trust that arise from prior interaction. It is not just the social context that matters, but what the parties have learned about each other's tendencies, ways of doing business and values that are important drivers of contract structure and relationship management.

Fourth, while it is important to understand individual contract terms, it is also necessary to examine how they fit together to become a coherent contract (Argyres et al., 2005). Contract terms fit together and affect one another, but we don't know enough about the nature of these relationships among terms. While notions of overall contract complexity can be difficult to create and even more difficult to link to specific contractual hazards, more work is needed on how contract terms work together to create effective contracts.

Conclusion

Contracts are important documents that have a significant bearing on the performances of alliances and other interorganizational relationships. One important role of a contract is to get the parties to share enough information so that they can understand each other's needs and ensure that their interests are protected. Some people argue that people do not need to codify this understanding in a contract. There are three reasons why important expectations, such as task description, should be in the contract. First, if there is turnover on the alliance management team, the contract serves as a clear indicator of what is expected from each firm without having to understand a bunch of 'loosely understood' deals between individuals from each firm. Second, the contract serves as a communication vehicle that will be read by most people involved in the alliance from both firms; including detailed task description ensures that higher level management and those who will be involved in executing the alliance all have a common understanding of what each firm will do. Third, formal contracts provide for more effective third-party enforcement.

The bottom line is that more detailed task descriptions are most valuable when the parties to the contract view the document as a framework to facilitate their deal – not a document that will be used against them later. A contract is a legal document and some of them do wind up in litigation. The most effective firms, while prepared for litigation, plan their contracts in such a way that they provide a solid framework for the exchange – particularly in the specification of roles and responsibilities – while also involving the lawyers to ensure that the firm's interests are protected.

Circumstances will change over the course of most exchanges – particularly alliances; adaptation will be required due to changing technology, regulation or competitive conditions. Additional detail is valuable in the presence of a solid relationship between the two firms because the relationship helps the firms adapt. They know each other so they know the other firm's processes and culture enough to work together more smoothly to facilitate change. More detailed task descriptions should be paired with a degree of flexibility. It takes time to convince other firms that you want the additional detail for planning reasons and not for litigation reasons. A reputation for fair dealing and flexibility will help in negotiating good, detailed contracts in which the parties are willing to codify their roles and responsibilities in the contract because they believe that their partner will work with them if circumstances change. In addition, firms often include extensive contingency planning in many of these contracts to ensure that their responsibilities will change if certain external events occur.

Contracts impact performance. They align expectations, create incentives and protect the firm's interests. It is important to consider carefully the detail used to describe tasks in contracts and consider involving managers and engineers, who have the necessary knowledge, to negotiate these parts of the contract.

Note

1. Kyle J. Mayer, University of Southern California, Marshall School of Business, Management & Organization Department, Bridge Hall 306, Los Angeles, CA 90089-0808, E-mail: kmayer@marshall.usc.edu

References

Alchian, A. and Demsetz, H. (1972) 'Production, Information Costs, and Economic Organization', *American Economic Review*, 62: 777–95.

Allen, Douglas W. and Lueck, D. (1992) 'Contract Choice in Modern Agriculture: Cash Rent versus Cropshare', *Journal of Law and Economics*, 34: 397–426.

Allen, Douglas W. and Lueck, D. (1993) 'Transaction Costs and the Design of Crop-share Contract', *RAND Journal of Economics*, 24: 78–100.

Argyres, N. A., Bercovitz, J. and Mayer, K. J. (2006) 'Complementarity and Evolution of Contractual Provisions: an Empirical Study of IT Services Contracts', forthcoming in *Organization Science*.

Argyres, N. and Liebeskind, J. (1999) 'Contractual Commitments, Bargaining Power, and Governance Inseparability: Incorporating History into Transaction Cost Theory', *Academy of Management Review*, 24(1): 49–63.

Baker, G., Gibbons, R. and Murphy, K. J. (1994) 'Subjective Performance Measures in Optimal Incentive Contracts', *Quarterly Journal of Economics*, 109: 1125–56.

Bamford, J. D., Gomes-Casseres, B. and Robinson, M. S. (2003) *Mastering Alliance Strategy*, San Francisco, CA: John Wiley & Sons.

Banerjee, A. V. and Duflo, E. (2000) 'Reputation Effects and the Limits of Contracting: a Case Study of the Indian Software Industry', *Quarterly Journal of Economics*, 115: 989–1017.

Corts, K. S. and Singh, J. (2004) 'The Effect of Repeated Interaction on Contract Choice: Evidence from Offshore Drilling', *Journal of Law, Economics and Organization*, 20: 230–60.

Daft R. L. and Lewin, A. Y. (1993) 'Where are the Theories for the "New" Organizational Forms? An Editorial Essay', *Organization Science*, 4: i–vi.

Dyer, J. and Singh, H. (1998) 'The Relational View: Cooperative Strategy and Sources of Interorganizational Competitive Advantage', *Academy of Management Review*, 23: 660–79.

Eisenhardt, K. M. (1985) 'Control: Organizational and Economic Perspectives', *Management Science*, 31: 134–49.

Eswaran, M. and Kotwal, A. (1985) 'A Theory of Contractual Structure in Agriculture', *American Economic Review*, 75: 352–67.

Granovetter, M. (1985) 'Economic Action and Social Structure: the Problem of Embeddedness', *American Journal of Sociology*, 91: 481–510.

Gulati, R. (1995) 'Social Structure and Alliance Formation Patterns: a Longitudinal Analysis', *Administrative Science Quarterly*, 40: 619–52.

Gulati, R. and Singh, H. (1998) 'The Architecture of Cooperation: Managing Coordination Costs and Appropriation Concerns in Strategic Alliances', *Administrative Science Quarterly*, 43(4): 781–814.

Holmstrom, B. (1979) 'Moral Hazard and Observability', *Bell Journal of Economics*, 10 (Spring): 74–91.

Holmstrom, B. and Milgrom, P. (1991) 'Multi-task Principal-agent Analysis', *Journal of Law, Economics, and Organization*, 7: 24–52.

Jones, G. R. (1987) 'Organization–Client Transactions and Organizational Governance Structures', *Academy of Management Journal*, 30: 197–218.

Kalnins, A. and Mayer, K. J. (2004) 'Relationships and Hybrid Contracts: an Analysis of Contract Choice in Information Technology', *Journal of Law, Economics and Organization*, 20: 207–29.

Kreps, D. M. (1990) 'Corporate Culture and Economic Theory', in J. E. Alt and K. A. Shepsle (eds), *Perspectives on Positive Political Economy*, Cambridge: Cambridge University Press, 90–143.

Lafontaine, F. (1992) 'Agency Theory and Franchising: Some Empirical Results', *RAND Journal of Economics*, 23: 263–83.

Macaulay, S. (1963) 'Non-Contractual Relations in Business', *American Sociological Review*, 28: 55–70.

MacNeil, I. R. (1974) 'The Many Futures of Contracts', *Southern California Law Review*, 47: 691–816.

MacNeil, I. R. (1978) 'Contracts: Adjustments of Long-Term Economic Relations under Classical, Neoclassical and Relational Contract Law', *Northwestern University Law Review*, 72: 854–906.

Mayer, K. J. (2005) 'The Role of Prior Relationships on Contract Design: an Analysis of Early Termination Provisions', Working Paper.

Mayer, K. J. (2006) 'Spillovers and Governance: an Analysis of Knowledge and Reputational Spillovers in Information Technology', *Academy of Management Journal*, 49: 69–84.

Mayer, K. J. and Argyres, N. (2004) 'Learning to Contract: Evidence from the Personal Computer Industry', *Organization Science*, 15: 394–410.

Mayer, K. J. and Bercovitz, J. (2005) 'Planning for the Future in Contract Design: the Extent of Contingency Planning in Information Technology Service Contracts', Working Paper.

Mayer, K. J. and Bercovitz, J. (2006) 'Inertia and Contract Design: the Extent of Contingency Planning in Information Technology Service Contracts', forthcoming in *Managerial & Decision Economics*.

Mayer, K. J., Nickerson, J. A. and Owan, H. (2004) 'Are Supply and Supplier Plant Inspections Complements or Substitutes? A Strategic and Operational Assessment of Inspection Practices in Biotechnology', *Management Science*, 50: 1064–81.

Mayer, K. J. and Weber, L. (2005) 'Designing Contracts that Help Develop Inter-Firm Relationships: the Use of Extendibility Provisions in Information Technology Contracts', Working Paper.

Peteraf, M. (1993) 'The Cornerstones of Competitive Advantage: a Resource-based View', *Strategic Management Journal*, 14: 179–91.

Pfeffer, J. and Nowak, P. (1976) 'Joint Ventures and Interorganizational Interdependence', *Administrative Science Quarterly*, 21: 398–418.

Poppo, L. and Zenger, T. R. (2002) 'Do Formal Contracts and Relational Governance Function as Substitutes or Complements?' *Strategic Management Journal*, 23(8): 707–25.

Rao, A. R. and Ruekert, R. W. (1994) 'Brand Alliances as Signals of Product Quality', *Sloan Management Review*, 36: 87–97.

Reuer, J. J. and Ariño, A. (2002) 'Contractual Renegotiations in Strategic Alliances', *Journal of Management*, 28: 47–68.

Ring, P. S. and Van de Ven, A. H. (1994) 'Developmental Processes of Cooperative Interorganizational Relationships', *Academy of Management Review*, 19(1): 90–118.

Ryall, M. and Sampson, R. (2005) 'Repeated Interactions and Contract Structure: Evidence from Technology Development Contracts', Working Paper.

Shapiro, C. (1985) 'Consumer Information, Product Quality, and Seller Reputation', *Bell Journal of Economics*, 13: 20–35.

Thompson, J. D. (1967) *Organizations in Action: Social Science Bases of Administrative Theory*, New York, McGraw-Hill.

Uzzi, B. (1996) 'The Sources and Consequences of Embeddedness for the Economic Performance of Organizations', *American Sociological Review*, 61: 674–98.

Wernerfelt, B. (1984) 'A Resource-based View of the Firm', *Strategic Management Journal*, 5: 171–80.

Wernerfelt, B. (1995) 'The Resource-based View of the Firm: Ten Years After', *Strategic Management Journal*, 16(3): 171–4.

Williamson, O. E. (1975) *Markets and Hierarchies: Analysis and Antitrust Implications*, New York: Free Press.

Williamson, O. E. (1985) *The Economic Institutions of Capitalism*, New York: Free Press.

Williamson, O. E. (1991) 'Comparative Economic Organization: the Analysis of Discrete Structural Alternatives', *Administrative Science Quarterly*, 36: 269–96.

Zollo, M., Reuer, J. and Singh, H. (2002) 'Interorganizational Routines and Performance in Strategic Alliances', *Organization Science*, 13: 701–13.

18
The Value of Patent Protection for Technology Development Alliances

Simon Wakeman[*1]

Introduction

An alliance with an established product firm is often the most efficient means by which a start-up firm can access the complementary capabilities necessary to commercialize a technological innovation (Teece, 1986; Gans and Stern, 2003). However, revealing its technology to an alliance partner enables the partner to replicate the innovation and potentially to take advantage of that innovation outside the alliance. Moreover, the amorphous nature of knowledge makes it difficult to write a 'complete' contract that delineates entirely how the partner may use the technology (Williamson, 1991). Hence, entering into a technology development alliance exposes the start-up firm to the risk that its partner will expropriate the returns from the innovation.

A patent grants the owner a legally enforceable property right over an invention, which enables it to prevent others from using the invention without its permission. In the contractual setting, the property rules attached to a patent right provide the start-up firm with additional remedies if its partner uses the technological innovation beyond the terms explicitly allowed under the contract (Arora and Merges, 2004). Therefore, patent rights provide an additional mechanism that the start-up technology firm can use to protect against expropriation and thereby to capture the rents from its innovation.

This chapter investigates how the strength of a start-up firm's patent rights affects the timing, choice of partner, and structure of the alliance contract. The next section analyses the effects that stronger patent rights have in the context of technology development alliances. The third section discusses how stronger patent rights may affect timing, choice of partner, and structure of technology development alliances. The final section describes the empirical context and gives a brief summary of the findings.

The effects of stronger patent rights in technology development alliances

Patent rights have three distinct effects in the context of technology development alliances:

1. Increasing the returns to technology development;
2. Strengthening the technology firm's bargaining power; and
3. Mitigating the risk of expropriation within the alliance relationship.

Increasing the returns to technology development

A patent gives the owner a right to prevent rivals from using the innovation either to develop a competing product or to launch a competing product on the market. Under the patent law, a 'utility' patent can apply to either a method or a composition. If the patent applies to a method for developing or manufacturing a product, it enables the patent holder to prevent a rival from using that technology to develop a competing product. Alternatively, if the patent applies to a composition then it enables the holder to stop rivals from copying a product described by the patent once it is launched on the final product market.

In an industry where a firm must innovate in order to maintain its revenue stream, a patent creates a hurdle that rivals must overcome. Rivals may overcome this hurdle either by inventing around the patent or by obtaining a licence from the patent holder (which is granted at the holder's discretion). However, inventing around a patent requires the rival to devote additional resources to another (often more difficult) research project and increases its expected time to market (O'Donoghue et al., 1998), while obtaining a licence increases the rival's costs directly. Because developing a product has an opportunity cost (which may be measured in terms of other projects the firm might pursue), raising a rival's expected cost, deflating its expected returns, and increasing its time to market increase the likelihood that the rival will abandon its project. Since the returns to an innovation are usually inversely related to the number of competitors, forcing a rival to abandon its project (or merely delaying its arrival on the final product market) increases the technology firm's expected returns from developing its innovation.

Strengthening the technology firm's bargaining power

Since the final stages of a contract negotiation are essentially a compromise between the two parties, the negotiation process can be characterized as a bargaining game. The economic theory of bargaining (Nash, 1950) conjectures that in a non-cooperative bargaining game the parties divide the surplus from cooperation, which is based on each party's outside options. Since stronger patent rights increase the expected returns from getting a product to market, they increase the potential returns to developing the technology outside of the alliance. If the technology firm has higher expected returns, it increases the likelihood that another firm will be willing to enter into an alliance to develop the technology or, alternatively, that the technology firm will be able to obtain alternative sources of funding such as venture capital in order to develop the technology itself (Merges, 1999). Hence, stronger patent rights increase the technology firm's outside options. Meanwhile, to the extent that the potential partner is also a potential rival, stronger patent rights held by the technology firm decrease the partner's expected returns from developing a rival product in the same field. Therefore, stronger patent rights simultaneously increase the technology firm's outside options and decrease those of the potential partner.

Mitigating the risk of expropriation within the alliance relationship

The expected return from joint technology development is highly contingent on the parties' actions during (and after) the alliance relationship, but the amorphous nature of knowledge makes it difficult to write a 'complete' contract that protects the start-up firm's technology entirely (Arrow, 1962). The difficulty of describing what is the knowledge that the technology firm brought to the alliance and distinguishing it from the knowledge that the partners produced during the alliance, as well as the weakness of contractual remedies (discussed below), mean contractual rights are a weak form of protection against expropriation. This exposes the start-up firm to the risk that if an unforeseen contingency arises the partner will be able to take advantage of the contract's incompleteness to expropriate the technology (Williamson, 1991).

Potentially the parties could prevent expropriation though hierarchical governance mechanisms (Williamson, 1991). By taking control of its partner (e.g. through an equity stake), the firm can prevent the partner from using the technology outside the alliance or, alternatively, can claim a share of the returns from its misappropriated technology as a return on equity. Oxley (1997) showed that strategic alliance partners choose more hierarchical alliances when appropriability hazards are higher. However, in alliances between a small technology firm and an established product firm, the relative firm sizes make it infeasible for the technology firm to obtain a sufficient ownership stake in its partner to exercise any control or capture the incremental returns the partner gains from using the technology outside the alliance.

Teece (1986) identified a range of mechanisms or 'appropriability regimes' – including patents, secrecy, bundling with complementary assets, and the tacit nature of the knowledge itself – that enable firms to mitigate the risk of expropriation in the commercialization of technology. In general, the stronger the appropriability regime, the better able the firm is to prevent others from expropriating its technology. However, appropriability regimes operate through different mechanisms. A regime's effectiveness in a specific case depends on the nature of the intellectual property being protected and the circumstances that generate the risk of expropriation.

When the knowledge needed to replicate the technology is codified then patent rights are more effective than either bundling with complementary assets or secrecy in mitigating the risk of expropriation. Patent rights can be enforced against any user who does not have explicit permission to use the technology. By contrast, bundling the technology with complementary assets only prevents those who do not have access to the necessary complementary assets, and because the reason for entering the partnership is usually to obtain access to the complementary assets, this mechanism may not be very effective in protecting against expropriation by a technology development partner. Secondly, patent rights apply to the technology even if the technology becomes common knowledge, while secrecy is only effective as long as the holder has made efforts to restrict dissemination of the knowledge, which does not apply when the technology firm has intentionally revealed the technology to its partner. Furthermore, it is inherently difficult to maintain a partnership based on secrecy because the partner is unable to monitor the technology firm's effort; it may become suspicious that the technology firm is not performing its obligations and the alliance may break down.

In principle, the technology firm could attempt to replicate the patent right by negotiating a contractual provision to prevent its partner from using the technology without permission. However, patent rights provide a more effective mechanism for mitigating expropriation in an alliance than any contractual arrangement could. Since patent rights cover the technological innovation itself, rather than the actions of the parties with respect to that innovation, they give the patent holder an enforceable right to stop – or 'injunct' – a partner from using the technology. By contrast, contract rights only give the injured party the right to claim damages for breach of a contractual term. Therefore, patent rights provide stronger and more flexible protection against expropriation than contractual rights and so the technology firm is likely to rely on patent rights to protect its technology when available.

The effect of stronger patent rights on alliance strategy

The effects of stronger patent rights set out in the previous section in turn impact strategic decisions that the technology firm makes in negotiating and entering into technology development alliances. In particular, stronger patent rights affect:

1. The timing of entering into an alliance;
2. The choice of an alliance partner; and
3. The structure of the alliance contract.

Timing of entering into an alliance

The timing of when to enter into technology development alliance is a critical factor in the profitability of technology commercialization. If the firm tries to enter into an alliance before the risks of the technology are known then typically it has to give up a large share of the returns from innovation to persuade its partner to sign the contract. But if it waits too long then it may run out of money to finance further development or slow the product development to the extent that it misses a market opportunity.

By mitigating the risk of expropriation by its alliance partner, stronger patent rights increase the incentive to enter into an alliance. This means stronger patent rights may induce the technology firm to enter into an alliance earlier. However, by increasing the expected value of the firm's technology and so the willingness of other investors to finance the technology development, stronger patent rights may delay the technology firm's need to enter into an alliance. Therefore stronger patent rights may either increase or decrease the probability of entering an alliance.

The choice of an alliance partner

Another important strategic decision the biotech firm makes is its choice of alliance partner. The ideal partner will have the capabilities that most closely complement the start-up firm's technology, without threatening to expropriate the technology for its own purposes. The level of complementarity – or 'fit' – between an alliance partner's capabilities and the start-up firm's technology is a function of the overlap between the firms' capabilities (Mowery et al., 1998). Other things being equal, a technology firm will obtain higher value from an alliance partner with higher technological overlap, and therefore is more likely to enter into an alliance with such a firm. However, technological overlap between potential partners also increases the risk of expropriation because the alliance partner can more easily absorb the firm's knowledge and apply it in other areas (Cohen and Levinthal, 1990). Because of the risk of expropriation, a technology firm may avoid entering into an alliance with a partner that has high technological overlap, or build in contractual safeguards against expropriation that make the alliance less efficient (relative to an alliance with a partner that has less technological overlap).

Patent rights provide a mechanism to mitigate the risk of expropriation by firms with high technological overlap, and therefore facilitate a start-up firm entering into an alliance with its ideal partner. Hence, stronger patent protection means that firms are more likely to choose partners with high overlap in their technological capabilities.

The structure of the alliance contract

In negotiating an alliance, the start-up firm must make numerous strategic decisions about the alliance structure. The structure of the alliance contract is a combination of financial and non-financial terms. The financial terms include consideration paid to the start-up firm in exchange for its technology, including upfront (i.e. cash) payments, fee-for-service, milestone payments, royalties and equity investments. Meanwhile, the non-financial terms include terms which determine various aspects of the alliance management, such as control over the product development process (including further development, manufacturing and marketing), limitations on the scope of the research project, the ownership of intellectual property and 'know-how', and the governance of the alliance.

As discussed in the previous section, stronger patent protection will simultaneously improve the expected value of the product developed with the technology (i.e. the size of the pie) and the bargaining power of the technology firm vis-à-vis the alliance partner (i.e. the share of the pie). Therefore, stronger patent rights are likely to be correlated with better financial terms and a larger share of control rights over the allocated to the technology firm. Nevertheless, the parties may change the way some control rights are allocated depending on the risk of expropriation. If the technology firm is exposed to the risk that its partner will divert its technology to another project, the technology firm is likely to insist on developing its technology separately until it has built up its patent portfolio sufficiently or it has developed other means to protect itself from expropriation. However, if the technology firm has strong patent protection then it may be more willing to share its technology during the alliance, which increases the chance of positive spillovers. Arora and Merges (2004) show that stronger patent rights improve the chances that a technology firm will enter a technology development alliance as an independent firm rather than integrating with a partner.

Hence, stronger patent rights mean that the parties are more likely to construct a more collaborative structure, including a technology transfer to the alliance partner.

Empirical context and summary of findings

In order to examine the predictions made in the previous section, I compiled a data set of alliance contracts from the biotechnology industry. Alliances are the predominant mode for commercializing innovations within this industry (Pisano et al., 1988); 80 per cent of the 100 or so pharmaceuticals commercialized by biotech firms over the past 25 years were partnered with a pharmaceutical firm at some stage in their development (Edwards, 2005). Meanwhile, patent rights are one of the primary forms – if not *the* primary form – of intellectual property protection in this industry (Cohen et al., 2000). Hence, if there is a systematic relationship between the strength of a technology firm's patent protection and the structure of a technology development alliance, then it is likely to be evident in this industry.

The data set includes information on the relevant patent rights that the technology firm brings to the alliance, the financial and non-financial terms of those contracts, and other characteristics of the technology firm and partners that may affect the structure of the contract. The primary data source is the Recombinant Capital ('Recap')'s Alliances database, which contains high-level summaries of almost 20 000 biotech alliances signed since 1973. I limited my sample of biotech-to-pharmaceutical-firm alliances for which Recap has obtained the full, unredacted version of the contract and for which the contract contains an appendix that lists all the relevant patent rights. This restricts my sample for analysis to approximately 170 alliances. Using the US Patent & Trademark Office (PTO)'s Public Patent Application Information Retrieval (PAIR) database, I traced the patent applications listed on the contract through to those patents that eventually issued, then used the NBER patent file (Hall et al., 2001) to extract the detailed information on the patents.

I performed statistical analyses on this data set to test the effect of patent rights on the technology firm's bargaining power in alliance negotiations. In order to distinguish the effect of stronger patent rights on the technology firm's bargaining power from their effect on the expected value of the alliance product, I constructed two different dependent variables that are related to the relative bargaining power but not to the expected value of the alliance product. The first dependent variable is the ratio of the upfront payments relative to the milestone payments that the technology firm receives. I argue that this variable reflects the relative bargaining power of the technology firm because of the different incentives that these two payment types give the technology firm and the alliance partner. The upfront payment gives the technology firm an incentive to sign the deal but does not provide any incentives that will affect its performance during the alliance. Therefore, the alliance partner does not benefit from a larger upfront payment and the technology firm's ability to negotiate such a payment will depend entirely on its bargaining power in negotiations.

By contrast, milestone (and royalty) payments give the technology firm incentives to exert additional effort during the alliance, and so the alliance partner receives compensating benefit that may make it willing to grant milestone payments regardless of the technology firm's bargaining power in negotiations. Hence, the impact of patent rights on bargaining power should be reflected in the ratio of upfront payments to milestone payments, and stronger patent rights will lead to a higher ratio of upfront payments to milestone payments (all other things being equal).

In addition, I construct a second dependent variable that reflects the allocation of control rights in the alliance. Following Lerner and Merges (1998), this variable counts how many of 25 specific control rights that commonly occur in alliances and are considered important to both parties in the contract are allocated to the alliance partner. The control rights relate to management of the product development process, the scope of the research project, the ownership of intellectual property and 'know-how', and the governance of the alliance. In theory, the expected value of the alliance product depends on efficiently allocating control rights to the firm whose marginal effort has the greater impact on the outcome of development (Grossman and Hart, 1986). However, in practice, a firm will attempt to maximize its share of the alliance returns by negotiating control rights that enable the firm it to direct the alliance in its favour (Lerner and

Merges, 1998). Therefore, the impact of patent rights on bargaining power should be reflected in the number of control rights that the technology firm obtains under the alliance contract.

The primary independent variable in my analysis is the 'strength' of the technology firm's patent portfolio. The strength of patent rights reflects the ability to prevent rivals from using the technology to develop a product or copy the final product. However, the strength of patent rights is not readily observable and is usually not revealed until the patent rights are tested in court. Moreover, despite the importance of patent strength for the returns that an inventor will receive for its innovation, the dimensions of the concept have not been explored in the academic literature on patents. Instead, using the detailed data available on issued patents and drawing clues from the prior literature (Lanjouw and Schankerman, 2004), I proxy for the strength of patent rights using several variables (including number of claims, patent classes, and forward citations) that are correlated with patent strength. I also control for the financial position of the technology firm at the time the alliance was signed, using information on the valuation of the technology firm obtained from Compustat (for publicly listed firms) and Recap's financing database (for privately held firms), the stage of technology development, and the nature of the technology.

The empirical tests provide some support for the argument that stronger patent protection over its technology increases the technology firm's bargaining power. On their own, the issued patents are weakly correlated with the ratio of upfront to milestone payments, but once the stage of development, financial position, and dummies for the type of technology are included, the variables that capture the dimensions of the issued patents all have the predicted sign (positive) and are highly significant. Moreover, consistent with predictions, the technology firm's issued patents have a significant negative effect on the number of control rights allocated to the alliance partner,[2] although the effects of patent applications are not significant. This result persists when the stage of development, financial position of technology firm, and dummies for the technology and year are included in the regression.

Future work will test how stronger patent right affects the other strategic decisions made in negotiating and entering into technology development alliances, including the timing, choice of partner, and collaborative structure of the alliance relationship. Exploratory interviews with biotech executives and transactional lawyers reveal that when patent protection is weak, the biotech firm attempts to negotiate separate operations (e.g. no technology transfer, research in separate facilities, biotech does manufacturing), outright control of alliance IP, or broad claims on revenues.

Notes

* I wish to thank Hank Chesbrough, Bronwyn Hall, Ben Hermalin, Jenny Lanjouw, Robert Merges, David Mowery, David Teece and participants in the Economics of

Innovation and the Business & Public Policy seminars at the Haas School of Business for their comments on earlier drafts of this paper. I would also like to thank Mark Edwards, Storn White and Mike McCully at Recombinant Capital for generously giving me access to their data, and John Wolpert of the Australian Innovation Exchange for facilitating a series of interviews related to this research. I gratefully acknowledge the support of the Institute for Innovation, Management, & Organization at the Haas School of Business for financial support of my research. All errors are my own.

1. Simon Wakeman, Haas School of Business, University of California, Berkeley, CA 94720-1900, USA, E-mail: wakeman@haas.berkeley.edu
2. The predicted sign is negative because the dependent variable is characterized in terms of alliance partner, while the independent variables are in terms of the patent rights assigned or licensed to the technology firm.

References

Arora, A. and Merges, R. P. (2004) 'Specialized Supply Firms, Property Rights and Firm Boundaries', *Industrial & Corporate Change*, 13(3): 451–75.

Arrow, K. (1962) 'Economic Welfare and the Allocation of Resources for Invention', in R. R. Nelson (ed.), *The Rate and Direction of Inventive Activity*, Princeton, NJ: Princeton University Press.

Cohen, W. and Levinthal, D. (1990) 'Absorptive Capacity: a New Perspective on Learning and Innovation', *Administrative Science Quarterly*, 35(1): 128–52.

Cohen, W. M., Nelson, R. R. and Walsh, J. P. (2000) *Protecting their Intellectual Assets: Appropriability Conditions and Why US Manufacturing Firms Patent (or Not)*, National Bureau of Economic Research, Inc.

Edwards, M. (2005) 'Partnerships and Licensing Between Pharma & Biotech Firms', paper presented at the Health Technology Finance & Strategy class, Haas School of Business, University of California, Berkeley.

Gans, J. S. and Stern, S. (2003) 'The Product Market and the Market for "Ideas": Commercialization Strategies for Technology Entrepreneurs', *Research Policy*, 32(2): 333–50.

Grossman, S. and Hart, O. (1986) 'The Costs and Benefits of Ownership: a Theory of Vertical and Lateral Integration', *Journal of Political Economy*, 94(4): 691–719.

Hall, B. H., Jaffe, A. B. and Trajtenberg, M. (2001) 'The NBER Patent Citation Data File: Lessons, Insights and Methodological Tools', *NBER Working Paper*.

Lanjouw, J. O. and Schankerman, M. (2004) 'Patent Quality and Research Productivity: Measuring Innovation with Multiple Indicators', *Economic Journal*, 114(495): 441–65.

Lerner, J. and Merges, R. P. (1998) 'The Control of Technology Alliances: an Empirical Analysis of the Biotechnology Industry', *Journal of Industrial Economics*, 46(2): 125–56.

Merges, R. P. (1999) *Intellectual Property Rights, Input Markets, and the Value of Intangible Assets*, Boalt School of Law, University of California, Berkeley.

Mowery, D. C., Oxley, J. E. and Silverman, B. S. (1998) 'Technological Overlap and Interfirm Cooperation: Implications for the Resource-based View of the Firm', *Research Policy*, 27(5): 507–23.

Nash, J. (1950) 'The Bargaining Problem', *Econometrica*, 18(2): 155–62.

O'Donoghue, T., Scotchmer, S. and Thisse, J.-F. (1998) 'Patent Breadth, Patent Life, and the Pace of Technological Progress', *Journal of Economics Management Strategy*, 7(1): 1–32.

Oxley, J. E. (1997) 'Appropriability Hazards and Governance in Strategic Alliances: a Transaction Cost Approach', *Journal of Law, Economics and Organization*, 13(2): 387–409.

Pisano, G., Shan, W. and Teece, D. (1988) 'Joint Ventures and Collaboration in the Biotechnology Industry', in D. Mowery (ed.), *International Collaborative Ventures in US Manufacturing*, Cambridge, MA: Ballinger Publishing Company.

Teece, D. J. (1986) 'Profiting from Technological Innovation', *Research Policy*, 15(6): 285–305.

Williamson, O. E. (1991) 'Comparative Economic Organization: the Analysis of Discrete Structural Alternatives', *Administrative Science Quarterly*, 36 (June): 269–96.

19
Do Prior Alliances Influence Alliance Contract Structure?

Micheal D. Ryall[1] and Rachelle C. Sampson[2]

Introduction

As the cost and risk of technological development grow, firms continue to look for alternatives to purely in-house R&D. R&D alliances represent one such alternative – a means by which firms can spread the risk and cost of new development and gain access to unique technologies. While such alliances are increasingly attractive to firms in technologically intensive industries, the attendant risks can be substantial. Firms entering into R&D alliances face considerable moral hazard problems, since partner behaviour is often unobservable and the costs of opportunism are potentially high. Firms anticipate such difficulties and often craft formal governance to address these issues.

Formal organizational structures, such as alliance contracts, serve to establish rights and obligations of partner firms and provide some documentation of the original agreement should the alliance go awry. The presumption is that the threat of legal enforcement will keep partners from behaving opportunistically.[3] Such formal devices are not the only means to protect against opportunism and create a cooperative environment, however.

Repeated interactions between firms have long been argued to lead to cooperative behaviour, even between competing firms.[4] Such prior interactions can lead to the development of trust between firms or may signal a firm's valuable reputation; in both cases cooperative behaviour becomes more attractive, since it serves to preserve either the relationship or the reputation.

Despite the growing literature on how firms select the organization form for their alliance activities (Pisano, 1989; Oxley, 1997; Sampson, 2004), we still know little about alliance contract structure and whether selection of this structure is systematic. Here, we examine technology alliance contracts, to explore if and how formal contract terms vary with prior alliances – either with a specific partner or generally. Extending the current literature on contracting to the context of alliances yields two competing predictions for the relationship between prior alliances and contract structure. Literature on relational governance suggests that prior relationships can substitute for costly, detailed contracts (for example, Macaulay, 1963; Larson, 1992). In contrast, recent empirical evidence suggests that formal contracts are in fact complementary to relational exchange; Poppo and Zenger (2002) find that as relationships between firms deepen, contracts become increasingly customized. Thus, a question arises: do prior relationships complement or substitute for formal governance?

In our analysis summarized below, we examine 52 technology alliance contracts in the telecommunications equipment manufacturing and microelectronics industries and discuss the empirical results from a test of the relationship between prior alliances and formal contract structure (Ryall and Sampson, 2004). Several interesting patterns emerge from this analysis. First, it appears that prior alliances generally (that is, with any firm) increase the extent to which a contract is well specified or more detailed. Prior alliances with the same partner appear to have a similar effect – contracts are more detailed when firms have allied with each other previously. However, concurrent alliances with the same partner have the opposite effect – contracts are less detailed under these circumstances, even when alliance duration and technology breadth are controlled for. One interpretation is that firms gain experience in drafting effective collaborative agreements with prior alliances, which allows these firms to specify rights, obligations and development processes at lower cost. In contrast, concurrent alliance relationships may operate as an informal means to deter non-cooperative behaviour, since such behaviour can affect the future prospects not only of the current alliance, but also of the concurrent alliance. Overall, these results suggest that prior relationships, via prior alliances, affect formal contract structure.

The remainder of this chapter is as follows. We first define the coordination and contracting problem in alliances in more detail and briefly review the organizational responses to these difficulties, according to prior literature. We also examine the relational contracting literature to understand the possible effect of prior alliances on contract structure. The contract sample, data sources, research context and results are then discussed in the following sections.

Coordination difficulties and solutions in technology alliances

Technology development across firm boundaries is difficult at best. The complexity and uncertainty surrounding collaborative R&D efforts create a fertile environment for partner opportunism. Firms often cannot directly observe their partner's efforts. Further, because of the idiosyncratic nature of R&D (see, for example, Holmstrom, 1989), it is frequently not possible to infer effort provided by observing outcomes. Partners may, for example, contribute fewer or lesser quality inputs to the alliance than origin-ally agreed. Further, since joint technological development often requires pooling or at least exposure to partner firm technologies, firms are naturally concerned about leakage of intellectual property outside the spirit of the alliance. Firms recognize these issues and often develop alliance governance mechanisms in response.

Researchers in organizational economics argue that the governance mech-anisms we observe reflect a rational attempt to induce either efficient ex ante investments (that is, property rights theory, as developed initially by Grossman and Hart, 1986) or to reduce ex post bargaining and hold-up threats (that is, transaction cost economics, Williamson, 1975). This current literature on the choice of alliance organizational form, while informative, has certain limitations. For example, current research in the transaction cost vein relies on discrete choice analysis, which assumes that average differ-ences exist between form choices and that the extent of variance within groups does not render the average differences meaningless. In other words, discrete choice analysis is problematic if there is very substantial overlap between groups such that it becomes difficult to argue that the groups are truly discrete choices. Property rights research, such as Lerner and Merges (1998), moves away from this discrete choice analysis to examine contract terms specifying control rights. However, given the fundamental assump-tions underlying the property rights literature,[5] this literature focuses almost exclusively on the allocation of residual control rights and equity among partners. Thus, we still lack information on other dimensions of contracting that may be relevant to solving the coordination problem in alliances.

There are two ways of thinking about contracting choice that differ from the current literature: first, there may be a wide variety of contract terms used to guard against non-cooperative behaviour and ensure effective collabora-tion, distinct from incentive alignment mechanisms like equity and residual control rights. Second, contracts may go beyond purely legal documents – their only value may not simply be to the extent that contract terms are enforceable – and these agreements may form blueprints for exchange and a means to plan the collaboration, set partner expectations and, consequently, reduce misunderstandings and costly missteps. Under either of these two approaches, we would expect that more detailed contracts would lead to better outcomes and, therefore, be preferable, because such contracts set clear expectations for behaviour or provide a means to identify and curtail opportunistic behaviour.

Formal contracting, though, is not the only solution to the coordination difficulties inherent in alliances. Means exist apart from such formal mech-anisms to curtail opportunism and encourage cooperative behaviour. The economics literature emphasizes how repeated interactions can, through implicit mechanisms, serve to mitigate moral hazard. For example, Green and Porter (1984) demonstrate that a cartel is sustainable when firms repeatedly interact. Telser (1980) also argues that agreements can be self-enforcing, even if not complete, when the parties value the future relationship sufficiently. Repeated interactions in the marketplace rather than with a specific firm may lead to development of reputation, which may also support economic exchange through less formal means (Kreps, 1990). Klein and Leffler (1981) lend empirical support to these arguments through simulation, finding that the threat of lost reputation is a means to enforce promises on quality, which are otherwise unenforceable.

Sociologists also discuss the role of repeated interactions in achieving cooperation. Macaulay (1963) argued that firms rarely rely on legal sanctions to uphold terms of economic exchange and that reputation or social norms may serve to ensure cooperative behaviour. Granovetter (1985: 490) notes that, 'individuals with whom one has a continuing relation have an economic motivation to be trustworthy, so as not to discourage future transactions; and departing from pure economic motives, continuing economic relations often become overlaid with social content that carries strong expectations of trust and abstention from opportunism.' Empirical evidence in the context of alliances provides some support for this link. Gulati and Singh (1998) find that firms with prior ties are less likely to choose more hierarchical controls for their alliance activities and suggest that trust developed over these prior ties may alleviate concerns of opportunism.

Given the cost of drafting more detailed contracts (see for example, Crocker and Reynolds, 1993), the impact of prior alliances on alliance contracting appears straightforward. Where alternative discipline mechanisms exist, contracts are less detailed or less 'complete'. Prior alliances between partners may serve to develop trust or may signal a high relative value for the specific relationship, leading to a reduced need for more formal governance. Similarly, prior alliances generally may signal a positive reputation that curtails a firm's opportunistic behaviour in the current alliance. However, recent evidence from Poppo and Zenger (2002) suggests the opposite, at least in the context of data entry outsourcing relationships; prior relationships between firms lead to more detailed or customized contracts, perhaps because prior relationships allow parties to learn more about each other. Via better information on likely partner behaviour or the contingencies that arise in particular types of deals, the cost of more detailed agreements is reduced, relative to those firms that have no repeated experiences.

On the basis of this literature, there appear to be two different, but equally logical, links between prior alliances and contract structure. Both the marginal benefit and marginal cost of additional contract precision decrease in the presence of prior deals, and the optimal level of contract detail depends upon the relative magnitude of these two effects. Given this ambiguous relationship, whether and how repeated deals affect contract structure becomes an empirical question that we investigate below.

Data: technology alliances in the telecommunications equipment and microelectronics industries

To examine whether and how contract structure varies with prior alliances, we examine technology alliance contracts in the telecommunications and microelectronics industries. These alliances take many forms, including cross-licensing arrangements, joint technology development agreements and formal joint ventures for development and manufacturing. Consistent with prior observations on the change in focus of cooperative R&D efforts, we do not see any examples of truly basic research in our sample contracts.

Our source of alliance contracts is SEC filings. Public firms, under SEC disclosure requirements, submit 'material contracts' as part of their 8K, 10K, 10Q and S-1 filings, including alliance contracts. From these filings, we obtained over 120 technology alliance contracts for the years 1991 to 2000, inclusive. However, we confine our consideration to those alliances involving some form of joint development (52 contracts), whether this joint development is very limited in scope or involves colocation of research personnel in the case of some joint ventures. These alliances cover a broad spectrum of purposes, from development of new microprocessor cores based on existing technology to developing a 'next-generation' ferroelectric chip.

To obtain information about pre-existing relationships between allying firms, or prior deals, we supplement this data with information on prior alliances from the Securities Data Company (SDC) Database on Alliances and Joint Ventures. The SDC database compiles information on a firm's alliance activity from news reports, SEC filings, industry and trade journals. Using SDC data, we capture all alliance activity for a firm and break this information down into two components: information on prior alliances with a specific partner (where we have a contract for a later alliance with the same firm) and all prior alliances for the firm, irrespective of partner. Prior alliances are counted for the five years prior to the focal alliance (the alliance where a contract has been collected). We begin with a broad description of our coding scheme developed via case analysis to categorize the variety of formal mechanisms used by alliance partners to deal with the underlying moral hazard and coordination problems (Ryall and Sampson, 2004). This coding scheme exposes the diverse clauses used to specify inputs and outcomes.

Coding scheme and empirical summary

In designing their contracts, allying firms have to devise means to make expectations explicit and facilitate cooperation while constraining non-cooperative behaviour. Here, we focus on the role of contract detail to better define cooperative behaviour. This contractual detail can be considered on multiple grounds, including whether specific development goals and benchmarks are set or whether goals are more general in nature. Several other dimensions of contract detail are identified via earlier case analyses, including: (1) the extent to which time frames for completion are set; (2) the specificity of intellectual property rights (for example, whether specific technology improvements are reserved for one firm, rather than equally shared); and (3) the extent to which partner contributions are defined. In addition, firms may also specify individuals to manage the alliance projects. The more detailed the contract is along these dimensions, the easier it is to observe failure to meet objectives and the more efficient is external enforcement. Presumably, more detailed contracts also facilitate greater cooperation between partners, by setting explicit expectations for firm behaviour and forcing the partners to agree in advance on what each hopes to contribute and achieve via collaboration.

To summarize, the terms we use to code contract detail are:

- Development specifications (such as tolerances) included
- Time frame for completion of each stage specified
- Number of employees to be contributed specified
- Specific persons stipulated for management or other development work
- Specific technologies to be contributed described
- Intellectual property rights defined over specific technologies

We expect that the greater the number of these mechanisms used, the 'tighter' the contract and the stronger the formal governance.

After identifying the coding scheme, the question becomes, can we link the strength of formal governance (in the form of contract detail) to the presence of prior alliances? On the basis of our case studies, contracts appear to be more specific when firms lack a pre-existing relationship. This may, however, reflect other alliance characteristics that we cannot control for with the case study approach. For example, greater uncertainty associated with broader technology development tasks may lead to less detailed contracts simply because firms cannot accurately anticipate the needs and outcomes of the collaborative development in advance. Firms may be more willing to enter into such broad technology collaborations where that firm has prior experience with a specific partner. Thus, comparisons between contracts with similar purposes become more important.

We code the contracts in our sample according to the scheme set out above and analyse the differences using standard regression techniques. In these regressions, we also include several other dimensions of the contracts. Generally, we expect that anything increasing the uncertainty or complexity associated with alliance activities will make contracts less detailed, since specifying development steps and time frames for completion of each step, etc., becomes more difficult under such circumstances. We identify four factors that we expect may increase uncertainty and/or complexity associated with the alliance: (1) technology breadth (that is, whether the technology development was largely incremental, for example customization of existing technologies for new uses, or next generation, where partners are focused on relatively radical changes to technology); (2) long duration of the alliance (greater than one year in duration); (3) manufacturing and/or marketing activities in addition to joint development; (4) cross-border coordination between partners (international alliance).

The average alliance in the sample is two years in length, of moderate technology breadth, involves manufacturing in addition to joint development, and is international (involving partners headquartered in different countries). Further, most alliances are between firms that have not previously allied – only 14 of the 52 alliances coded involve firms that have collaborated together previously (according to the SDC data). However, most firms have some degree of prior alliance experience with, on average, 25 alliances in the five years prior to the focal alliance.

Several interesting patterns emerge from our coding. First, the contracts exhibit substantial variance. Alliance contracts in this sample are far from identical, utilizing different combinations of detailed specifications, termination clauses, and division of property rights, for example. A few details are worth mentioning: (1) most contracts have fixed termination dates; (2) the majority of allying firms choose to divide the intellectual property rights based upon who is the primary developer, rather than sharing the new intellectual property equally; and (3) development work is infrequently colocated.

We estimate the choice of contract detail clauses as a function of prior alliances and variables capturing alliance task complexity or uncertainty. We rank the contracts according to how many 'detail' clauses each contract contains and distinguish between prior alliances with the same partner (that is, the same firms as in the contract) and prior alliances generally with other partners (that is, firms other than in the contract). From this analysis, two patterns emerge. First, prior or concurrent alliances appear to decrease the degree of contract detail. This result is consistent with the argument that firms develop 'trust' (Gulati and Singh, 1998) or a desire to maintain the relationship with the current partner that may curtail noncooperative behaviour and reduce the need for more formal governance mechanisms. However, when we break these alliances down into their prior and concurrent counterparts, another interpretation is possible. Prior alliances between partners in the focal alliance increase the probability that firms draft detailed contracts, while concurrent alliances decrease this probability. Firms may learn about their partners from their experience with them such that more detailed or customized contracts become less costly. This finding is consistent with Poppo and Zenger (2002), who argue that formal and relational governance are complementary. This is consistent with MacNeil's (1981: 1041) observation that, 'the exercise of choice [about contract content] is thus an incremental process in which parties gather increasing information and gradually agree to more and more as they proceed.' When firms have prior relationships, they have more opportunities to work through agreed terms, which are then embodied in later alliance agreements. Concurrent alliances, in contrast, may operate to reduce the need for formal governance by creating a 'mutual hostage' – the potential for reciprocity may curtail the threat of non-cooperative behaviour (Williamson, 1985). Thus, in this sense prior alliances may facilitate learning between partners, while concurrent alliances provide mutual hostages.

Prior alliance experience with any partner consistently increases the customization and detail of alliance contracts. This suggests that a firm's ability to draft more detailed contracts improves with alliance experience. Thus, while extensive prior experience may signal a strong firm reputation that may curtail non-cooperative behaviour in the current alliance, we do not find the negative effect of such experience on detail that would be consistent with this argument.

Control variables behave largely as expected. Broad technology alliances are less likely to have detailed contracts; the greater uncertainty and complexity surrounding broader technology development likely makes detailed specification of rights, obligations and time frames more difficult. International alliances are more likely to have more detailed contracts. Given that international collaborations are more challenging to coordinate because of, for example, geographic distance, firms may place more importance on drafting detailed contracts before collaborating.

Conclusion

In this chapter, we examine technology alliance contracts in detail not only to explore such contracts, but also to determine whether prior alliances affect contract structure. Prior literature in organizational economics and sociology suggests that, given the cost of complete contracting, detailed contracts are less likely in the presence of implicit governance mechanisms, such as trust or the desire to maintain a valuable relationship. Our earlier analysis of 52 alliance contracts in the telecommunications equipment and microelectronics industries suggests that prior alliances do indeed affect formal contract structure (Ryall and Sampson, 2004). However, this relationship is more nuanced than previously expected. Firms draft more detailed contracts when they have prior alliance experience, whether with the same partner or not. In contrast, less detailed contracts result when firms have concurrent alliances with the same partner. Thus, it appears that the informal governance inherent in interfirm relationships has different effects on formal governance depending upon whether these relationships are on-going or past.

In addition to these empirical results, our exploration of contracts reveals that such documents are highly heterogeneous and often incorporate terms that are not readily explained by traditional contract theory. Firms often include contract terms that are legally unenforceable, suggesting that the purpose of such contracts goes beyond providing guidance to the courts in the case of breach. The fact that firms include such detailed terms even when they will not be upheld in a court of law argues that one role of contracts is to provide a blueprint for collaboration. Via the contract, partners not only set out rights, obligations and contingencies to the extent possible, but also plan how they will collaborate and what their expectations are with respect to the identity of managerial inputs (for example). By defining expectations, even if not legally enforceable, firms may be able to avoid costly misunderstandings. If formal contracts are indeed such a blueprint, they are especially important for technology alliances, given the substantial difficulties of development across firm boundaries. As such, further work is required to better understand whether the quality of such blueprints affects the success of the venture.

Naturally, there are important limitations to our work here. First, the substantial heterogeneity makes true comparison between contracts difficult at best. While we attempt to control for sources of heterogeneity, our measures are blunt instruments, which cannot perfectly capture, for example, the breadth of the underlying technologies developed in the alliance. Further, while access to actual contracts permits more detailed analysis, the difficulty in accessing these contracts prevents collection of large samples. Fruitful directions for future work include further coding to enlarge our sample size and analysis of monitoring and penalty clauses in addition to contract detail. Further access to contracts (for example, all of the alliance contracts for a single firm) would allow us to better control for within-firm boiler plate terms and firm experience. On-going research (for example, Mayer and Argyres, 2004) is particularly encouraging in this area.

Notwithstanding these limitations and the need for further research efforts, this study provides some evidence of the link between prior alliances and contract structure. Further, our data facilitate a greater understanding of how firms organize their alliance development activities and respond to thorny coordination difficulties. Hopefully, this detailed examination of alliance contracts will lead to a better understanding of how firms can more effectively collaborate and, ultimately, the role of contracts in business exchange.

Notes

1. Michael D. Ryall, Melbourne Business School, 200 Leicester St., Carlton, VIC 3053, Australia, E-mail: m.ryall@mbs.edu
2. Rachelle C. Sampson, RH Smith School of Business, Van Munching Hall, 3301, University of Maryland, College Park, MD 20742, E-mail: rsampson@rhsmith.umd.edu
3. As Crocker and Masten (1991: 71) note, 'the presumption is clear that courts will either direct specific performance or apply appropriately measured damages to assure that the intentions of the parties are fulfilled.'

4. See, for example, Macaulay (1963), Green and Porter (1984), Gulati and Singh (1998).
5. That is, that contracts are substantially incomplete, largely unenforceable and, thus, the primary means to ensure investment efficiency is allocation of control rights.

References

Crocker, K. J. and Masten, S. E. (1991) 'Pretia ex Machina? Prices and Process in Long Term Contracts', *Journal of Law and Economics*, 34: 69–99.

Crocker, K. J. and Reynolds, K. J. (1993) 'The Efficiency of Incomplete Contracts: an Empirical Analysis of Air Force Engine Procurement', *Rand Journal of Economics*, 24: 126–46.

Granovetter, M. (1985) 'Economic Action and Social Structure: the Problem of Embeddedness', *American Journal of Sociology*, 91: 481–510.

Green, E. J. and Porter, R. H. (1984) 'Noncooperative Collusion Under Imperfect Price Information', *Econometrica*, 52: 87–100.

Grossman, S. J. and Hart, O. D. (1986) 'The Costs and Benefits of Vertical Ownership: a Theory of Vertical and Lateral Integration', *Journal of Political Economy*, 94: 691–719.

Gulati, R. and Singh H. (1998) 'The Architecture of Cooperation: Managing Coordination Costs and Appropriation Concerns in Strategic Alliances', *Administrative Science Quarterly*, 43: 781–814.

Holmstrom, B. (1989) 'Agency Costs and Innovation', *Journal of Economic Behavior and Organization*, 12: 305–27.

Klein, B. and Leffler, K. B. (1981) 'The Role of Market Forces in Assuring Contractual Performance', *Journal of Political Economy*, 89: 615–41.

Kreps, D. M. (1990) 'Corporate Culture and Economic Theory', in J. E. Alt and K. A. Shepsle (eds), *Perspectives on Positive Political Economy*, Cambridge: Cambridge University Press: 90–143.

Larson, A. (1992) 'Network Dyads in Entrepreneurial Settings: a Study of the Governance of Exchange Relationships', *Administrative Science Quarterly*, 37: 76–104.

Lerner, J. and Merges, R. P. (1998) 'The Control of Technology Alliances: an Empirical Analysis of the Biotechnology Industry', *Journal of Industrial Economics*, 46: 125–56.

Macaulay, S. (1963) 'Non-Contractual Relations in Business: a Preliminary Study', *American Sociological Review*, 28: 55–67.

MacNeil, I. R. (1981) 'Economic Analysis of Contractual Relations: Its Shortfalls and the Need for a "Rich Classificatory Apparatus"', *Northwestern University Law Review*, 75: 1018–63.

Mayer, K. J. and Argyres, N. (2004) 'Learning to Contract: Evidence from the Personal Computer Industry', *Organization Science*, 15(4): 394–410.

Oxley, J. E. (1997) 'Appropriability Hazards and Governance in Strategic Alliances: a Transaction Cost Approach', *Journal of Law, Economics and Organization*, 13: 387–409.

Pisano, G. (1989) 'Using Equity Participation to Support Exchange: Evidence from the Biotechnology Industry', *Journal of Law, Economics and Organization*, 1: 109–26.

Poppo, L. and Zenger, T. (2002) 'Do Formal Contracts and Relational Governance Function as Substitutes or Complements?' *Strategic Management Journal*, 23: 707–25.

Ryall, M. D. and Sampson, R. C. (2004) 'Formal Contracts in the Presence of Relational Enforcement Mechanisms: Evidence from Technology Development Projects', Working Paper.

Sampson, R. C. (2004) 'The Cost of Misaligned Governance in R&D Alliances', *Journal of Law, Economics and Organization*, 20(2): 484–526.

Telser, L. G. (1980) 'A Theory of Self-Enforcing Contracts', *Journal of Business*, 53: 27–44.

Williamson, O. E. (1975) *Markets and Hierarchies: Analysis and Antitrust Implications*, New York: Free Press.

Williamson, O. E. (1985) *The Economic Institutions of Capitalism*, New York: Free Press.

20
Learning to Govern by Contract
Nicholas Argyres[1] and Kyle J. Mayer[2]

Introduction

Strategic alliances almost always involve the development of contracts of some kind, especially in high technology industries. Yet while contracts may play an important role in defining and governing alliances, until very recently strategy and organization scholars have not been much concerned with studying their design of such contracts much. In this chapter, we discuss the research we have been conducting recently into how firms learn to design their contracts. We discuss the evidence our work provides suggesting that firms in young high technology industries only learn efficient contracting practices over time, and that learning time can be quite long. We also suggest ways in which patterns of learning to contract are reflected in the evolution of contractual provisions over time. We highlight the implications of these findings for the possibility that firms may develop firm-specific contract design capabilities, and that such capabilities can serve as one source of a firm's competitive advantage. Finally, we argue that the possibility that governance more generally is subject to learning suggests a new link between evolutionary and transaction cost economics, and therefore a connection between the different views of competitive advantage suggested by those theories.

Learning to contract

Whereas strategy scholars have largely ignored contract design until recently (e.g. Ariño and Reuer, 2004; Reuer and Ariño, 2005), economists have studied contract design extensively. The economists' approach, however, has generally been to analyse a contract as an equilibrium solution to an incentive problem between a principal and an agent. Alternatively, contract designs are seen as solutions to the problem of governing an exchange relationship over time, when some contingencies cannot be anticipated. In the latter case contracts are analysed as efficient solutions to ex post governance problems (such as potential hold-up, etc.). Rarely has the question been asked, however, how do firms actually arrive at an efficient contract? Are firms always well prepared to design efficient contracts for new types of exchanges which they may not have experienced previously?

Our research suggests that in fact firms may take a significant time before arriving at a set of contractual provisions that adequately anticipate and address the relevant contingencies that could adversely impact the exchange. The first piece of our research that makes this suggestion was based on extensive field interviews with two firms that contracted with each other over an eleven-year period (Mayer and Argyres, 2004). The supplier in the relationship we studied was a developer of custom software; the buyer was a large firm that produced personal computers, along with a range of other electronics. The two partners signed about a dozen contracts with each other over this period for various kinds of custom software. The period we studied began in 1988, still fairly early in the history of the personal computer industry.

Our research showed how these two firms repeatedly agreed to contractual designs that failed to anticipate emergent contingencies, and failed to deal with them adequately even when anticipated. It was clear from the context, however, that the managers and engineers developing these contracts were not incompetent. Instead, it appeared that they did not have a good grasp of the kinds of contingencies they were likely to face, nor a good sense of the kinds of contractual provisions that could adequately address these contingencies. After all, the personal computer industry was new and still in flux. Areas that were particularly problematic were communication protocols between the parties, and scheduling. How should the content of different software versions be defined? How should engineering changes be communicated, by whom, and by when? These questions turned out to raise challenging problems of contracting, yet the parties could not anticipate them until they actually experienced the negative consequences of failing to consider them. Once these negative experiences occurred, the parties attempted to enhance their follow-on contracts, though occasionally the initial contractual solutions that were proposed to correct some communication or task definition problem were inadequate, and had to be reworked in later contracts. We estimated that it required roughly nine years before the parties arrived a stable set of provisions for inclusion in their contracts. Clearly, the partners we studied were not well prepared to organize the new kinds of transactions in which they were engaged, nor were they prepared to quickly learn how to do so.

The evidence analysed in Mayer and Argyres (2004) comes from one relationship only. Can broader evidence be found for the importance of learning behaviour in contracting? Moreover, do particular categories of contractual provisions evolve in systematic ways as a result of such learning behaviour? These questions motivated a second piece of research we carried out, this time examining a larger sample of 386 contracts between a single IT services firm and 162 different partners over a twelve-year period (Argyres et al., 2006). These contracts were relatively short – usually five pages or less – and included payment terms, a duration clause, more or less detailed task descriptions, and in some cases contingency planning provisions. The task description provisions were technical statements of the nature of the work to be carried out. A detailed set of task description provisions for an applications migration project might include:

(1) The criteria used to determine which projects should be migrated first.
(2) A detailed task list.
(3) The number and types of personnel required to complete the project.
(4) Scheduling initiation of work, and duration of various aspects of the project.
(5) Provisions for testing converting applications.
(6) Information and resources required from the customer in order to determine the software applications that need to be migrated.

Contingency planning provisions, on the other hand, identify possible contingencies that could disturb the relationship or lead to conflict, and sometimes contain guidelines for how parties are expected to behave if those contingencies occur. An example of a fairly detailed contingency planning provision is the following:

> During code conversion, it may be determined that structural changes will be necessary to port a specific function to UTS. In such cases, the [Compustar] technical staff will discuss the situation & possible alternatives with [Customer]. The selection of viable alternatives will be a joint decision between [Compustar] and [Customer]. A list of all such changes will be kept and those changes will be documented as to 'what the change was' and 'why it was made'. During the course of code modification porting [Customer] applications to UTS, it is likely that situations will be found where restructuring of code would significantly enhance performance or reliability. In such cases, it will be noted and documented for future evaluation and disposition by [Customer].

The question we posed in this second piece of research was whether, as firms learn about the characteristics of the transactions they undertake – that is, as they learn about the kinds of incentive and governance problems that are embedded in these transactions – this learning is reflected in the design of task description and contingency planning provisions. We hypothesized that as firms learned about the nature of their transactions and how to govern them, we would observe learning spillovers between task description and contingency planning provision development, so that the relationship between these two categories would be one of complementarity. We conjectured that as firms develop more knowledge about their transactions, task descriptions would become more detailed, and contingency planning provisions would become more extensive (controlling for key transaction characteristics expected to affect each of these provision categories independently). Moreover, highly detailed task descriptions for one contract would lead to more extensive contingency planning provisions for the next contract, since a better understanding of how to describe the task to be undertaken would improve knowledge about the critical contingencies that could upset transactions involving this type of task. We expected this kind of inter-provisional learning spillover to operate in the reverse direction as well, with more extensive contingency planning provisions in one contract leading to more detailed task descriptions in the next. The idea here is that as partners gain a better understanding of potentially problematic contingencies that could affect their exchanges, they can partly deal with such contingencies through more detailed and appropriate task descriptions in later contracts. Our data allowed us to examine these kinds of inter-provisional spillovers across contracts between the same two partners over time, but not between different pairs of partners.

Our hypotheses were strongly supported in the contract data we examined. Testing for endogeneity between task description and contingency planning detail, and correcting for it econometrically where it is present, we found that our two categories of contractual provisions were positively associated with each other in a given contract (controlling for several key characteristics of the transactions). We also found that more extensive task description in one contract was associated with more detailed contingency planning in the next contract, and vice versa. These findings indicate a pattern in which learning within each of the contractual provision categories we studied spilled over to the other, and in which the two categories therefore co-evolved in a 'balanced' way within the overall contract design.

Contract design capabilities

One set of implications that follows from this observation of learning-to-contract behaviour concerns the development of firm-level contract design capabilities. If contracting in young industries is subject to a learning curve, then firms may learn at different rates, and faster learners may develop superior contract design capabilities than rivals. This can be important if firms with superior contract design capabilities are better able to deal with problematic contingencies in their relationships with various partners, and otherwise improve the performance of those relationships, whereas firms with inferior capabilities experience repeated problems managing their relationships with contractual partners. Contract design capabilities are of course of special interest to firms (and to strategy scholars) if they can serve as a source of competitive advantage for the firm. (So far our research has focused on the role of contract capabilities in creating value in a transaction, rather than capturing it, although the latter may be important as well.)

A natural question that arises, however, is that if a firm finds itself with underdeveloped contract design capability, can it not simply hire the appropriate lawyers, and rely on them to work out an efficient contract design? In a third piece of research, we argue that the answer to this question – especially in high technology industries – is often 'no' (Argyres and Mayer, 2006). Contracts in high technology industries often contain quite technical provisions for task descriptions and contingency planning, the development of which requires significant input from the engineers and managers actually involved in implementing the project. Indeed, even provisions for communication, intellectual property allocations, and other provisions must often take into account the technical characteristics of the project at hand, and require heavy involvement of the managers and engineers. We suggest that lawyers will often take on a less important role in development certain of these provisions such as task description and communication, even as they perhaps take a stronger role in the development of, say, dispute resolution procedures. Moreover, because the development of communication, task description and contingency planning provisions are more likely to benefit from the tacit and/or firm-specific knowledge of engineers and managers regarding technologies and production processes than provisions such as payment terms or dispute resolution procedures, we argue that firm-level contract design capability with regard to the former is more likely to serve as a source of competitive advantage than such capability with regard to the latter.

Transaction cost economics, evolutionary economics and competitive advantage

The research we have been describing on learning to contract and contract design capabilities carries a number of implications for bridging transaction cost economics and evolutionary economics, with an eye towards contributing to a theory of competitive advantage. Transaction cost economics (TCE) is of course concerned with the ways in which various governance mechanisms can make a discriminating match with transactions with different kinds of characteristics (Williamson, 1985). TCE assumes that these kinds of efficient matches occur either through initial (boundedly) rational choices of managers, or through the progressive elimination of inefficient matches as market pressures are brought to bear on the firms responsible for making them. But while the logic supporting TCE's efficient matches has found much (indirect) empirical support, the actual processes by which efficient matches might come about have not been much studied.

Meanwhile, evolutionary economics has been specifically concerned with disequilibrium processes, and with understanding how market competition can work as a selection force (Nelson and Winter, 1982). According to evolutionary economics, market pressures act upon firms, not particular transactions, and selection occurs on a relative basis, rather than on an absolute basis. Therefore, firms may carry a few inefficient matches – inefficiently organized transactions – for some time. Market competition will not quickly and automatically lead to the elimination of such inefficient matches. Moreover, managers tend to behave according to predefined organizational routines, and when they search for solutions to problems, that search tends to be local. This behaviour can therefore cause them to miss opportunities to discover more efficient matches.

These assumptions featured in evolutionary economics seem to describe the patterns of learning to contract we observed in our studies. Certainly the behaviour we observed seems more consistent with local search than with far-sighted contracting. Evolutionary economics, however, was of little help in predicting the directions in which learning to contract would occur. That is, evolutionary economics has little to say about efficient governance matches – what forms of governance will eventually efficiently match with what kinds of transactions, once the learning process has run its course. This is perhaps because evolutionary economics has tended to focus on production rather than exchange (Winter, 1988).

Our research, however, suggests that TCE is important in understanding the content of governance choices, while evolutionary economics is important for understanding the processes through which these choices come to be made over time. Our research showed that matching governance mechanisms to transaction characteristics may require significant time for the parties to learn – both about the characteristics and the efficient matching. While this learning process is occurring, many mismatches may be observed, and they may persist for some time. Eventually, however, efficient matches will emerge, as underlying relationships are better understood. Before equilibrium 'matches' appear, however, some firms may learn faster than others, thereby reducing the ratio of efficient to inefficient matches they experience. In these learning periods, which may be quite long in high technology industries, some firms may be governing their exchange relationships more efficiently than others, and be earning rents on the contract design capabilities they are developing. These learning periods are the ones in which firm-level contract design capabilities may contribute to a firm's competitive advantage.

Williamson (1999) argued that one could think of integrating governance and competence perspectives on the firm by recognizing that governance choices may be conditional on the a priori distribution of competences across firms, where 'competence' is thought of as competence in production. Our own research on learning to contract, however, suggests that this approach is insufficient. We suggest that by studying how firms learn to contract, we can achieve a deeper integration of transaction cost and evolutionary economics – one that recognizes that governance can itself be a competence that is unequally distributed across organizations. This recognition, we further suggest, promises to enhance our understanding of the sources of competitive advantage in emerging industries.

Notes

1. Nicholas Argyres, Boston University School of Management. 595 Commonwealth Avenue, Boston, MA 02215. E-mail: nargyres@bu.edu. Tel: 617-353-4152. Fax: 617-353-5003
2. Kyle J. Mayer, Marshall School of Business, Management and Organization Department, University of Southern California, Los Angeles, CA 90089-0808. E-mail: kmayer@marshall.usc.edu. Tel: 213-821-1141. Fax: 213-740-3582.

References

Argyres, N. and Mayer, K. (2006) 'Contract Design as a Firm Capability: an Integration of Transaction Cost and Learning Perspectives', forthcoming in *Academy of Management Review*.

Argyres, N., Bercovitz, J. and Mayer, K. (2005) 'Complementarity and Evolution of Contractual Provisions: an Empirical Study of IT Services Contracts', conditionally accepted for publication in *Organization Science*.

Ariño, A. and Reuer, J. (2004) 'Negotiating and Renegotiating Strategic Alliance Contracts', *Academy of Management Executive*, 18: 37–48.

Mayer, K. and Argyres, N. (2004) 'Learning to Contract: Evidence from the Personal Computer Industry', *Organization Science*, 5: 394–410.

Nelson, R. and Winter, S. (1982) *An Evolutionary Theory of Economic Change*, Cambridge, MA: Belknap Press.

Reuer, J. and Ariño, A. (2005) 'Contractual Complexity in Strategic Alliances', manuscript.

Williamson, O. E. (1985) *The Economic Institutions of Capitalism*, New York: Free Press.

Williamson, O. E. (1999) 'Strategy: Governance and Competence Perspectives', *Strategic Management Journal*, 20: 1087–99.

Winter, S. (1988) 'On Coase, Competence and the Corporation', *Journal of Law, Economics and Organization*, 4: 163–80.

21
Contractual Renegotiations in Entrepreneurial Alliances

Africa Ariño,[1] Roberto Ragozzino[2] and Jeffrey J. Reuer[3]*

Introduction

Strategic alliances hold out numerous potential benefits for small firms in particular, including the ability to tap into new markets, access scale economies, obtain complementary resources in under-developed value chain activities, respond to environmental uncertainties, and receive endorsements from reputable incumbents, among others (for instance, Deeds and Hill, 1996; Eisenhardt and Schoonhoven, 1996; Gomes-Casseres, 1997). It is equally clear, however, that small firms encounter their share of challenges in formulating and implementing collaborative strategy (Doz, 1988).

In attempting to understand firms' experiences with alliances, it is worth beginning with the observation that the value that a firm ultimately derives from a collaborative agreement hinges upon its ability to manage a number of distinct, yet interrelated, stages, including scanning for partners, negotiating the alliance terms and design, implementing the agreement and specifying the ways in which it may change or eventually terminate (for instance, Zajac and Olsen, 1993). It is also important to consider the unique challenges and attributes of small firms in alliances because failing to do so may lead to generalized statements that do not map well into the resource-constrained context faced by small firms.

Despite the wealth of research on strategic alliances, comparatively little work has considered the post-formation stages of collaboration, however (Reuer and Ariño, 2002; Reuer et al., 2002). In recent years, more research has analysed termination rather than just alliance formation, but the events and collaborative dynamics preceding termination have gone relatively unexplored in empirical research (Ariño and de la Torre, 1998). However, it is likely that in these stages of collaboration entrepreneurial firms will often face significant challenges in managing their collaborative relationships effectively (Niederkofler, 1991). Doz and Hamel (1998) argue that how firms manage an alliance over time is a more important determinant of the alliance's ultimate success or failure than how the collaboration is initially set

224

up. Other researchers have similarly acknowledged the importance of the dynamic aspects of collaborative processes (for instance, Deeds and Hill, 1999; Weaver and Dickson, 1998).

This chapter examines the experiences of small firms in strategic alliances as they evolve, focusing on contractual renegotiation as one type of post-formation change in these collaborative agreements. The bulk of the existing empirical research has tended to assess firms' governance choices under the assumption that a selection environment acts to weed out inefficient structures before managers have the opportunity to adapt them (for instance, Williamson, 1991). By contrast, we allow for managerial discretion to remedy alliances subject to governance misalignment. Additionally, we analyse the extent to which small firms differ from others in their propensity to use contractual changes and in their exposures to the hazards of hold-up in alliances, which allows us to isolate the mechanisms behind alliance dynamics as they are experienced uniquely by this category of firms.

After providing a more detailed motivation for the present study, we report data on the dynamics of alliances experienced by small and large firms. We then proceed to a discussion of the findings, which demonstrate that although small firms are no more or less likely to renegotiate alliances than their counterparts, they tend to adjust their alliances less in the face of governance misalignments. Moreover, small firms make higher levels of transaction-specific investments without implementing appropriate contractual safeguards, which can trigger ex post changes in alliances.

The evolution of small firms' alliances

Contractual changes in alliances may be viewed either as an outcome of a collaborative relationship or as a specific post-formation governance decision made by a partner. In the first scenario, several considerations suggest that contractual renegotiations may be expected to be more likely for small firms: small firms typically lack extensive alliance experience, which allows partners to anticipate some of the contingencies that may arise later in the agreement and include appropriate provisions, in order to avoid the need for ex post adjustments. As another illustration, the lack of information available on small firms may make them prone to misrepresent their abilities in alliances early on, leading to necessary adjustments over time (Zacharakis, 1997). Finally, small firms' lack of financial resources can cause sub-optimal allocations of control rights ex ante, which then lead to subsequent shifts in the terms of the agreement (Lerner and Merges, 1998).

If contractual changes are viewed as decisions or actions taken by the firm, the differences between small and large firms become less clear, because such decisions or actions depend both on firms' willingness to take them and on their ability to do so. For instance, collaborative experience may facilitate ex post adjustments in alliances by enabling the firm to know when and how changes are warranted. Thus, the lesser alliance experience held by small firms suggests that they may be less likely to take such actions when they are needed. Additionally, their lower bargaining power in a relationship also suggests that such changes may be difficult to effect in practice. This set of considerations, along with the logic developed previously, lead to two competing predictions on the likelihood of contractual renegotiation for small firms versus others.

Although we wish to test the effects of firm size on the likelihood of contractual changes in alliances, the competing arguments noted above indicate the importance of developing a deeper analysis, in order to clarify the mechanisms that bring about contractual renegotiations and determine whether the experiences of small firms are truly unique. Below we discuss two explanations for contractual renegotiations in alliances. First, alliance partners may wish to renegotiate to eliminate inefficiencies of a previously developed design that no longer suits the realities of the relationship. The more severe the governance misalignment, the greater the incentive to bear the costs of renegotiation to adjust the alliance's structure. Second, a firm will be willing to renegotiate when its significant transaction-specific investment in an alliance provides a partner firm with the opportunity to appropriate this value. In this case, contractual renegotiation may reflect the presence of contractual hazards and ex post hold-up risks.

While the first explanation implies that contractual renegotiations in alliances can be efficiency-enhancing, in the second scenario a transfer of value occurs between the parties and inefficiencies can be exacerbated in the process of renegotiating the alliance's terms. Two questions therefore arise: are small firms more or less able to respond to governance misalignments, and are they more or less susceptible to alliances' contractual hazards that lead to contractual renegotiations? It is plausible that small firms will be less able to reap the benefits of alliance adaptation, and that the changes that occur in alliances over time will not always coincide with the small firm's interests. We consider these possibilities in turn in the next two sections.

Governance misalignment and contractual renegotiation

Because our goal is to focus on the post-formation setting, it is important to point out two related propositions that help in the development of our predictions. First, the efficiency of a transaction will be positively related to the alignment between the chosen governance structure (and the 'syndrome' of properties it represents) and the fundamental attributes of the transaction in the broader contracting environment (Williamson, 1991). The implication that follows is that no one governance structure for alliances is universally more or less efficient than others. Second, and closely related to the proposition of discriminating alignment, empirical research has often used a selection approach to fit, whereby efficiency implications are drawn from reduced-form models of firms' governance choices (for instance, Drazin and

Van de Ven, 1985). This is made possible by the assumption that competitive forces in the selection environment weed out inefficient governance decisions, yet it is plausible that misaligned transactions may exist and even persist (for instance, Argyres and Libeskind, 1999). In studying ex post contractual changes in alliances, we therefore relax this assumption to allow for managerial discretion, which can enable firms to refine an alliance's governance before a maladapted collaborative relationship is selected out by competitive forces.

More precisely, inefficiencies generated by two types of governance misalignment may prompt firms to renegotiate their collaborative relationships. First, it is possible that 'excessive' governance was put in place for a comparatively simple exchange relationship, which can lead to an overly bureaucratic and slow decision-making process. Second, inefficiencies may arise if inadequate governance mechanisms are instituted in complex relationships that present a high threat of opportunism. Here, parties' rights and obligations can be very difficult to specify up front, monitoring and control can be impeded by the lack of a board to coordinate activity, and incentive alignments can be attenuated. Again, the costs of governance misalignment may prompt firms to renegotiate the alliance.

The question is whether small firms will be more or less able to improve upon their alliances' initial governance structures through contractual changes. We anticipate that they will be less likely to adapt their alliances, because the lack of alliance experience by small firms suggests that they may be less able to detect the need for contractual renegotiation, or the direction and the magnitude of these changes. Moreover, since realignments can be costly, small firms' inferior slack financial resources may make them unable to undertake such adjustments. Furthermore, the fact that small firms are often dependent on their alliance partners (Larson, 1991) suggests that they may not wish to run the risk of disrupting their existing relationship, even if inefficiencies arise. We wish to test these hypotheses to determine if governance misalignment contributes to contractual renegotiations in alliances and if small firms experience greater difficulties in managing alliances over time due to this factor.

Contractual renegotiation as a manifestation of hold-up

Although firms may make post-formation governance decisions to alleviate alliance inefficiencies, they may also undergo contractual changes that are imposed upon them when they have made transaction-specific investments in the alliance and a partner attempts to appropriate this value from the firm via renegotiations. In such situations, the gap between these assets' first and second best use values provides a motivation to incur costs to renegotiate the alliance's terms and obtain less favourable terms. Thus, to the extent that such transfers of value are possible and stimulate haggling, contractual renegotiations may contribute to, rather than ameliorate, inefficiencies in strategic alliances. In short, contractual renegotiation can be a manifestation of hold-up behaviour.

As before, the question that arises is whether small firms are more or less sensitive to such hazards in alliances. To the extent that they have less extensive experience with interfirm collaboration, small firms' hazard mitigating capabilities are likely to be lower (Delios and Henisz, 2000), which suggests that these firms are more exposed to contractual hazards for a given level of asset specificity. Moreover, when small firms have lower levels of bargaining power in alliances, the increased expected payoff from appropriation encourages their partners to engage in hold-up. We therefore test whether asset specificity contributes to contractual renegotiations in alliances and whether small firms are more susceptible to these hazards.

Analysis and results

Our data collection started from the 674 dyadic alliances by Spanish firms between the years 1986 and 1992. This time window begins with Spain's adhesion to the EC and ends with the start of the Single European Market, which is a fertile period in which the external opportunities and threats posed by deregulation and heightened competition likely stimulated interfirm collaborations. We sent questionnaires for the 189 alliances in which a knowledgeable respondent could be identified, which, after accounting for missing data, resulted in data on 71 alliances involving 63 firms.

We defined small firms as firms with less than 500 employees, as per the US Department of Commerce. To measure governance misalignment, we first developed a typology of alliances by distinguishing equity from non-equity collaborative agreements (for instance, Gulati, 1995; Pisano, 1989) as the former involve more extensive control rights as well as the introduction of incentive alignment through joint residual claimancy (Hennart, 1988). Then, we estimated a model to compare firms' actual alliance governance decisions with those implied by the underlying attributes of the collaboration (Anderson, 1988; Silverman et al., 1997). The set of attributes we used to predict each alliance's governance form included asset specificity, the number of other potential partners available to the focal firm, whether prior ties existed between the alliance partners prior to the agreement, whether the alliance was cross-border and whether the focal firm was a small entity as defined above.

Turning to the model estimating the ex post likelihood of renegotiation, aside from the attributes listed above, we included a few other controls, such as the alliance age, the level of contractual safeguards in the alliance contract, whether the collaboration was domestic or international, and whether the alliance experienced changes in the environment or in the firm's strategy.

Forty-five per cent of the collaborative agreements involved equity, and one-fifth of the collaborators had prior alliances with their partners. Eighty-four per cent of the alliances were between firms from different countries and slightly under half of the firms were classified as small. While small firms might be expected to economize on search costs in establishing alliances, they are no more likely to take on domestic partners than larger organizations, which might be attributable to the economic threats and opportunities posed by economic integration in Europe.

The results for the equity-versus-non-equity model reveal that small firms were no more prone to use either governance solution than their counterparts. Equity alliances were used when making transaction-specific investments and when a small number of alternative partners were available. Interestingly, firms with prior ties used equity alliances, while cross-border agreements did not seem to induce firms to implement the controls and incentives offered by equity structures. Both of these findings run counter to trust-based explanations of firms' governance choices (Gulati, 1995). Moving to the contractual renegotiation variables, our data show that roughly one-fifth of the alliances underwent a change, and that small firms were equally likely to experience one as their counterparts were. However, small firms made greater transaction-specific investments in their alliances, but they did not place greater safeguards in their collaborative agreements to aid in the enforcement and coordination of the alliance.

The estimation of our final model for contractual renegotiation demonstrates that firm size does not affect the likelihood of contractual renegotiation or the firm's exposure to a given level of asset specificity. However, asset specificity appears to be a key driver of alliance renegotiation, and it is evident that small firms tend to make greater transaction-specific investments in their alliances. Our models also demonstrate that smaller firms bore the inefficiencies associated with governance misfit, because they were less able to adapt misaligned alliances.

Turning to our controls, the models indicate that the alliances with less complete contracts were more likely to be renegotiated, while the likelihood of renegotiation was the same for domestic and cross-border deals. There was mixed evidence that environmental changes surrounding a collaboration prompted contractual changes, while the results clearly show that changes in a firm's strategy often led to alliance renegotiations. Interestingly, further analysis revealed that the effects of these ex post contingencies generalized to small firms and others in alliances, and no differences were evident that would suggest that small firms were more or less sensitive to such changes.

Discussion

While research has historically focused on the formation of alliances and, more recently, has given more attention to alliance termination, our findings demonstrate the relevance of studying the evolution of strategic alliances and how small firms manage the stages of these interfirm collaborations. Since this chapter focused solely on contractual renegotiations, future work could consider other types of post-formation changes in alliances and develop a

taxonomy of them in order to allow managers to understand their altern
atives and the trade-offs. Some changes, such as changing a joint venture's
board or its scope will tend to be more formal, whereas other changes in
collaborative agreements may be more informal in nature.

Our results indicate the value of maintaining the fundamental proposition of discriminating alignment while relaxing assumptions concerning
the selection environment (Williamson, 1991). We allow for managerial
discretion and for the possibility that firms can adapt their relationships
and refine the governance of their strategic alliances through contractual
renegotiations. Based on the empirical results we present, it is interesting
to note that in many respects, small firms' experiences in alliances parallel
those of larger organizations. However, further investigation underscores the
importance of relating the unique features of small firms to the likelihood
of ex post alliance renegotiations. Although generally firms respond to the
inefficiencies associated with governance misalignment, it is apparent that
small firms are less likely to make contractual adjustments in their alliances
in the face of such inefficiencies. Extensions to the present study could
consider the specific attributes of small firms, and whether less extensive alliance experience or the lack of other resources account for their lower degree
of responsiveness to governance misalignment. Clinical research would be
helpful in this effort, allowing researchers to examine situations in which
firms attempt to adapt their relationships yet fail and to sort out why such
changes are difficult for some firms.

Despite the fact that small firms will often lack bargaining power or
extensive alliance experience that can provide hazard-mitigating capabilities,
the results indicate that they are no more exposed to contractual hazards
than other firms, for a given level of asset specificity. A firm's transaction-
specific investment in alliances emerges as a key variable affecting the
dynamics of collaborations, however. Thus, while contractual renegotiation
may be used to mitigate inefficiencies due to governance misalignment, it
also may exacerbate inefficiencies due to opportunities for hold-up. While
small firms are no more exposed to such contractual hazards for a given
level of asset specificity, they do tend to make more transaction-specific
investment in alliances without incorporating commensurate contractual
safeguards into their collaborative agreements. The completeness of the alliance contract as well as the level of transaction-specific investment both in
turn relate to the likelihood of contractual renegotiations.

In attempting to bring transaction cost theory into the post-formation
setting and examine the experiences of small firms as their alliances evolve,
our study has limitations that present additional opportunities for future
research. For instance, in common with most studies of alliances, our
research involved collecting data on one firm per alliance. Collecting sufficient data on both sides of alliance dyads is challenging, but it would
allow for a more complete assessment of partners' renegotiation efforts by

considering parties' differing perceptions, roles, and outcomes. As another illustration, our models are also limited by their cross-sectional construction based on survey data. Recent conceptual research on alliance evolution has proposed frameworks including feedback loops (for instance, Ariño and de la Torre, 1998; Zajac and Olsen, 1993), so data sets with access to longitudinal information would be helpful to test these predictions on the causes and consequences of alliance dynamics. Finally, our study ultimately is silent on the performance implications of ex post changes in alliances. Although indirect inferences may be made concerning efficiency from the linkages between governance misalignment and contractual renegotiations or between asset specificity and contractual renegotiations, it would be attractive to study the implications of contractual renegotiations more directly. Future research could examine how such changes affect the longevity of alliances or shape collaborators' performance outcomes, possibly drawing insightful conclusions on the relative importance of different alliance life-cycle stages. Relative to other areas of research on alliance formation and termination, the topic of alliance dynamics remains relatively uncharted territory and presents many new avenues for inquiry in entrepreneurship research.

Notes

* In developing this research, we have benefited from discussions with Peter Ring and Maurizio Zollo. We gratefully acknowledge the financial support of the Anselmo Rubiralta Center for Research on Globalization and Strategy at IESE and of the Spanish Ministerio de Ciencia y Tecnología (grant SEC2003–09533).

1. Africa Ariño, Avda. Pearson, 21, 08034, Barcelona, Spain, E-mail: afarino@iese.edu
2. Roberto Ragozzino, College of Business Administration, University of Central Florida, P.O. Box 161400, Orlando, FL 32816-1400, E-mail: roberto.ragozzino@bus.ucf.edu
3. Jeffrey J. Reuer, Kenan-Flagler Business School, University of North Carolina, Campus Box 3490, McColl 4603, Chapel Hill, NC 27599-3490, E-mail: reuer@unc.edu

References

Anderson, E. (1988) 'Strategic Implications of Darwinian Economics for Selling Efficiency and Choice of Integrated or Independent Sales Forces', *Management Science*, 34: 599–618.

Argyres, N. S. and Liebeskind, J. P. (1999) 'Contractual Commitments, Bargaining Power, and Governance Inseparability: Incorporating History into Transaction Cost Theory', *Academy of Management Review*, 24: 49–63.

Ariño, A. and de la Torre, J. (1998) 'Learning from Failure: Towards an Evolutionary Model of Collaborative Ventures', *Organization Science*, 9: 306–25.

Armstrong, J. S. and Overton, T. S. (1977) 'Estimating Nonresponse Bias in Mail Surveys', *Journal of Marketing Research*, 14: 396–403.

Deeds, D. L. and Hill, C. W. L. (1996) 'Strategic Alliances, Complementary Assets and New Product Development: an Empirical Study of Entrepreneurial Biotechnology Firms', *Journal of Business Venturing*, 11: 41–55.

Deeds, D. L. and Hill, C. W. L. (1999) 'An Examination of Opportunistic Action within Research Alliances: Evidence from the Biotechnology Industry', *Journal of Business Venturing*, 14: 141–63.

Delios, A. and Henisz, W. J. (2000) 'Japanese Firms' Investment Strategies in Emerging Economies', *Academy of Management Journal*, 43: 305–23.

Doz, Y. L. (1988) 'Technology Partnerships between Larger and Smaller Firms: Some Critical Issues', in F. J. Contractor and P. Lorange (eds), *Cooperative Strategies in International Business*, Lexington, MA: D. C. Heath: 317–38.

Doz, Y. L. and Hamel, G. (1998) *Alliance Advantage: the Art of Creating Value through Partnering*, Boston, MA: Harvard Business School Press.

Drazin, R. and Van de Ven, A. H. (1985) 'Alternative Forms of Fit in Contingency Theory', *Administrative Science Quarterly*, 30: 514–39.

Eisenhardt, K. M. and Schoonhoven, C. B. (1996) 'Resource-based View of Strategic Alliance Formation: Strategic and Social Effects in Entrepreneurial Firms', *Organization Science*, 7: 136–50.

Gomes-Casseres, B. (1997) 'Alliance Strategies of Small Firms', *Small Business Economics*, 9: 33–44.

Gulati, R. (1995) 'Does Familiarity Breed Trust? The Implications of Repeated Ties for Contractual Choice in Alliances', *Academy of Management Journal*, 38: 85–112.

Harman, H. H. (1967) *Modern Factor Analysis*, Chicago: University of Chicago Press.

Hennart, J.-F. (1988) 'A Transaction Cost Theory of Equity Joint Ventures', *Strategic Management Journal*, 9: 361–74.

Larson, A. (1991) 'Partner Networks: Leveraging External Ties to Improve Entrepreneurial Performance', *Journal of Business Venturing*, 6: 173–88.

Lerner, J. and Merges, R. P. (1998) 'The Control of Technology Alliances: an Empirical Analysis of the Biotechnology Industry', *Journal of Industrial Economics*, 46: 125–56.

Niederkofler, M. (1991) 'The Evolution of Strategic Alliances: Opportunities for Managerial Influence', *Journal of Business Venturing*, 6: 237–57.

Pisano, G. P. (1989) 'Using Equity Participation to Support Exchange: Evidence from the Biotechnology Industry', *Journal of Law, Economics and Organization*, 5: 109–26.

Reuer, J. J. and Ariño, A. (2002) 'Contractual Renegotiations in Strategic Alliances', *Journal of Management*, 28: 51–74.

Reuer, J. J., Zollo, M. and Singh, H. (2002) 'Post-formation Dynamics in Strategic Alliances', *Strategic Management Journal*, 23: 125–51.

Salancik, G. R. and Pfeffer, J. (1977) 'An Examination of Need-satisfaction Models of Job Attitudes', *Administrative Science Quarterly*, 22: 427–56.

Silverman, B. S., Nickerson, J. A. and Freeman, J. (1997) 'Profitability, Transactional Alignment, and Organizational Mortality in the US Trucking Industry', *Strategic Management Journal*, 18 (Summer Special Issue): 31–52.

Weaver, K. M. and Dickson, P. H. (1998) 'Outcome Quality of Small- to Medium-sized Enterprise-based Alliances: the Role of Perceived Partner Behaviors', *Journal of Business Venturing*, 13: 505–22.

Williamson, O. E. (1991) 'Comparative Economic Organization: the Analysis of Discrete Structural Alternatives', *Administrative Science Quarterly*, 36: 269–96.

Zacharakis, A. L. (1997) 'Entrepreneurial Entry into Foreign Markets: a Transaction Cost Perspective', *Entrepreneurship Theory and Practice*, 21: 23–39.

Zajac, E. J. and Olsen, C. (1993) 'From Transaction Cost to Transaction Value Analysis: Implications for the Study of Interorganizational Strategies', *Journal of Management Studies*, 30: 131–45.

Index

847487

DH

658.
044
STR

00012014873

DH owl

WITHDRAWN